UNIVERSITY OF WESTMINSTER

D1391208

Failure to return or renew over
borrowing rights at all Universi

UNIVERSITY OF WESTMINSTER
HARROW IRS CENTRE

22 0262909 3

What is an author?

In 1968, Roland Barthes declared the death of the Author and the birth of the Reader. This volume has brought together an international group of authors, including Terry Eagleton, Nancy Miller and Gayatri Spivak to respond to the persistent and politically-charged question: 'What is an Author?'

The structuralist onslaught on agency has thrown into question the humanistic certainties of biography and literary authority. Intellectual developments in psychoanalysis and literary theory have meanwhile signalled the collapse of the unified subject and the need to challenge authority by stressing the slipperiness of language and meaning. Studies of the role of the reader have multiplied.

Yet the author has not gone away. The cult of the author, perhaps especially the cult of the poststructuralist authors themselves, persists. Recent thinking on race, gender and sexuality has rearticulated the need to position authors who write from a 'different' perspective within specific historical frameworks. The challenge of dealing with authorship in the postmodern world is both serious and urgent.

Readership: graduate students and academics working in the fields of literature and critical theory

Nicola Miller is Lecturer in Latin American History at University College London

Maurice Biriotti is Lecturer in Hispanic Studies at the University of Birmingham

RIDING HOUSE STREET LIBRARY
UNIVERSITY OF WESTMINSTER
37-49 Riding House St., W1P 7PT

22526 29093

808.02 WHA

What is an author?

edited by Maurice Biriotti and Nicola Miller

MANCHESTER UNIVERSITY PRESS
MANCHESTER and NEW YORK

distributed exclusively in the USA and Canada by ST. MARTIN'S PRESS, New York

Copyright © Manchester University Press 1993

While copyright in the volume as a whole is vested in
Manchester University Press, copyright in individual chapters
belongs to their respective authors, and no chapter may be
reproduced wholly or in part without the express permission in
writing of both author and publisher.

Published by Manchester University Press
Oxford Road, Manchester M13 9PL, UK
and Room 400, 175 Fifth Avenue,
New York, NY 10010, USA

Distributed exclusively in the USA and Canada
by St. Martin's Press, Inc.,
175 Fifth Avenue, New York, NY 10010, USA

British Library Cataloguing-in-Publication Data
A catalogue record for this book is available from the British Library

Library of Congress Cataloging-in-Publication Data
What is an author? / edited by Maurice Biriotti and Nicola Miller.
       p.   cm.
    Includes bibliographical references.
    ISBN 0-7190-3372-1 (hardback)
    1. Authorship.   2. Authors.   I. Biriotti, Maurice.   II. Miller, Nicola.
PN145.W44   1993
801' .95 – dc20   92-43924

ISBN 0 7190 3372 1 *hardback*

Printed in Great Britain
by Biddles Ltd, Guildford and King's Lynn

Contents

Part V Authorship and the academic world

Contributors

Philippa Berry is a Fellow of King's College, Cambridge, where she lectures in English.

Maurice Biriotti is University Lecturer in Latin-American Cultural Studies at the University of Birmingham.

Thomas Docherty is Professor of English, Trinity College, Dublin.

Terry Eagleton is Wharton Professor of Poetry and Fellow of Linacre College, Oxford.

Simon Goldhill is University Lecturer in Classics and Fellow of King's College, Cambridge.

Graham McCann is University Lecturer in Social and Political Science and Fellow of King's College, Cambridge.

Nancy K. Miller is Distinguished Professor of English, Lehman College and the Graduate Center, CUNY.

Henrietta Moore is Lecturer in Social Anthropology, London School of Economics.

Gayatri Chakravorty Spivak is Professor of Women's Studies at Columbia University, New York.

Andrew Wernick is Professor of Cultural Studies at Trent University, Ontario and Director of the Graduate Program in Methodologies for the Study of Western History and Culture.

Steve Woolgar is Reader in Sociology, Centre for Research into Innovation, Culture and Technology, Brunel the University of West London.

Introduction: authorship, authority, authorisation

Maurice Biriotti

Introducing the author

Roland Barthes announced the 'Death of the Author' in 1968.[1] The traditional, humanist concept of a single, human source of all meaning was discarded amid the clamour of disturbances and manifestations against authority all over Europe. Although Barthes was later to refine his categorical assertion, the declaration became arguably the most famous slogan for the fast-growing field of 'theory'. With the jettisoning of the Author as the source and guarantor of all meaning, the path was clear for the proliferation of questions about the process of reading. A revolution in thought had begun.

A year later, Foucault published the piece that lends its title to this collection.[2] In it, he challenges the notion that the author can simply disappear, and he posits the existence of a number of author-functions which are still current in the way people approach texts. These functions are historically-determined and culturally-specific categories whose effects persist. But Foucault calls for a time when authorship, and along with it the limitations on meaning that the author-functions impose, will no longer be regarded as a necessary idea, when there will be nothing more than the repeated refrain 'What difference does it make who's speaking?'

Foucault's analysis is based on an interrogative: 'What is an Author?' challenges 'The Death of the Author'. Despite his questioning of the Death, however, it is Foucault's evocation of an authorless world, rather than his insistence that we have not yet arrived at it, that dominates readings of the essay. As Gayatri Spivak puts it (in Chapter 6), 'Foucault's question "What is an Author?" has been construed by most readers as a rhetorical question to be answered in the negative.'

There is nothing new in the idea of the disappearance of the author: a tradition of textual exegesis that does not depend on a monolithic authorial source of meaning has existed for centuries, particularly in Biblical scholarship. But since the 1960s, part of the academy has been seduced by 'theory': the Death of the Author has become a commonplace among its practitioners.

Although new theoretical positions have emerged in the last few years which avoid a return to the old humanist conception of the Author, little has been published since 1969 that deals with authorship directly. This book invites a number of scholars (authorities) who work in different academic disciplines and from different theoretical perspectives to take up Foucault's challenge again. Written some twenty years after Barthes' dramatic declaration and Foucault's considered response, the essays collected here are sometimes complementary, sometimes contradictory. They all work with 'theory'. The aim of this introduction is to show how the pieces in this volume are part of a continuing debate on the nature of Authorship. There is no single way that 'theory' approaches this debate, but a multiplicity of strategies, of opinions, of intellectual and political commitments.

'Theory' and the author

The success of the declaration of the Death of the Author can be traced to a number of interrelated but different, and not necessarily complementary, developments in late twentieth-century thought. In order to understand the debates that follow, it is necessary to have some idea of these different strands. The following summary is not exhaustive (there are many other movements, and combinations of movements, which have appeared in the last twenty or thirty years). Nor does it hope to cover any of these strands adequately (the literature for each of them is vast), but simply to draw some of the lines of engagement which run through this collection.

1 Perhaps the earliest theoretical impulse to remove the Author was based on a discrediting of the concept of intentionality.[3] Traditionally, an author's intentions were considered the basis

for the 'meaning' of a text: a text meant literally what its author intended it to mean. Romantic notions of the individual and of the creative genius of the author dominated literary criticism.[4] Biographies were scrutinised for clues on the way the mind of the author functioned, on the personal and historical triggers that might have motivated the creation of the text.

The belief that the intentions of an author can be determined adequately in the first place, or, even if gleaned in some way, used to shed light on a text, has come under attack since Beardsley and Wimsatt published their influential essay 'The intentional fallacy' in 1954.[5] The problem of intentionality is a complex philosophical issue; Barthes' description of writing as an oblique space where all identity is lost provides a way of approaching texts that avoids some of the most profound problems generated by traditional criticism.

2   Barthes' declaration was part of a broader project in the 1960s: structuralism. Much has been written on this movement and I will not venture to summarise its roots and its different branches here.[6] But two strands relevant to this discussion can be outlined: first of all, structuralism, following the work of Saussure[7] in the early part of the century, insisted that the linguistic sign (e.g. word) was arbitrary and that therefore the link between language and the 'real world' was not straightforward. Secondly, concentrating on a socially determined structure rather than the intentional acts of individuals, structuralism launched an assault on the notion of human agency. This had obvious implications for approaches to authorship.

3   'The birth of the reader must be at the cost of the death of the author.'[8] Barthes' bold formulation can be read as part of a general move towards reader-based studies of texts. Barthes' insistence that the Death of the Author would make way for the pre-eminence of another subject, the reader, proved to be true only for some branches of 'theory': reception theory, hermeneutics and semiotics[9] all develop strategies in which the author is no longer the source of all meaning, but the processes of interpreting the text are the focus of critical attention. Studies which dealt with the role of the reader multiplied, especially in the 1970s and early 1980s.

4   Some contemporary critics, such as Teresa de Lauretis,[10] retain
    an interest in the position of the reader (in de Lauretis' case,
    especially the woman reading film narrative) within the text,
    but others have turned their attention elsewhere. A large number
    of critics have neither author nor reader in their sights, but the
    text itself.[11] For these critics, within the text, the signs play
    against each other in a chain of signification and difference.
    'Writing', or *écriture* is seen as slippery and evasive of any one
    stable meaning which could be attributed to any one author(ity).
    The notion of authority itself, with its investment in Being and
    Presence, is subjected to the most relentless scrutiny, in a philo-
    sophical tradition that owes much to Nietzsche and Heidegger.
    'Deconstruction' has shown that 'writing' is infinitely complex,
    infinitely susceptible to readings and misreadings, ironies and
    contradictions. Its analyses have challenged fixity in favour
    of a constant and uncompromising interrogation, a rigorous
    questioning that at once opens up and undermines (even its own)
    avenues of interpretation.

5   Underpinning many of these intellectual movements are political
    concerns. Through the institutional practices that govern the
    formation of the literary canon, and the establishment of taste
    and value, Authors come to acquire authority.[12] The naming of
    the author is ideologically overdetermined by the institutions of
    Literature. For those who take issue with the constructions of
    authority, combating the bourgeois values enshrined in the
    canon, and overturning the hierarchical distinction between high
    and low culture, become political imperatives in which the death
    of the humanist Author is one useful move.

        Traditionally, Western thinking has constructed the subject
    as white, male and bourgeois. Subjectivity, and indeed authorship
    itself, have been denied for huge portions of the population: those
    oppressed on the grounds of race, gender and sexuality. The death
    of the author, an attack on the humanist subject, with his im-
    plications in racism, sexism and imperialism, can therefore be
    seen as part of a strategy of political liberation.[13]

6   Since Freud, to speak of the subject has been to invoke a set
    of problems thrown up by contemporary debates in psycho-
    analysis.[14] Freud's work on the functioning of the unconscious,

of its desires and repressions, revolutionised beliefs on the nature of human subjectivity. It no longer seems possible to believe in a motivation based on straightforward intentions, or in simple relationships between the human character and its actions. Early attempts at incorporating these ideas into the processes of criticism focused on the Author's psyche, locating it as a site for speculation in an attempt to understand the complex motivation that lay behind the text. Developments in linguistics, however, undermined the notion that language could be used to understand intentions in such a straightforward way. Meanwhile, following new readings of Freud by such thinkers as Lacan and Deleuze,[15] the subject itself is now seen as 'split'. The notion of a single intending psyche which exists before and beyond language now seems hopelessly inadequate. Critical attention shifts instead to language itself, with all its slipperiness, its leakages, its ironies.

The 'Death of the Author'?

In very schematic form, the points above suggest just some of the changes in the intellectual landscape that have allowed the 'Death of the Author' to become such a powerful notion in contemporary 'theory'. These positions, as I have already indicated, may contradict one another, as is evidenced by Nancy Miller's piece, 'Changing the subject', already a feminist classic, which opens this collection.

Feminism's contribution to 'theory' is central. It is in feminist thought that the political consequences of 'theory' are most rigorously examined, that the critique of authority is at its most biting, that the most innovative work on subjectivity and the self is being produced. Significantly, perhaps, its contribution is frequently represented as marginal in the various key texts that seek to 'disseminate' literary theory.

Feminist theory rapidly became associated with the changes in the literary canon that the death of the Author made possible. With the demise of the male, humanist Author (lionised, canonised, anthologised) new possibilities for challenging the male-dominated literary canon emerge. But ironically, just at the time when different voices were being heard (black voices, women's voices, the voices of those in the margins), the Author's death denied authorship precisely to those who had only recently been empowered to claim it. Miller argues that the Death of the Author, therefore, should not apply to those subjects to whom subjectivity had, historically and traditionally, been denied. Miller's commitment to feminism causes her to question the consequences of poststructuralist 'theory' in the practice of writing and reading.

Miller's challenge to the Death of the Author questions the 'monolith of anonymous textuality' in favour of a recognition of the need not to foreclose the question of agency for women, but to recognise that, in history, women have 'not, I think (collectively), felt burdened by *too much* Self, Ego, Cogito, etc.' The article does not, however, imply a return to unexamined notions that underpinned traditional ideas about the subject writing. In the first place, it draws on contemporary ideas in psychoanalysis to suggest that new approaches to authorship must, as her title suggests, change the subject: that is to say take into account fragmentation, ambiguity, complexity. Secondly, Miller's turn to feminism does not imply an invocation of universalised notions of Woman which themselves derive from the representations and constructions of traditional readings. Miller's hope that 'we are becoming feminists' is therefore not a rallying call for identity politics, rather it is a suggestion of the complex work that is involved in challenging tradition 'beyond the always already provided identity of Woman with which we can only struggle'.

For Terry Eagleton, poststructuralist approaches to texts have potentially disastrous results: having usefully removed the author, and concentrating instead on 'difference' within the text, they banish the subject from the processes of making a meaning. At the same time as doing away with the author, 'poststructuralism thus managed to erase the true author or meaning-donor, which is the reader, interlocutor or audience'.

Eagleton's argument is based on an exploration of the political consequences of adopting such theoretical strategies to deal with authorship and the subject. In contrast to Nancy Miller's focus, however, the issue here is not the identity of the subject, but the implications that theories of the subject have for agency and political action. The piece is predicated on an insistence that political analysis must inform cultural criticism: it is this insistence that has made Eagleton's work controversial not only among scholars who oppose 'theory' but also among those whose work has a 'deconstructive' or psychoanalytic investment.

'Self-authoring subjects' traces the trajectory of Western notions of the subject between two extreme formulations: from Fichte's grounded idealism to contemporary notions of the 'decentred' subject inspired by Nietzsche. Eagleton is critical of both extremes. He questions Fichte's bourgeois humanism for its persistent call for fixity and its failure to take on board the slippery relationship between meaning, subjectivity and language. Postmodern formulations of the subject, meanwhile, are attacked for their failure to define a subject sufficiently centred to be capable of any sort of agency or action: '[W]e can't simply turn back to the old, largely discredited bourgeois-humanist subject; yet the sorts of subjects we have mostly been offered in its place would seem hardly capable of toppling a bottle off the wall, let alone of bringing down the state.'

In addition, Eagleton suggests that the Nietzschean notion of a 'ceaseless self-production', without the restraint of the authority of God, the family, religion, etc. (an impulse that aestheticises everything), may even have sinister implications, such as 'the riding of one's chariot over the decaying and diseased races'. Inextricably linked to the controversy surrounding the subject, theories of authorship are, according to Eagleton, always implicated in the most pressing political questions: each strategy may have profound consequences.

The responsibility of the critic

What both Nancy Miller and Terry Eagleton do, in very different ways, is to challenge the currency of the slogan 'The Death of the Author' on the grounds that its consequences precisely contradict the liberation from the shackles of authority which its declaration had so triumphantly heralded. The political stakes are clearly very high, and critics who have addressed these issues, wrestling with the responsibility that their engagement involves, can come up with startlingly different solutions.

For Thomas Docherty, there is little compromise. He argues that Modernist conceptions of the Author, in their idealist focus, are always implicated in the processes of legitimating texts. They thereby not only reinforce the institutional authority that feeds the creation of a literary canon, of bourgeois taste, etc., but also preclude a reading of the text that accords it its proper status in history. Docherty further argues that resorting to standard critical procedures associated with 'theory' – procedures that posit a notion of a transgressive authority – fare little better, resisting transgression even at the point at which it is invoked. The all-pervasive processes of authorisation are seen as an impediment to the liberating potential of criticism.

On the other hand, postmodernism, for Docherty, with its *mélange* of styles, its 'inherent drive [...] to deterritorialisation and immaterialisation', its confusion of tastes and genres, provides a way out of this impasse. It offers hope because it bypasses the rigid categories which dominate the institutionalised values of modernity. It allows, therefore, for a criticism that is not grounded in class-based, imperialist categorisations, but that defies rigid categories. The resulting displacement allows, according to Docherty, for a criticism that is 'divorced from the totalising pretensions of a modernist knowledge with its drive to power and mastery', and which will release the true historicity of texts and subjects.

According to this analysis, the mastery of being an author, of being implicated in the strategies of authorship, implies slavery. The solution conjures a radical decentring: a postmodern world in which the distinctions of taste and value are thoroughly undermined. For many critics the kind of picture Docherty paints raises fundamental questions. For instance: is ditching the authority of the author, and with it the literary canon, 'terrorism' as René Girard[16] puts it, in that it destroys what is of genuine value along with what is politically reprehensible? In the name of liberation, in other words, do we put too much at risk?

Such questions may lead to a rejection of postmodern values. Graham McCann, adopting a principled and ethical high ground, argues that '[c]riticism is oriented towards the future: the critic must believe that the conduct of other people can conform more closely to a moral standard than it does now [...] or that their institutions can be more justly organised than they are now. This belief is now under threat' from what McCann sees as the 'entrenched academic dogma' of 'theory'.

Drawing on the work of George Steiner, 'Distant voices, real lives' argues against the replacement of the authored text with an authorless 'textuality' for two reasons: Firstly, to kill the 'concept of the self because the self may kill does not extricate one from the cycle of violence.' Secondly, McCann insists that the removal of the author as a category from language removes also the responsibility of the subject writing. This responsibility is onerous. (It is an irony, for example, that just as poststructuralist debates that focus on the text and not the author gain currency, the power of language to represent, to do violence or to perpetuate prejudice has never been more clearly understood. The author's responsibility to avoid language that is racist, sexist, homophobic, etc., has never been articulated more insistently.) Theories of textuality, according to McCann, undermine such moral imperatives, and threaten the notion that the critic writes to do good.

The Rushdie affair: responses

In 1989/90, as the articles in this collection were being delivered as seminars at Cambridge, the publication of Salman Rushdie's *The satanic verses* was causing an international furore. Rushdie's novel, read by the religious authorities in Iran as insulting to Islam, led to an extraordinary *fatwa* or death sentence being meted out against Rushdie the individual. Rushdie went into hiding, and as the seminar series progressed, grim jokes on 'The Death of the Author' multiplied in bars and common rooms, as people discussed the latest paper.

Graham McCann's argument suggests that poststructuralist and, by implication, 'deconstructionist' approaches to texts, leave the question of authorship and responsibility out of the practice of reading. When the *fatwa* was declared against Salman Rushdie, McCann's two moral challenges became evident: firstly, how could one deal with the fact that this authorship affected 'real lives'?;

and secondly, how would critics (particularly poststructuralist critics) face up to the responsibility of writing about the case?

Responding to the Rushdie affair, Gayatri Spivak demonstrates that a poststructuralist approach need not be depoliticised: 'Reading *The satanic verses*' does not avoid the political implications of dealing with authorship, but confronts them head-on. Reading the Ayatollah as the author of the text, and Rushdie as merely the writer-performer, Spivak produces an analysis that is both 'deconstructive' and highly politically engaged.

Spivak's argument is complex, and it would be impossible to reduce it to a few bold traces here. But that is exactly my point: critics of poststructuralism often write as if 'theory' were some monolith which rested on a foundation of unexamined dogma. The reality is very different and much more complicated: Derrida's approach to the politics of authorship, which informs Spivak's reading, jettisons liberal humanist ideas of the author, but does not do away with the author altogether. Spivak makes a key distinction between Barthes' announcement of the death of the author and its subsequent adoption as 'a metropolitan aphorism' on the one hand, and Derrida's work on the autobiography of Nietzsche on the other. Far from insisting on the 'nothingness of the Author', Derrida views the author as present in excess, staged 'as author by the author' within the text. In Spivak's use of Derrida to shed light on a peculiarly sensitive instance of twentieth-century authorship, she has shown the subtlety and complexity of Derridean thought: 'deconstruction' has not denied the political implications of authorship. Quite the reverse. It has insisted that the proper name has, precisely, a politics.

The politics of the proper name, of the signature, functions not only in critical interpretations of the text, but also in the way the text operates within a literary market. Put crudely, the author's name sells books. For Andrew Wernick, adopting an approach that owes much to development in cultural studies, authorship today operates within the specific framework of the capitalist market and its promotional strategies. At the heart of his analysis is the notion that the author's name functions as a kind of brand-name, guaranteeing the value of the goods (the text) which one consumes (reads).

Wernick posits the idea that promotion can operate as a 'supplement' in our understanding of authorship. Like any supplement, it can either be taken in isolation (as a discreet theory of authorship) or in conjunction with other theories of the author. Through a close reading of some of the texts and events that emerged from the Rushdie affair, Wernick shows how this strategy can be deployed, and how the functioning of the name of the author in the literary market-place can be brought to the fore of literary theory. Wernick's argument does not reinstate the authority of the author as the humanist source of all meaning. But it does provide a way of dealing with the undeniable authority of the author (as an institution). As Spivak puts it, 'the Author function dies hard'; and Wernick's analysis provides a framework for a postmodern critique of that function.

Authorship and the literary tradition ʎ

What is clear from all this is that, since the declaration of the Death of the Author, the critical landscape has changed dramatically. An unquestioning acceptance of the authority of the canonical Author has come under attack. Several alternative strategies for dealing with authorship have been put in place. But, in schools and universities, in the media and even among some of the various branches of literary theory, the canon persists, and the names of authors (Shakespeare, Cervantes, Flaubert ... I choose at random) continue to exercise great authority. To conjure up these names is to authorise and legitimise one's own discourse. Literary authority is still current. Wernick's suggestion that these names function as promotional strategies is, perhaps, part of the story; but it still leaves the question of how precisely we approach the texts, how we read them within the canonical tradition.

Simon Goldhill argues that, although the insights of the master-theoreticians have challenged the very notion of authority, 'it is not by chance that Derrida, Foucault, Barthes, Freud, those modern masters who feature so strongly in this book, turn and return to what a recent commentator on Foucault has called the "tyranny of Greece"'. The classics are invoked time and again as the foundation

of contemporary thought, the basis upon which even the most
radical theory rests, the most canonical of all canons.

Through a close reading of three texts from the corpus of classical
literature, Goldhill shows that, while the citation of a series of
classical references is 'all too often a series of authoritative and
authorising quotations: the tag, the motto', classical texts resist
simple readings and sociological categorisations. 'As language
leaks, so texts go beyond the lines on the map.' In the crossfire of
irony, humour, subversion and contradiction, how can one position
the author's voice?

Through an analysis of the interplay between the texts and their
elements of parody and of citation, Goldhill draws a general
theoretical conclusion about the processes of authorship, of authorising a voice, of dealing with the authority of texts of the past.
'There is', Goldhill argues, 'an inevitable gap between the author's
voice and the voice of authority. This gap opens a space – *un écart*
in which writing as an author takes place.' No longer, in Goldhill's
analysis, is the author's voice perceived as a monumental authority,
but it is precisely in the 'gap' between that voice and authority
(the authority of the past, of the canon, etc.) that authorship can
be articulated.

Philippa Berry's argument is also based on a close reading of
canonical texts. Her focus is the late Renaissance period. This has
come to be regarded as a key moment in the development of modern
authorship: a moment at which attention shifts towards an 'increasingly complex awareness of language'. For obvious reasons, this
period has been especially interesting to literary critics influenced
by poststructuralism.

There is a suggestion that this interest in language replaces an
earlier fascination for images, colour, vision. Berry disputes this
and posits instead the emergence in this period of a new 'vision,
where motifs of substance as well as spirit are improbably interwoven in the critique of authorial identity'. The authorial crisis
which Berry describes is complex, 'dark'. Her argument links this
crisis with the themes of sexual difference that dominate late
Renaissance writing: authorial death reworked and redefined by
the experience of woman. The feminine shadows in Berry's reading
are suggestive of a new way of understanding the author: a way

that challenges traditional male thinking. These figures, therefore, 'dimly foreshadow the possibility of another kind of authorship, able to relinquish its ties to historical forms of authority'. In a new analysis of a canonical past, Berry (like Goldhill) indicates the complexity of the canon, the crises and paradoxes of authority.

Authorship and the academic world

For the critic, then, dealing with the author presents a number of complex problems. But these problems are compounded by the fact that the critic also writes, is also an author, is also implicated in the very structures of authority about which he or she writes. All disciplines have been subjected to analyses that question the strategies which authorise the academic text (and with it the academic author): its citation of the names of other authors, its legitimating rhetoric, its institutionally-sanctioned critical apparatus. The challenges of, among others, Ricoeur and de Certeau, Kuhn and Feyerabend[17] have problematised the notion of an 'objective' academic authority in history, in philosophy, in sociology, in science.

Steve Woolgar's contribution addresses the changes that post-structuralist thought has made to the study of science, perhaps the most authoritative of all discourses. Foucault identifies a divergence in the fate of science and literature: in the Middle Ages, it was science and not literature that required the name of an Author to legitimate it. In the seventeenth and eighteenth centuries, these roles are reversed: the literary text becomes, as a rule, authored, whereas for the scientific text, the role of the author disappears as a guarantee of truthfulness. In its quest for 'objectivity', science eliminates the subject; the Author in one sense disappears.

Woolgar examines the development of a new field: the sociology of scientific knowledge. This field has, he argues, been ready to associate itself with poststructuralist strategies to undermine authority. It is striking to note that, in contrast to literary criticism's adoption of the Death of the Author, one move in this endeavour is to reposition the author within the scientific text: this undermines science's claim to 'objectivity', and reinstates the subject at the centre of discourse.

Woolgar points out a key paradox in all this. The sociology of scientific knowledge is itself a science (a social science) whose practice is governed by the same rules of legitimation as the science it examines. The invocation of 'objectivity' is therefore a key factor in its own articulation, in its own rhetorical armoury. To effect the reinstatement of the Author of Science, the Author of Social Science must vanish.

Such problems are legion when one begins to examine authorship. How does one include oneself, one's own authorship, in the analysis one makes? More pertinently: how does one attack authority, even one's own, without becoming an authority figure oneself? Questions like these dominate this collection of essays, and lead to a number of different strategies (Thomas Docherty's constant reference to his own implication in the processes he denounces, for instance).

The authority of ethnography is perhaps the most politically-charged academic authority to invoke. A key discourse in the development of imperialism, it was used to bolster racist and colonialist ideologies in the nineteenth and early twentieth centuries. (Some might argue, despite the changes in anthropological methodology, that its involvement has not diminished.) It is not surprising to find that attacks on the authority of the white, male, colonialist ethnographer, marking out the peculiar 'primitive' otherness of peoples he studied were, and continue to be, so virulent.

Henrietta Moore's argument traces the development of anthropological authorship from missionaries' narratives in the nineteenth century to contemporary attempts to write a postmodern ethnography, which purport to avoid the authoritative attitudes to writing that had characterised the work of earlier scholars. In a sophisticated survey of the narrative strategies adopted by ethnographers, Moore analyses the key devices and metaphors which dominate the discipline.

Among other things, Moore's argument articulates some of the problems raised by postmodern ethnography: in particular, she argues that, however disjointed these narratives are, however complex and obscure, however decentred, they are still supremely authoritative, supremely male: 'We are no longer objective, comparative scientists, but self-reflexive, self-critical connected individuals. This newly valorised subject-position is no less male than the one which preceded it and its liberal credentials should be viewed with the same scepticism.'

The point that Moore makes has implications for the whole of 'theory'. To articulate a critique of authority is always itself an authoritative gesture. The names of 'theory's' favoured authors proliferate in this collection, in all their often unexamined mastery: Nietzsche, Heidegger, Freud, Lacan, Barthes, Foucault, Derrida, Deleuze ... These names inspire the same fears and desires as any roll-call from the old humanist canon: desire to read, to know, to master: fear of ignorance, fear of error, fear of 'theory' itself.

In attempting to explain some of the issues and arguments which run through this collection, this introduction has no doubt fallen prey to the perils of oversimplification and misinterpretation. Such are the problems of reading and writing. It is no doubt also implicated in all the processes of authorisation which the pieces in this volume criticise. As Simon Goldhill puts it, 'there's no eluding one's implication in authority, its strategies, ruses and institutions'. But the essays in this volume all demonstrate that it is imperative that the reader rigorously challenges the most commonsensical assumptions about authority. In the complex crossfire of their strategies and counter-strategies, together they suggest why it is that we return so insistently to the question: What is an Author?

Notes

1 R. Barthes, 'The death of the author', in R. Barthes, *Image–music–text*, trans. S. Heath (Glasgow: Fontana/Collins, 1977). See also his 'From work to text', in J. V. Harari, ed., *Textual strategies* (London: Methuen, 1979).

2 M. Foucault, 'What is an author?', in Harari, *Textual strategies*.

3 For a philosophical discussion of intentionality and its complexities, see J. R. Searle, *Intentionality. An essay in the philosophy of mind* (Cambridge: Cambridge University Press, 1983).

4 See P. Bourdieu, 'L'invention de la vie d'artiste', *Actes de la recherche en sciences sociales*, 2 mars 1975.

5 M. C. Beardsley and M. K. Wimsatt, 'The intentional fallacy', in *The verbal icon. Studies in the meaning of poetry* (Lexington, Ky: University of Kentucky Press, 1954).

6 For a fuller survey, see F. Jameson, *The prison house of language: a critical account of structuralism and Russian formalism* (Princeton: Princeton University Press, 1972), and R. Scholes, *Structuralism in literature* (New Haven: Yale University Press, 1974). See also C. Levi-Strauss, *Structural anthropology*, vol. 1 (London: Allen Lane, 1963).

7 See F. de Saussure, *Course in general linguistics*, trans. R. Harris (London: Duckworth, 1915).

8 Barthes, 'Death of the author', 148.

9 W. Iser, *The art of reading* (Baltimore: Johns Hopkins University Press, 1978); P. Ricoeur, *Interpretation theory* (Fort Worth: Texas Christian University Press, 1976); S. R. Suleiman and I. Crossman, eds, *The reader in the text* (Princeton: Princeton University Press, 1980); J. Kristéva, *Desire in language*, trans. L. Roudiez (Oxford: Basil Blackwell, 1980). See also J. Fish, *Is there a text in this class?* (Cambridge, Mass.: Harvard University Press, 1980).

10 T. de Lauretis, *Technologies of gender: essays on theory, film and fiction* (Bloomington: Indiana University Press, 1987). See also L. Mulvey, 'Visual pleasure and narrative cinema', in *Screen*, 16, 3 (1975).

11 See especially J. Derrida, *Writing and difference* (London: Routledge, 1978), and also G. C. Spivak, *In other words: essays in cultural politics* (London and New York: Routledge, 1987).

12 See R. Williams, *Marxism and literature* (Oxford: Oxford University Press, 1977), and also his *Problems in materialism and culture* (New York: Schoken, 1981) and *Culture* (New York: Schoken, 1982). See also T. Eagleton, *Marxism and literary criticism* (Berkeley and Los Angeles: University of California Press, 1976), and P. Bourdieu, *Distinction: a social critique of the judgment of taste*, trans. R. Nice (London: Routledge, 1984).

13 For challenges to the canon and traditional interpretations of it, see, among others, S. Gilbert and S. Gruber, *The madwoman in the attic: the woman writer in the nineteenth century literary imagination* (New Haven: Yale University Press, 1979) and H. L. Gates, ed., 'Race, writing and difference', special issue of *Critical Inquiry*, 12, 1 (1985).

14 See S. Freud, especially *On metapsychology: the theory of psychoanalysis*, vol. 10 (London: Pelican Freud Library, 1984).

15 See J. Lacan, *Ecrits: a selection* (London: Tavistock, 1977), especially 'The mirror stage as a formative of the function of the I'; G. Deleuze and F. Guattari, *Anti-Oedipus* (New York: Viking, 1977). Also J. Mitchell and J. Rose, eds, *Feminine sexuality: Jacques Lacan and the école Freudienne* (London: Macmillan, 1982); J. Gallop, *The daughter: seduction* (Ithaca: Cornell University Press, 1982); and T. Brennan, *Between feminism and psychoanalysis* (London: Routledge, 1980) for some of the most incisive and informative criticism.

16 R. Girard, 'Theory and its terror', in T. M. Kavanagh, ed., *The limits of theory* (Stanford, Ca.: Stanford University Press, 1989).

17 See P. Ricoeur, especially *Time and narrative*, vol. 3, trans. K. Blamey and D. Pallauer (Chicago and London: Chicago University Press, 1988); M. de Certeau, *L'écriture de l'histoire* (Paris: Editions de Seuil, 1975); T. Kuhn, *The structure of scientific revolution* (Chicago: Chicago University Press, 1962); and P. Feyerabend, *Farewell to reason* (London: Verso, 1987).

PART I

The death of the author?

Changing the subject:
authorship, writing and the reader

Nancy Miller

*In the spring of 1985 I wrote 'Changing the subject' for two con-
ferences that provided me with an occasion after 'Arachnologies'
to elaborate my thinking about the woman writer and her feminist
reader in relation both to questions of feminist theory and to the
various poststructuralist discussions of writing and sexual difference. The first of these events was held at the Pembroke Center,
Brown University, in March 1985; its agenda was flagged in the
punctuation of its title, 'Feminism/theory/politics'; the second,
held at the Center for Twentieth-Century Studies of the University
of Wisconsin-Milwaukee in April 1985, was entitled 'Feminist
studies: reconstituting knowledge'.*

*The session at which I spoke at the Pembroke conference was
called 'The feminist politics of interpretation', and the panellists
were asked to reflect upon a crux of issues very similar to the
general charge of the Milwaukee conference as Teresa de Lauretis
described it in her opening remarks (now the introduction to*
Feminist Studies/Critical Studies). *Both call for an interrogation
of the current state of feminist projects: 'What is specifically
feminist about the varieties of feminist critical practice? Are
feminist strategies of reading written and visual texts transferable
to the study of such things as social and political institutions?'
(Pembroke conference, emphasis added). In de Lauretis's letter to
participants: 'there are a general uncertainty, and among feminists,
serious differences as to what the specific concerns, values and
methods of feminist critical work are, or ought to be ... Speakers
will seek to identify the specificity of feminism as a critical theory'
(Milwaukee conference, emphasis added).*

These are not easy questions, and in this essay I have not attempted to describe the specificity of feminist theory and practice directly. Instead I have chosen to rehearse a certain number of positions against, from, and through which feminist critical theory might define itself as it emerges within the discourse of literary studies. This rehearsal identifies two chronologies, poststructuralist and feminist; two rhetorics, dilatory and hortatory; and, to return to the figure of the 'exquisite dance of textual priorities' named by Hortense Spillers and evoked by de Lauretis at the opening of the conference (13), two moves, or rather a hesitation between, say, the calls of a square dance and the ritual of a minuet, as the dance searches for the right steps and rhythm, perhaps the waltz satirised by Dorothy Parker, or as one of the participants suggested after the conference, the foxtrot (which has interesting possibilities).[1]

Though I may indeed be looking for a third tropology (in the feminist spirit of always mapping the territory of future perspectives), I want just as strongly to leave the hesitation in place, and refuse the temptation of a synthesis, because the question forming before us is none other than the question of female subjectivity, the formation of female critical subjects. And this, in face of the current trend toward the massive deconstitution of subjectivity, is finally the figure I'm looking for.

Authorship, writing and the reader

The question of authorship has been on the agenda of intellectuals and literary critics in France since at least 1968, a date that also marks a certain theoretical repositioning in political and social chronologies. In 1968, for example, Roland Barthes contended in 'The death of the author' that the author, as we have known him, has lost what was thought to be a 'natural' authority over his work. The author gives way to *writing*, a theory and practice of textuality which, Barthes argued then, 'substitutes language itself for the person who until then had been supposed to be its owner' (p. 143). From such a perspective, the emergence of this disembodied and ownerless *écriture* in fact requires the author's suppression.[2] In the structuralist and poststructuralist debates about subjectivity, authority, and the status of the text that continue to occupy and preoccupy the critical market-place, the story of the author's disappearance has remained standard currency.

Now, to the extent that the author, in this discourse, stands as a kind of shorthand for a whole series of beliefs about the function of the work of art as (paternally authorised) monument in our culture, feminist criticism in its own negotiations with mainstream hegemonies might have found its positions joined by the language of those claims. It is, after all, the author anthologised and institution-alised who by his (canonical) presence excludes the less-known works of women and minority writers and who by his authority justifies the exclusion. By the same token, feminist criticism's insistence on the importance of the reader – on positing the hypothesis of her existence – might have found affinities with a position that understands the Birth of the Reader as the necessary counterpoint to the Death of the Author. (Barthes actually puts it a good deal more apocalyptically: 'the birth of the reader must be at the cost of the death of the Author' (p. 148).)

The political potential of such an alliance, however, has yet to be realised. The removal of the author has not so much made room for a revision of the concept of authorship as it has, through a variety of rhetorical moves, repressed and inhibited discussion of any writing identity in favour of the (new) monolith of anonymous textuality or, in Foucault's phrase, 'transcendental anonymity' (p. 120). If 'writing', then, as Barthes describes it, 'is that neutral, composite, oblique space where our subject slips away, the negative where all identity is lost, starting with the very identity of the body writing' (p. 142), it matters not *who* writes. In the same way, the shift that moves the critical emphasis from author to reader, from the text's origin to its destination, far from producing a multiplicity of addressees, seems to have reduced the possibility of differentiating among readers altogether: 'the reader', Barthes declares, 'is without history, biography, psychology' (p. 148). What matters who reads? The reader is a space and a process. The reader is only '*someone*' written *on*. (I also think that the failure of an effective critical alliance is more generally due to the fact that the relationship between mainstream feminism and the practices and positions that have come to be grouped together under the label of deconstruction or poststructuralism in US academic scenes has

not been one of a *working* complicity: of fighting the same institutional battles. But this deserves a discussion of its own.)

*I want none the less to make a distinction between the asymmet-
rical demands generated by different writing identities – male and
female, or more perhaps more usefully, hegemonic and marginal.
It is inarguable that the destabilisation of the paternal – patriarchal,
really – authority of authorship (Milton's, for example) brought
about through deconstruction has been an enabling move for
feminist critics. But it does not address the problem of his 'bogey'
at the level of subjectivity formation. The effect of his identity and
authority on a female writing identity remains another matter and
calls for other critical strategies. The psychological stress of that
negotiation in literature for the nineteenth-century woman writer
has been formulated dramatically by Gilbert and Gubar in Madwoman in the Attic. Here I am trying to resituate that question at
the level of theory itself, or rather theory's discourse about its own
project.*

So why remember Barthes, if this model of reading and writing
by definition excludes the question of an identity crucial to feminist
critical theory? Well, for one thing because Barthes' interest in the
semiotics of literary and cultural activity – its pleasures, dangers,
zones, and codes of reference – intersects thematically with a
feminist emphasis on the need to situate, socially and symbolically,
the practices of reading and writing. Like the feminist critic, Barthes
manoeuvres in the spaces of the tricky relations that bridge the
personal and the political, the personal and the critical, the interpersonal and the institutional (his seminar, for example). Barthes
translates seductively from within French thought the more arduous
writings of Derrida, Lacan, Kristéva, for or into literature; and in
the same gesture represents metonymically outside the Parisian
scene (or in North American literature departments) most of the
concepts that animate feminist (and other) literary critics not
hostile to Theory's stories: currently, the poststructuralist epistemologies of the subject and the text, the linguistic construction of
sexual identity.

In the preface to *Sade, Fourier, Loyola* (1971) Barthes returns to
the problem of authorship: 'For if,' he writes, 'through a twisted
dialectic, the Text, destroyer of all subjects, contains a subject to

love – *un sujet à aimer* – that subject is dispersed, somewhat like the ashes we strew into the wind after death' (p. 8). And he continues poignantly in the same sentence, 'were I a writer, and dead [*si j'étais écrivain, et mort*] how I would love it if my life, through the pains of some friendly and detached biographer, were to reduce itself to a few details, a few preferences, a few inflections, let us say: to "biographemes"' (p. 9). What interests me here, more than yet another nomination, another code, is Barthes' acknowledgement of the persistence of the subject as the presence in the text of perhaps not some*one* to love in person, but the mark of the need to be loved, the persistence of a peculiarly human(ist?) desire for connection. It is as though thinking of a writer's life – a 'life' of Sade, a 'life' of Fourier appended to a reading of their writing – generated a thinking of self: for Barthes then imagines himself 'a writer'.[3] But we have just seen the writer is already dead, his ashes scattered to the winds; and the self fatally dispersed. Thus no sooner is the subject restored metaphorically to a body through love, than he is dispersed figuratively through death. If one is to find the subject, he will not be in one place, but modernly multiple and atopic.

Will *she*?

The postmodernist decision that the Author is Dead and the subject along with him does not, I will argue, necessarily hold for women, and prematurely forecloses the question of agency for them. Because women have not had the same historical relation of identity to origin, institution, production that men have had, they have not, I think, (collectively) felt burdened by *too much* self, ego, cogito, etc. Because the female subject has juridically been excluded from the polis, hence decentred, 'disoriginated', deinstitutionalised, etc., her relation to integrity and textuality, desire and authority, displays structurally important differences from that universal position.

In Breaking the Chain, *Naomi Schor takes up Barthes' analysis in S/Z of the cultural discourse on 'femininity', which he locates for the sake of argument in a passage from Balzac's* Sarrasine. *Curiously, this is also the passage that serves as the opening citation of 'The death of the author': 'This was woman herself...' (etc.). Following Schor's lead, it is interesting to puzzle the*

connections that for Barthes join écriture *and 'woman' in a defini-*
tion of textuality that refuses a coherent subjectivity.

In 'Mapping the postmodern' Andreas Huyssen asks: 'Isn't the
"death of the subject/author" position tied by mere reversal to the
very ideology that invariably glorifies the artist as genius, whether
for marketing purposes or out of conviction and habit? ... [D]oesn't
poststructuralism, where it simply denies the subject altogether,
jettison the chance of challenging the ideology of the subject (as
male, white, and middle-class) by developing alternative and
different notions of subjectivity?' (p. 44).*

*In 'Women Who Write Are Women', Elaine Showalter, arguing
against Cynthia Ozick's belief (subsequently rearticulated by Gail
Godwin in the same publication) that 'writing transcends sexual
identity, that it takes place outside of the social order', pointedly
observes that in the gender asymmetry of dominant culture 'the
female witness, sensitive or not, is still not accepted as first-person
universal' (p. 33).*

It seems to me, therefore, that when the so-called crisis of the
subject is staged, as it generally is, within a textual model, that
performance must then be recomplicated by the historical, political,
and figurative body of the woman writer. (That is, of course, if we
accept as a working metaphor the location of women's subjectivity
in female authorship.) Because the discourse of the universal
historically has failed to include the testimony of its others, it
seems imperative to question the new doxa of subjectivity at this
juncture of its formation.

Feminist critics in the United States have on the whole resisted
the fable of the author's demise on the grounds that stories of
textuality which trade in universals – the author or the reader –
in fact articulate marked and differentiated structures of what
Gayatri Spivak has called masculine 'regulative psychobiography'.
Feminist critics, I argue in 'The text's heroine', have looked to the
material of the female authorial project as the scene of perhaps a
different staging of the drama of the writing subject. But what does
it mean to read (for) the woman writer when the Author is Dead?
Or, how can 'reading as a woman' – a deconstructionist phrasing
of a reconstructionist feminist project – help us rethink the act
of reading as a politics? I'd like to see a more self-conscious and

deliberate move away from what I think remains in dominant critical modes, a *metaphysics* of reading. As Foucault asks in 'What is an author': 'In granting a primordial status to writing (*écriture*), do we not, in effect, simply reinscribe in transcendental terms the theological affirmation of its sacred origin?' (p. 120).

In her presentations at both the Pembroke and the Milwaukee conferences, Spivak contrasted the psychobiography of a male subjectivity based on naturalised access to dominant forms of power with that of the 'postmodern female subject' created under late capitalism (emblematised by the hegemony of the computer chip): women of colour whom imperialism constructs as a permanent casual labour force doing high-tech work for the multinationals. Her relation to networks of power is best understood through the concept of 'women in the integrated circuit', which Donna Haraway describes as 'the situation of women in a world ... intimately restructured through the social relations of science and technology' (pp. 84–5). It is not self-evident what form testimony would take in such an economy.

Speaking from within a certain 'new French feminism', Hélène Cixous makes a homologous argument for the need to recognise a deuniversalised subjectivity: 'until now, far more extensively and repressively than is ever suspected or admitted, writing has been run by a libidinal and cultural – hence political, typically masculine – economy' (p. 879). This definition of a sexually 'marked writing' that expresses and valorises masculine access to power emerges from the critique of phallogocentrism, but because of its place in the network of Derridean operations, it remains at odds with the reconstructive impulses of much feminist literary criticism in the United States: the analysis of canon formation and reformation through the study and valorisation of women's writing.

Thus, in his concluding remarks to the section of On deconstruction *devoted to feminist criticism, Jonathan Culler builds on Peggy Kamuf's troping of signature and identity in 'Writing as a woman': 'For a woman to read as a woman is not to repeat an identity or an experience that is given but to play a role she constructs with reference to her identity as a woman, which is also a construct, so that the series can continue: a woman reading as a woman reading as a woman' (p. 64). The question for feminist critical theory is how to imagine a relation between this logic of deferral and the immediate complexities of what Adrienne Rich calls 'a politics of location' (Blood, bread, and poetry, p. 215).*

I want to offer one kind of political reading with a passage from a famous account of a female 'psychobiography'. I take it as an example of what has been characterised as the 'first moment' or first stage of feminist criticism, a criticism Jonathan Culler describes as 'based on the presumption of continuity between the reader's experience and a woman's experience' (p. 46). The account is Adrienne Rich's 'When we dead awaken: writing as re-vision', which, she explains in a retrospective frame, was originally given as a talk on 'The woman writer in the twentieth century' in a forum sponsored by the Commission on the Status of Women in the Profession at the MLA in 1971. I cite Rich's return to the context of her talk by way of suggesting that we review these issues *both* in 'women's time' and in men's, the Eastern Standard Time of mainstream events. (I'm referring here to Elaine Showalter's personal take on the history of feminist criticism.)[4]

Rich notes:

A lot is being said today about the influence that the myths and images of women have on all of us who are products of culture. I think it has been a peculiar confusion to the girl or woman who tries to write because she is peculiarly susceptible to language. She goes to poetry or fiction looking for *her* way of being in the world, since she is looking eagerly for guides, maps, possibilities; and over and over ... she comes up against something that negates everything she is about: she meets the image of Woman in books written by men. She finds a terror and a dream, she finds a beautiful pale face, she finds La Belle Dame Sans Merci, she finds Juliet or Tess or Salomé, but precisely what she does not find is that absorbed, drudging, puzzled, sometimes inspired creature, herself, who sits at a desk trying to put words together. (p. 39)

Rich's woman 'susceptible to language', like Roland Barthes, goes to literature as a *writing subject*: she does not, however, find there 'un sujet à aimer'. She finds instead, a terror and a dream. To find 'somebody to love', as the song goes, Rich, like Barthes, would have to find someone somehow *like her* in her desire for a place in the discourse of art and identity from which to imagine and image a writing self – 'absorbed, drudging, puzzled' – at a desk. For the girl 'susceptible to language' the words have established a split she cannot overcome: Woman whose image, whose 'beautiful pale face' has installed in her place a regime of the specular and excluded her from production.[5] Woman leaves the woman poet in exile.

In her 1983 essay, 'Blood, bread, and poetry: the location of the poet' (where she outlines the borders of scenes of writing in North America and in Central America), Rich returns to the biography of her reading, or the history of its subject, to develop in more explicitly political terms the implications of the split between the girl and the poet, 'the girl who wrote poems, who defined herself in writing poems, and the girl who was to define herself by her relationships with men' (p. 40). To close 'the gap between poet and woman', Rich argues here, the fragmentation within the writing subject requires the context of a 'political community' (p. 536). For Rich, on *this* side of identity, the condition of dispersal and fragmentation Barthes valorises (and fetishises) is not to be achieved, but overcome:

> I write for the still-fragmented parts in me, trying to bring them together. Whoever can read and use any of this, I write for them as well. I write in full knowledge that the majority of the world's illiterates are women, that I live in a technologically advanced country where forty per cent of the people can barely read and twenty per cent are functionally illiterate. I believe that these facts are directly connected to the fragmentations I suffer in myself, that we are all in this together. (p. 540)

In 'Blood, bread, and poetry', Rich maps the geopolitics of a poetics of gender. This vision of a global context for women's writing emerges from a programme of text production as a collective project. In the 1960s, under the logic of 'the personal is the political', the communication with the community involved writing 'directly and overtly as a woman, out of a woman's experience', taking 'women's existence seriously as theme and source for art' (p. 535). In 'When we dead awaken', Rich had contrasted this euphoric turn to feminocentric production – a more prosaic, or rather less lyrical account of the agenda valorised by Cixous (in 'The laugh of the Medusa') – with the anxieties of the 1950s where, she writes,

'I began to feel that my fragments and scraps had a common consciousness and a common theme, one which I would have been
very unwilling to put on paper at an earlier time because I had
been taught that poetry should be "universal", which meant, of
course, nonfemale' (p. 44). In the 1980s, the formula 'the personal
is the political' requires a redefinition of the personal to include
most immediately an interrogation of ethnocentrism; a poetics of
identity that engages with the 'other woman'.[6] If for Rich in 1971
the act of women's reading as a critique of the dominant literature
was seen not merely as 'a chapter in cultural history' (p. 135) but
as 'an act of survival', in 1983 the act of women's writing became
inseparable from an expanded definition of, and expanded attention
to, the social field in which the practices of reading and writing
are located and grounded. Now the question arises, if the ethics
of feminist writing involve writing for the woman who doesn't
read – to push this model to its limits – then what would be
required of a responsive, responsible feminist reading?

The question will remain open and generate other questions.
Does the specificity of feminist theory entail reading for the other
woman? Would this mean reading *as* the other woman? In her place?
Wouldn't this assumption reinstate a universal or an interchange-
ability of women under the name of woman and thereby 'collapse',
as Denise Riley put it to me at the Pembroke conference, 'the
different temporalities of "women"' which she glosses as 'the
uneven histories of the different formations of different categories
of "women" from the side of politics'? In more strictly literary
terms, I would now say that we must think carefully about the
reading effects that derive from a poetics of transparence – writing
directly from one's own experience, especially when doubled by
an ethics of wholeness – joining the fragments.

*Rich speaks in this essay of her discovery of the work of con-
temporary Cuban women poets in a book edited by Margaret
Randall called* Breaking the silences. *And it is in part because
of reading this book (her* tolle e lege*) that she decides to go to
Nicaragua (a decision which provides the occasion for 'Blood,
bread, and poetry'). To what extent does this active/activist model
of reading establish the grounds for a prescriptive esthetics – a
'politically correct' programme of representation – of the sort that*

shaped the arguments of Barbara Smith and Sondra O'Neale at the Milwaukee conference? [7]

Against the necessarily utopian rhetoric of an unalienated art that Rich reads in Cuban women poets ('the affirmation of an organic relation between poetry and social transformation' (p. 537), I want now to juxtapose the discourse with which I began this discussion of critical strategies. On the back jacket to *Sade, Fourier, Loyola* Barthes states the 'theoretical intention' of his project. It is a kind of self-referential challenge: to discover 'how far one can go with a text speaking only of its writing (*écriture*); how to suspend its signified in order to liberate its materialist deployment'. 'Isn't the social intervention achieved by a text', he asks rhetorically, located in the 'transport' of its writing, rather than in the 'message of its content'? In the pages of the preface, Barthes addresses the problem of the 'social responsibility of the text', maintaining that since there is 'today no language site outside bourgeois ideology', 'the only possible rejoinder' to, say, the establishment, is 'neither confrontation, nor destruction, but only theft: fragment the old text of culture, science, literature, and change its features according to formulae of disguise, as one disguises (*maquille*) stolen goods' (p. 10). We see here the double move we saw earlier in 'Death of the author': on the one hand disperse the subject, on the other, fragment the text, and repackage it for another mode of circulation and reception.

Dispersion and fragmentation, the theft of language and the subversion of the stereotype attract Barthes as critical styles of desire and deconstruction, rupture and protest. Certain women writers in France like Hélène Cixous, Luce Irigaray, and I would argue, paradoxically, Monique Wittig, have also been attracted to this model of relation: placing oneself at a deliberately oblique (or textual) angle to intervention. Troped as a subversion – a political intertextuality – this positionality remains in the end, I think, a form of negotiation within the dominant social text, and ultimately, a local operation.

Because it is also my sense that the reappropriation of culture from within its own arenas of dissemination is still a political urgency, I will recast my earlier question about the female subject in feminist theory to ask more narrowly now: what does it mean to read and write as a woman *within* the institutions that authorise and regulate most reading and writing in the university?

'Oubliez les professeurs'

In Charlotte Brontë's *Villette* acute attention is paid to the construction of female subjectivity, and in particular to the way in which female desire as quest aligns itself uneasily with the question of mastery (including, importantly, mastery of the French language), mastery and knowledge within an academy necessarily, in 1853, a female one. In the scene I will review here, the heroine, Lucy Snowe, is dragged off to be examined by two professors, 'Messieurs Boissec and Rochemorte' (the etymology is of course motivated). This examination perceived by Lucy as a 'show-trial' set up to prove that she indeed was the author of a remarkable essay the men suspected their colleague M. Emmanuel, Lucy's professor/friend, of having written for her (forging her signature in order to document his pedagogical agency) provides us with a vivid account of the institutional power arrangements that historically have constructed female experience. These two specimens of deadwood interrogate Lucy:

> They began with classics. A dead blank. They went on to French history. I hardly knew Mérovée from Pharamond. They tried me in various 'ologies, and still only got a shake of the head, and an unchanging 'Je n'en sais rien.' (p. 493)

Unwilling or unable to reply, Lucy asks permission to leave the room.

> They would not let me go: I must sit down and write before them. As I dipped my pen in the ink with a shaking hand, and surveyed the white paper with eyes half-blinded and overflowing, one of my judges began mincingly to apologize for the pain he caused. (p. 494)

They name their theme: 'Human Justice'.

> Human Justice! What was I to make of it? Blank, cold abstraction, unsuggestive to me of one inspiring idea … (p. 495)

Lucy remains blocked until she remembers that the two examiners were in fact known to her; 'the very heroes' who had 'half frightened (her) to death' (p. 495) on the night of her arrival in Villette. And suddenly, thinking how little these men deserved their current status as judges and enforcers of the law, Lucy falls, as she puts it, 'to work'.

> 'Human Justice' rushed before me in novel guise, a red, random beldame with arms akimbo. I saw her in her house, the den of confusion: servants called to her for orders or help which she did not give; beggars stood at her door waiting and starving unnoticed; a swarm of children, sick and quarrelsome, crawled round her feet and yelled in her ears appeals for notice, sympathy, cure, redress. The honest woman cared for none of these things. She had a warm seat of her own by the fire, she had her own solace in a short black pipe, and a bottle of Mrs Sweeny's soothing syrup; she smoked and she sipped and she enjoyed her paradise, and whenever a cry of the suffering souls about her pierced her ears too keenly – my jolly dame seized the poker or the hearth-brush ... (pp. 495–6)

Writing 'as a woman', Lucy Snowe domesticates the public allegories of Human Justice. Her justice is not blind (hence serenely fair), but deaf to the pathetic cries that invade her private space: arbitrary and visibly self-interested, marked not by the sword and scales of neo-classical iconography, Lucy's 'red, random beldame' smokes her pipe and sips her syrup.

However perversely, I am tempted to take this scene in which a woman is brought forcibly to writing as a parable of – which is not to say a recommendation for – the conditions of production for female authorship (or for the practice of feminist criticism). Because she reappropriates the allegory of timeless indifference particularised through the identification of the men and fictionalised through the imagined body of an ageing woman, Lucy both overcomes the terror of the blank page and undermines the regime of a universal self-reference.

I should perhaps have mentioned that the chapter in which this writing out takes place opens with a line rich in implications for the conclusion of my argument: 'Oubliez les professeurs'. Now in context, this imperative is a warning issued by Mme Beck that Lucy not think of M. Paul for herself. But clearly in this collegial psychodrama the relation to *him* is not only a question of female rivalry and the love plot. As I have just suggested, the scene asks more generally the question of women's relation to the arbitrariness of male authority, to the grounds of their power and their laws.

Lucy, we know, can't forget her particular professor, for she is moved more than she will say by his offer of friendship. But in her apprenticeship to the world of work, she has learned to make distinctions. To accept M. Paul does not mean that she accepts the system of institutional authorisation in which their relation is inscribed. Nor is the point of her essay, its style, lost on M. Paul who, having read the exam paper, calls her 'une petite moqueuse et sans coeur' (p. 496). Lucy's mockery, which is the flip side of her pathos, could also be figured as irony, which is, I think, a trope that by its status as the marker of a certain distance to the truth, suits the rhetorical strategies of the feminist critic.[8]

The chapter in which the scene of writing is staged is called 'Fraternity', for it is here that M. Paul asks Lucy to be the 'sister of a very poor, fettered, burdened, encumbered man'. His offer of 'true friendship' (p. 501), of a 'fraternal alliance' (p. 503), while not exempt from its own ironies, none the less announces a less depressing mode of relations between women and institutional authorities than that of the 'daughter's seduction' diagnosed by Jane Gallop, for it figures a working ground of parity.[9] At the end of Brontë's novel, through the enabling terms of the alliance, Lucy Snowe has not only her own seat by the fire but her own house and school for girls. Within that space, she makes Paul a 'little library'; he whose mind, she had said earlier, was her library, through which she 'entered bliss' (p. 472). And of course, in his absence, and in his place, she writes the narrative of *Villette*.

This being said, one might, in the final analysis, do better to restore to the fraternal its historical dimensions. Women writers' idealisation of fraternity belongs to a long and vexed tradition of feminist discourse about equality and difference that in 1949 provided Simone de Beauvoir with the last words of *The second sex*: 'To gain the supreme victory, it is necessary ... that by and through their natural differentiation men and women unequivocally affirm their brotherhood' (*fraternité*) (p. 814).

Subject to change

In 1973, in an essay called 'Toward a woman-centered university', Adrienne Rich described her vision of a future for feminist studies. In it we read: 'The university I have been trying to imagine does not seem to me utopian, though the problems and contradictions to be faced in its actual transformations are of course real and severe' (p. 153). Yet looking back over the past ten to fifteen years of women's studies, can we say that 'masculine resistance to women's claims for full humanity' (as Rich defines the project) has been overcome in any serious way? Nothing could be less sure.

In fact, I think that though we may have our women's studies programmes, our centres, journals, and conferences, feminist scholars have not succeeded in instituting the transformative claims we articulated in the heady days of the mid-1970s. Supported by the likes of William Bennett, Rochemorte and Boissec are going strong: they continue to resist, and to attack, feminism's fundamental understanding that the deployment of the universal is inherently, if paradoxically, partial and political. And the M. Pauls, who like Terry Eagleton *et al.* offer friendship and the promise of 'fraternal alliance', seem to be saying at the same time: 'feminism is theoretically thin, or separatist. Girls, shape up!' (Spivak, 'The politics of interpretations', p. 277). More serious, perhaps, because it is supported by the prestige of philosophy, the ultimate purveyor of universals, is the general failure on the part of most male theorists, even those most interested in 'feminine identity', to articulate sufficiently in the terms of their own enunciation what Rosi Braidotti calls 'the radical consciousness of one's own complicity with the very power one is trying to deconstruct' (Ms.). Like the humanists, they have not begun to question the grounds on which they stand, their own relation to the 'sexual differential' that inhabits '*every* voice' (Spivak, p. 277); their own difference from the universal, from the institution which houses them and from which they speak.

But we have of course participated in our own failure to challenge the ''ologies' and their authorities in a significant way. Our greatest strength in the 1970s, I would argue, was our experience, through consciousness raising, of the possibility of a collective identity resistant to but intimately bound up with Woman – in fact our account, analysis, and valorisation of experience itself (de Lauretis makes the point forcefully at the end of *Alice doesn't*). For reasons I cannot fully articulate here, but which have to do on the one hand with the difficulty of constructing theoretically the discourse of women's experience, a difficulty derived in part from the feminist bugaboo about essentialism – which can only be understood in relation to a massively theorised 'antiessentialism' (Russo, p. 228); and on the other, particularly for those of us working in things French, with the prestige of a regime of accounts of post-gendered subjectivities, we seem to have become stuck between two varieties of self-censorship.

In the face of a prevailing institutional indifference to the question of women, conjoined with a prevailing critical ideology of the subject which celebrates or longs for a mode beyond difference, where and how to move? On what grounds can we remodel the relations of female subjects to the social text? In the issue of *Tulsa Studies* devoted to the current state of feminist criticism (republished in *Feminist Issues in Literary Scholarship*) there is at least one pressing call to forget the professors, theorists masculine and feminine, to 'reject male formalist models for criticism' in the belief, Jane Marcus writes, that 'the practice of formalism professionalizes the feminist critic and makes her safe for academe' ('Still practice', p. 90). We must, I think, see this as too simple. Not only because, as Nina Auerbach argues in the same issue, 'whether we like it or not, we live in one world, one country ... one university department with men' (p. 155), but because we don't. If women's studies is to effect institutional change through critical interventions, we cannot afford to proceed by a wholesale dismissal of 'male' models. Rather, like Lucy in the school play (in another forced performance), who refuses to play a man's part dressed in men's clothes and instead assumes '*in addition*' to her 'woman's garb' the signifiers of masculinity (p. 209, emphasis added), the effectiveness of future feminist intervention calls for an ironic manipulation of the semiotics of performance.[10]

Earlier in *Villette*, Ginevra pressed Lucy to explain herself, to reveal some deeper truth that seems to elude her grasp: 'Who *are* you, Miss Snowe?' And Lucy, 'amused at her mystification', replies,

'Who am I indeed? Perhaps a personage in disguise. Pity I don't look the character' (pp. 392–3). But Ginevra is not satisfied with this flip account: 'But *are* you anybody?' This time Lucy is slightly more forthcoming, supplying information, at least, about her social insertion: 'Yes ... I am a rising character: once an old lady's companion, then a nursery-governess, now a school-teacher' (p. 394). Ginevra persists in thinking there is more to Lucy than Lucy will say, but Lucy will offer nothing more. If we take Lucy Snowe's account of herself at face value, not persisting like Ginevra in a hermeneutics of revelation that is structured, Barthes has taught us, on oedipal narratologies, we begin to take the measure of Brontë's radical achievement in this novel: creating a heroine whose identity is modulated through the cadences of work; through the effects of institutions. This is not to suggest that Lucy's subjectivity is recontained by a work history, circumscribed by its hierarchies of class. On the contrary, we have seen Ginevra's conviction that despite the institutional inscription, Lucy somehow continues to escape her, not only because Ginevra is looking for a social language she can understand – 'a name, a pedigree' – but because in some palpable and troubling way, Lucy, like the Lacanian subject she anticipates, also resides elsewhere in the 'field of language' which constitutes her otherness to herself (Mitchell, p. 241).

I want to float the suggestion, then, and by way of a gesture towards closure, that any definition of the female writing subject not universalised as Woman that we try to theorise now must include Lucy Snowe's ambiguities: in work, in language. This is a process that recognises what Elizabeth Weed describes as the 'impossible ... relation of women to Woman' (p. 74) and acknowledges our ongoing contradictions, the gap and (and perhaps permanent) internal split that makes a collective identity always a horizon, but a necessary one.[11] It is a fragmentation we can, however, as feminist readers work with and through. This is the move of resistance and production that allows Lucy to find language 'as a woman' despite the power of the ' 'ologies', despite the allegory of *human* justice.

At the end of 'Femininity, narrative, and psychoanalysis' (1982), an essay in which she takes as her example Emily Brontë's

Wuthering heights, *Juliet Mitchell outlines a question by way of*
providing herself with a solution of closure to her discussion of
the female (writing) subject and a critique of Kristéva's valorisation
of the semiotic, the heterogeneous space of the subject-in-process.
To her own question of what identity and text might mean con-
strued along the lines of such a theoretical model – 'in the process
of becoming what?' – *Mitchell responds: 'I do not think that we*
can live as human subjects without in some sense taking on a
history; for us, it is mainly the history of being men or women
under bourgeois capitalism. In deconstructing that history, we
can only construct other histories. What are we in the process of
becoming?' (p. 294).

Mitchell shrewdly leaves the question open, but since this is my
essay and not hers, I have felt it important to risk a reply. At the
Pembroke conference, I ended by saying: I hope we are becoming
women. Because such a reply proved too ironic to occupy the
privileged place of the last word, I will now say: I hope we are
becoming feminists. In both phrases, however, the hope I express
for a female future is a desire for all that we don't know *about what*
it might mean to be women beyond the always already provided
identity of Women with which we can only struggle; the hope for
a negotiation that would produce through feminism a new 'social
subject', as de Lauretis puts it in Alice doesn't *(p. 186), and that I*
have figured here as the work of female critical subjects.

Notes

N.B. This chapter was first published in N.K. Miller, *Subject to change* (New
York: Columbia University Press, 1988), 102–21. With the exception of the introductory remarks, which I read in slightly different form at Milwaukee, the material
that appears in italics was written after the events of the paper as discursive end-
notes; not so much as side issues, as asides pointing to the limits of the essay's
rhetorical space. Its place here in dialogic relation to the main body of the text
is the result of an experiment brought about by the always imaginative critical
judgement of the editor of the volume in which it first appeared, *Feminist Studies/
Critical Studies*, Teresa de Lauretis. Once I saw it in print, I decided to reproduce
it here in that form, with a few editorial changes of my own.

  1 The foxtrot is defined in Webster's Third as 'a ballroom dance in duple time
    that includes slow walking steps, quick running steps, and two steps'. What
    appeals to me here is the change of pace, the doubleness of moves within the

shape of the dance, and the collaborative requirement. The latter will re-emerge at the end of this paper, but really runs through the argument: the dead-endedness of the one-way street that bears the traffic (to mix a few metaphors) between feminist and dominant critics.

This figuration of the problem bears a certain resemblance to my discussion of shoes and tropes in 'The text's heroine' (Chapter 3 in my *Subject to Change*). My current position has been reformulated for me by Biddy Martin, who said at the Milwaukee conference that indeterminacy (what I am thematising here as the denegation and denigration of identity) is no excuse for not acting; that we must find a way to ground indeterminacy so that we can make political interventions. The question before us then becomes how to locate and allow for particularities within the collective.

2 Barthes' essay should be situated within the discussion of changing definitions of art in conjunction with the laws governing authorship in France, in particular a 1957 law which attempted to account for new kinds of artistic and authorial production not covered by the copyright law (*droits d'auteur*) of 1793. I am indebted to Molly Nesbit's 'What is an author', for an illuminating explanation of this material. Nesbit points out that the death of the author for Barthes seems to have meant 'really the imprinting author of 1793'; she also describes the original occasion for the essay: 'in 1967 in America for *Aspen* magazine, nos. 5 + 6 ... dedicated to Stéphane Mallarmé'. It is boxed (literally) along with all kinds of 'authorial work, much of it technologically based' (pp. 241–3). See also 'Le Droit d'auteur s'adapte à la nouvelle économie de la création', in *Le Monde*, 3 August 1985. These are pieces of a more contextual history of criticism.

3 At the Cerisy colloquium of which he was the 'prétexte', this phrase drew a certain amount of attention. In his comments on the meaning of the phrase Barthes situated his own relation to the historical context of writing *Sade/Fourier/Loyola*: 'It was the heyday of modernity and the text; we talked about the death of the author (I talked about it myself). We didn't use the word writer (*écrivain*): writers were slightly ridiculous people like Gide, Claudel, Valéry, Malraux' (pp. 413–14).

4 In 'Women's time, women's space: writing the history of feminist criticism,' Showalter adopts Julia Kristéva's 'genealogy' of subjectivity; of a *space* of generation which is both 'European *and* trans-European' (p. 15). In writing the history of American feminist criticism, she wants 'to emphasize its specificity by narrating its development in terms of the internal relationships, continuities, friendships, and institutions that shaped the thinking and writing of the last fifteen years' (p. 30). As examples of asymmetrical events in these non-parallel chronologies, Showalter contrasts the 1966 conference on 'the Structuralist Controversy and the Sciences of Man' (Johns Hopkins University) with 'the first feminist literary session at the Chicago MLA in 1970' (p. 32), neither of which I attended. In 1971 I was reading Roland Barthes, not Adrienne Rich. The discovery of Rich, for me a belated one, comes from being involved with a women's studies programme; this trajectory, I think, figures an inverse relation to the reading habits of much mainstream American feminist criticism, while remaining outside the classical reading patterns of women in French; which may or may not explain the feeling people have had that I am mixing things – Barthes and Rich – that somehow don't belong together. What is worrisome to me is the way in which conferences in literary studies continue to follow

their separate paths: though women are invited to English Institute (for which Showalter wrote this essay), Georgetown, etc., and men to Pembroke and Milwaukee, there is no evidence yet that feminist critical theory has affected dominant organisations and theorisations.

5 The stories of readers and writers emerge in both Rich and Barthes from a gendered poetics of sexual difference and family romances. For Barthes, like Rich, the author is male, and in his effects, patriarchal: 'As an institution, the author is dead: ... dispossessed, his (identity) no longer exerts the formidable paternity over his work that literary history, teaching, opinion had the responsibility of establishing ... but in the text, in a certain way *I desire the author*: I need his figure (which is neither his representation, nor his projection)' ('The death of the author', pp. 45–6). In Barthes' model of desire the reader and the writer participate in a system of associations that poses the masculine experience as central and universal. This 'I' who desires the author, and desires to be desired by him, who worries about the return of the father (having banished him), who takes his pleasure in a fragmented subjectivity, desires, worries, enjoys within an economy as (he of course says it himself) a son. The failure to differentiate (the question, for example, of the daughter's desire) becomes more than a matter of philosophy or style when allied with the authority – of the intellectual, writer, teacher – that supports the concept of indifference in the first place. On the politics of indifference, see Naomi Schor's 'Dreaming dissymmetry: Barthes, Foucault and sexual difference'.

6 This move corresponds to Gayatri Spivak's insistence on 'a simultaneous other focus: not merely who am I? but who is the other women? How am I naming her? How does she name me?' 'French feminism in an international frame', p. 179. On the 'other woman', see also Jane Gallop's 'Annie Leclerc writing a letter, with Vermeer'.

7 Smith wrote in her 1977 essay, 'Toward a black feminist criticism', from which she read at the Milwaukee conference: 'I finally want to express how much easier both my waking and sleeping hours would be if there were one book in existence that would tell me something specific about my life. One book based in black feminist and black lesbian experience, fiction or nonfiction. Just one work to reflect the reality that I and the black women who I love are trying to create. When such a book exists then each of us will not only know better how to live, but how to dream' (p. 184). For O'Neale's position, see her 'Inhibiting midwives, usurping creators: the struggling emergence of black women in American fiction'.

In the *New York Times Book Review*, 2 June 1985, Gloria Naylor, in a survey of writers' favourite opening passages, comments on the beginning of Toni Morrison's *The bluest eye*. Naylor writes: 'While the novel handles a weighty subject – the demoralization of black female beauty in a racist society (also the subject of O'Neale's paper) – it *whispers* in the mode of minimalist poetry, thus resulting in the least common denominator for all classics: the ability to haunt. It alerts my students to the fact that fiction should be about storytelling, the "why" of things is best left to the sociologists, the "how" is more than enough for writers to tackle ...' (p. 52). It seems to me that we are in desperate need of a specifically text-based discussion between black and white feminist critics and writers on the relations between the why and the how, between reference and representation. Without it we run the risk of a devastating repolarisation of the sort that at times during the Milwaukee conference resulted in bitter asides and accusations of racism.

8 At the Milwaukee conference Jane Gallop asked about the implicit risk one runs that irony can misfire. In *A handlist of rhetorical terms* Richard Lanham describes this problem under the rubric of 'rhetorical irony' (p. 61). He points out that the 'relationship of persuader and persuaded is almost always self-conscious to some degree', and goes on to make the claim that 'every rhetorical posture except the most naive involves an ironical coloration, of some kind or another of the speaker's *Ethos*'. To the extent that the ethos (character, disposition) of feminism historically has refused the doubleness of 'saying one thing while it tries to do another' (the mark of classical femininity one might argue), it may be that an ironic feminist discourse finds itself at odds both with itself (its identity to itself), and with the expectations its audience has of its position. If this is true, then irony, in the final analysis, may be a figure of limited effectiveness. On the other hand, since non-ironic, single, sincere, hortatory feminism is becoming ineffectual, it may be worth the risk of trying out this kind of duplicity on the road.

In 'A manifesto for cyborgs', Donna Haraway, calling for a greater use of irony 'within socialist feminism', argues: 'Irony is about contradictions that do not resolve into larger wholes, even dialectically, about the tension of holding incompatible things together because both or all are necessary and true' (p. 65).

9 The task of 'dephallicizing the father', as Gallop puts it in *The daughter's seduction*, to succeed must break out of the limits of the family circle (p. xv).

10 If Lucy in the classroom writes her way out of humiliation and into agency, on stage the use of language becomes a question of voice. The difficulty, Lucy discovers, once she begins to speak, lies not in the audience but in her performance: 'When my tongue got free, and my voice took its true pitch, and found its natural tone, I thought of nothing but the personage I represented' (p. 210). In both instances, Lucy's performative subjectivity is structured through a text and in another language. I have a more sustained analysis of this phenomenon in the Chapters 7 and 9 of *Subject to change*, on *Corinne* and *The vagabond*.

11 In 'A man's place', a talk she gave at the 1984 MLA session on 'Men in feminism', which has been published in the volume *Men in feminism*, Elizabeth Weed brilliantly outlined many of the issues with which I struggle here.

References

Auerbach, Nina (1984), 'Why communities of women aren't enough', *Tulsa Studies in Women's Literature*, 3, 1–2 (spring–autumn), 153–7; rpt. (1987) in Shari Benstock (ed.), *Feminist issues in literary scholarship* (Bloomington: Indiana University Press).

Barthes, Roland (1971), *Sade, Fourier, Loyola* (Paris: Seuil); trans. Richard Miller (1976), *Sade–Fourier–Loyola* (New York: Hill and Wang).

Barthes, Roland (1977), 'The death of the author', in *Image/text/music*, trans. Stephen Heath (New York: Hill and Wang).

Beauvoir, Simone de (1976), *Le deuxième sexe* (Paris: Gallimard-Folio); trans. H. M. Parshley (1970), *The second sex* (New York: Bantam).

Braidotti, Rosi, 'Patterns of dissonance: women and/in philosophy' (manuscript).

Brontë, Charlotte (1983; 1st ed., 1853), *Villette* (New York: Penguin).

Cixous, Hélène (1976), 'The laugh of the Medusa', trans. Keith Cohen and Paula Cohen, *Signs*, 1, 4, 875–94.

Culler, Jonathan (1982), *On deconstruction* (Ithaca: Cornell University Press).

De Lauretis, Teresa (1984), *Alice doesn't: feminism, semiotics, cinema* (Bloomington: Indiana University Press).

De Lauretis, Teresa (ed.) (1986), *Feminist studies/critical studies* (Bloomington: Indiana University Press).

Foucault, Michel (1980), 'What is an author?', in Donald F. Bouchard (ed.), *Language, counter-memory, practice* (Ithaca: Cornell University Press).

Gallop, Jane (1982), *The daughter's seduction* (Ithaca: Cornell University Press).

Gallop, Jane (1986), 'Annie Leclerc writing a letter, with Vermeer', in Nancy K. Miller (ed.), *The poetics of gender* (New York: Columbia University Press).

Gilbert, Sandra and Gubar, Susan (1979), *Madwoman in the attic: the woman writer and the nineteenth-century literary imagination* (New Haven: Yale University Press).

Haraway, Donna (1985), 'A manifesto for cyborgs: science, technology, and socialist feminism in the 1980s', *Socialist Review* 15, 2 (March–April), 65–107.

Huyssen, Andreas (1984), 'Mapping the postmodern', *New German Critique*, 33 (autumn), 5–52.

Kamuf, Peggy (1980), 'Writing like a woman', in Sally McConnell-Ginet, Ruth Borker and Nelly Furman (eds), *Women and language in literature and society* (New York: Praeger).

Lanham, Richard A. (1969), *A handful of rhetorical terms* (Berkeley and Los Angeles: University of California Press).

Marcus, Jane (1984), 'Still practice, a/wrested alphabet: toward a feminist aesthetic', *Tulsa Studies in Women's Literature* 3, 1–2 (spring–autumn), 79–98; rpt. (1987) in Shari Benstock (ed.), *Feminist issues in literary scholarship* (Bloomington: Indiana University Press).

Mitchell, Juliet (1984), 'Femininity, narrative, and psychoanalysis', in *Women: the longest revolution* (New York: Pantheon).

Naylor, Gloria (1985), 'Famous first words', *New York Times Book Review*, 2 June, p. 52.

Nesbit, Molly (1987), 'What is an author?', *Yale French Studies* 73, 229–57 (special issue on 'Everyday life', ed. Alice Y. Kaplan and Kristin Ross).

O'Neale, Sondra (1986), 'Inhibiting midwives, usurping creators: the struggling emergence of black women in American fiction', in Teresa de Lauretis (ed.), *Feminist studies/critical studies* (Bloomington: Indiana University Press).

Rich, Adrienne (1979), 'When we dead awaken: writing as revision (1971)' and 'Toward a woman-centered university (1973–74), in *On lies, secrets, and silence: selected prose, 1966–1978* (New York: Norton).

Rich, Adrienne (1986), 'Blood, bread, and poetry: the location of the poet', in *Blood, bread, and poetry: selected prose, 1979–1985* (New York: Norton).

Russo, Mary (1986), 'Female grotesques: carnival and theory', in Teresa de Lauretis (ed.), *Feminist studies/critical studies* (Bloomington: Indiana University Press).

Schor, Naomi (1985), *Breaking the chain: women, theory, and French realist fiction* (New York: Columbia University Press).

Schor, Naomi (1987), 'Dreaming dissymmetry: Barthes, Foucault, and sexual difference', in Alice Jardine and Paul Smith (eds), *Men in feminism* (New York and London: Methuen).

Showalter, Elaine (1984), 'Women's time, women's space: writing the history of feminist criticism', *Tulsa Studies in Women's Literature* 3, 1–2 (spring–autumn), 29–44; rpt. (1987) in Shari Benstock (ed.), *Feminist issues in literary scholarship* (Bloomington: Indiana University Press).

Showalter, Elaine (1984), 'Women who write are women', *New York Times Book Review*, 16 December, pp. 1, 31–3.

Smith, Barbara (1977), 'Toward a black feminist criticism', *Conditions: Two*, 1, 2 (October); rpt. (1985) in Elaine Showalter (ed.), *The new feminist criticism: essays on women, literature, theory* (New York: Pantheon).

Spivak, Gayatri Chakravorty (1981), 'French feminism in an international frame', *Yale French Studies*, 62, 154–84.

Spivak, Gayatri Chakravorty (1982), 'The politics of interpretations', *Critical Inquiry*, 9, 1 (September), 259–78.

Weed, Elizabeth (1987), 'A man's place', in Alice Jardine and Paul Smith (eds), *Men in feminism* (New York and London: Methuen).

Self-authoring subjects

Terry Eagleton

Like Mark Twain's obituary notice, the death of the author has been much exaggerated. Michel Foucault never set out to deny the reality of authorship, simply to insist that it was best grasped as a legal, political and historical category rather than as some transcendental source of meaning. Jacques Derrida never intended to deny the reality of intentions, simply to expose the ideological character of assuming that authorial intentionality is always and everywhere the *dominant* determinant of textual signification, or of imagining that any such intention, deferred and refracted as it is by the play of signs, could ever be fully present to itself. Even so, poststructuralism has damagingly suppressed the fact that meaning always has an author at least in this sense: that you can't move *directly* from difference to signification. You can do so only by the relay of an interpretation, and there's no interpretation without a subject. Difference, diacritical spacing, is the necessary but not sufficient condition of significance; without someone to identify this difference *as* difference, and as *making* a difference, there can be no meaning. In usefully toppling the all-privileged author, post-structuralism thus managed to erase along with him or her the true author or meaning-donor, which is the reader, interlocutor or audience.

We have been told many times by now that the human subject as self-authoring, self-generative, self-determining is the very lynchpin of bourgeois humanist ideology. My belief is that this assertion can only be made with the most stringent qualifications. Indeed you might well claim that one of the very marks of the 'modern', of post-Hegelian philosophy, is the insistence that there is always something which precedes or grounds or underlies the human subject. Even for the Kantian project, which aims to reconstruct the whole of objective reality from within the perspective of that subject, the subject itself could be said to be no more than a function of the celebrated categories. You can't get more undeconstructed than J. G. Fichte's philosophy of so-called Transcendental Egoism; but even for Fichte the force by which the self ceaselessly 'posits' itself is an unconscious determinant which eludes representation, and the same is true in a different style for the philosophy of Schelling. German idealism was well aware of the paradox that to assert the transcendental 'I' or subject as the founding principle of reality, itself utterly undetermined and self-grounding, is to undo your own declaration at a stroke, since there can be no 'I' without differentiation, no ego without an Other or not-I. The subject as absolute is thus ruined as soon as it reflects. Nor can the act of self-reflection be itself claimed as the absolute, since we stumble here on yet another paradox which makes itself felt all the way down to the Lacanian mirror phase: how can the subject recognise its reflection as its own, thus coming to full presence to itself, unless somehow it has *already* recognised itself? How do I know that the image in the mirror is me, unless I have already identified myself by an act of reflection? This much-vaunted grounding principle – consciousness, in a word – turns out to involve a dizzying infinite regress, and turns out, moreover, to be entirely vacuous. For subjectivity is simply that which is in no sense whatsoever an object, the absolute other of all such lowly facticity; and this means that subjectivity can never become *determinate*, since if it did so it would lapse in that moment to the degraded status of thinghood. The grand grounding principle of the entire enterprise thus turns out to be utterly elusive and evanescent: if subjectivity is to be determinate, then there must be some ground beyond it from which it can be determined, thus destroying its absolute status at a stroke. But if this is so then this slippery, quicksilver process known as subjectivity threatens to slip entirely through the net of representative knowledge, leaving us grasping at empty space. How can philosophy find sure anchorage in this elusive spectre of a subject, this ghostly parody of a phenomenon which is gone as soon as we give name to it, this untheorisable source of all our actions which is fully present in none of them?

It didn't, in other words, take us until 1968, or 1972 (or was it the publication of Saussure?) to recognise the aporias of transcendental

subjectivity. Schleiermacher is already speaking early in the nineteenth century of the feeling of 'absolute dependency' which the
subject endures the moment it comes to consciousness; and for
Schopenhauer that which makes me uniquely, essentially myself,
the stealthy workings of the voracious will within me, is as blankly
alien and indifferent to my individual consciousness as the force
which stirs the waves or spins the globe. Kierkegaard stakes all on
the intense, agonised inwardness of subjectivity, but the guilt of the
subject is its awareness of being sunk in the crime of historicity,
its abject dependency on that which has always gone before it.
Heidegger will later recapitulate this theme as the subject's
'thrownness', its emergence into being within a facticity it never
chose. Before this we have of course Nietzsche, for whom the
subject is a mere illusory function of the will to power, and Freud,
for whom I speak only because It does. The consciousness which
Husserlian phenomenology seeks to recover as its grounding
principle is now irredeemably intentional, ineluctably bound up
with its object. The same is true of Sartre's *être-pour-soi*, that
empty, nauseated thing-without-a-name which has all the privileged
originality of classical idealist consciousness but absolutely none
of its replete self-presence.

To put the point another way: the cultural left parodies the rich,
conflictive heritages of bourgeois humanism at its political peril.
Humanism was always more capable of acknowledging the internal
and external determinations of subjecthood than the editors of
Screen sometimes found it convenient to think. If consciousness
is the ground, then it must itself remain groundless and so indeter-
minable. As Schelling puts it, subjectivity is a light which shines
only forwards, not backwards; it can't lift itself up by its own boot-
straps, round upon its own murky origins, because one would need
an infinite regress of meta-subjects in order to do so. And if the
cultural left has, in its theory, made something of a convenient
straw target of this whole intellectual tradition, it has done so,
much more damagingly, in its politics. Those who have now been
correctly programmed to reach for their decentred subjectivities at
the mere mention of the dreaded phrase 'liberal humanist' repress
the courageous struggles of the early revolutionary bourgeoisie of
the Enlightenment against the brutalities of feudal absolutism –

struggles for which concepts of autonomy, self-determination, self-grounding and the rest were crucial political weapons. If we are able today to be critics of Enlightenment, it is Enlightenment which has empowered us to be so.

The subject as self-authoring is in any case a peculiarly tragic, self-thwarting creature. It knows only two ways of coping with external reality − either to thrust it into the limbo of absolute alterity, as that which is not and never can be subjective; or to devour and introject such recalcitrant objectivity, absorb it into the structure of the self. But in doing that it simultaneously cuts from beneath its own feet any objective grounds by which its own privilege might be validated. The psychical structure of this subject is that of manic depression: at the very acme of its exuberant powers it finds itself bereft and desolate, having swallowed up the very universe which might reflect back to it a consolatory, confirmatory image of itself. The megalomaniac cry of this subject − 'I take value from myself alone!' − is thus never far from a despairing groan: 'I am so lonely in this world!' If the subject is to be ground and author of itself, then it will have to conjure all value out of its own depths, spring at each moment fully-fledged from its own loins; but this value will be, accordingly, sickeningly fictional and contingent, as pointlessly self-generative and self-valorising as the work of art (on which, indeed, the bourgeois subject is modelled). The bourgeois subject requires some Other to assure it that its powers are more than hallucinatory, yet such otherness is in-tolerable to it, and must be either expelled or introjected. There can be no sovereignty without someone to lord it over, yet his or her very presence offers instantly to underdo one's mastery, so that the subject ends up exercising its capacities in empty space. If the essence of subjecthood is freedom, then bourgeois man seems con-demned to self-blindness at the very peak of his powers, since such freedom, as Kant brings home to us, is by definition indefinable. The subject, then, can figure only negatively, as some mute presence or pregnant silence, as empty excess or transcendence of any objective particular. As far as the system it authors is concerned, it is at once source and supplement, lynchpin and leftover, squeezed out of its own creation.

If transcendental subjectivity is tragically self-undoing in this sense, so is it in another. In a society of self-authoring subject, objectivity comes to mean something like: 'You respect my property and I'll respect yours'. To impose a limit on another's freedom is thus to impose one, unthinkably, on my own. (Unthinkably, since it's of the very essence of this freedom, of this ceaseless self-positing or creative act by which the subject conjures itself at each moment into being, that it can't be curtailed.) The bourgeois subject, just in order to be self-authoring, can't survive without a whole objective system of metaphysical guarantees that this freedom will be respected; but this whole legal, ethical and political superstructure will then come to inhibit its own freedom with respect to others. In this sense, one might claim, the productive 'base' of bourgeois society is at odds with its supportive superstructure. It was left to Friedrich Nietzsche to show that society a way out of this dilemma, but a way out so hair-raisingly radical that the bourgeoisie could not possibly contemplate taking it. What Nietzsche did was to announce the death of God, or the death of the superstructure, which comes to much the same thing. Nietzsche said: forget about trying to justify and guarantee your activities, stop trying to ground them metaphysically, just accept that will to power is all there is and live joyfully, self-productively, changeably, experimentally, in the rich fullness of your ephemeral powers. The *Übermensch* is thus post-metaphysical bourgeois man, the meta-capitalist who is prepared, in a supremely reckless gesture, to sacrifice his security to his liberty. Nietzsche sees that bourgeois society can't have it both ways, and proclaims that extreme solution to its impasses which we now call post-modernism. Forget about law and morality and religion and meta-narrative and live your life like a work of art, aestheticise everything away, dare to exist without meta-physical grounds. For the work of art is, mysteriously, its own absolute ground, gives the law unto itself in the manner of the Superman, provides its own internal rationale and stoops slavishly to no heteronomous command in what for Nietzsche is the squalid Judaeo-Christian style.

This is much too iconoclastic a solution for bourgeois society to stomach. For without deity and family, without the stout meta-physical subject of the domestic hearth, the religious assembly and the scientific laboratory, how is the true, frenetically decentred subject of bourgeois production ever to justify itself? If you generate your values directly from that process of ceaseless self-production, as Nietzsche cavalierly advocates, then you risk ending up with all the worst values, as indeed does Nietzsche himself: hardness, aggressivity, competitiveness, struggle, domination, the riding of one's chariot over the decaying and diseased races (as Nietzsche actually advocates, though you won't hear about that in Jacques Derrida or Gilles Deleuze). Bourgeois society simply can't dispense with the metaphysical in this way, even though the structural disparity between that and its sordid market-place practices, between appealing to God and Freedom and Family and having your hand in the till, will bulk farcically, embarrassingly large. (The common name for that structural disparity is, of course, the United States of America.) But at the same time those metaphysical values *will* be inexorably eroded, and not in the first place by the intellectual left. The metaphysical superstructure of this social order, which is utterly indispensable to its ideological legitimation, will be undermined precisely by its own ruthlessly rationalising, secularising 'infrastructural' activities. Like the lonely humanist subject, the more successful such a society is, the more it will eat away at its own supportive foundations, leaving itself revolving in empty space, turned in upon itself like the aesthetic artefact. Postmodernism is radical in so far as it turns the actual productive, pluralistic, decentred energies of such a regime against its deceptive metaphysical pieties, now grasped as a mere hangover from an earlier, more classical epoch of capitalist production. It is reactionary, by the same token, in that it uses the form of the commodity itself to carry out that essential subversion, passes the shattering force of the economic through the sacrosanct arena of the symbolic.

There is an interesting logical dilemma in the work of Nietzsche. He believes that it is possible either to affirm or to deny the will to power; he thinks, for instance, that Schopenhauer is a good instance of the latter. But at the same time will to power in Nietzsche would seem coterminous with everything there is. If, then, the act of choosing the will to power is already included within that will, it is difficult to see how it can figure as a genuine choice; but if it *is* a genuine choice, then it would seem to fall outside the

purview of the will to power, which for Nietzsche would simply
be impossible.

Nietzsche's canny response to this conundrum is to deconstruct
at a stroke the opposition between free will and necessity, which
is for him entirely metaphysical. And the supreme instance for him
of this deconstruction is artistic production. 'Artists', Nietzsche
writes, 'know only too well that precisely when they no longer do
anything "voluntarily" but do everything of necessity, their feeling
of freedom, subtlety, full power, of creative placing, disposing and
forming reaches its peak – in short, that necessity and "freedom
of the will" then become one in them' (Beyond good and evil,
p. 196). There is, of course, nothing particularly original in this
formulation, which as it stands is the merest commonplace of
Romantic 'inspiration'; but there is a chance that, suitably transformed, it might indicate some way out of our current political
dilemmas over the question of authorship. One might summarise
that political dilemma like this: that in order to develop some
adequate notion of political *agency* we can't simply turn back to
the old, largely discredited bourgeois-humanist subject; yet the sorts
of subjects we have mostly been offered in its place would seem
hardly capable of toppling a bottle off a wall, let alone of bringing
down the state. We have subjects of a bulging Bakhtinian repleteness
who seem too enraptured by their own orifices to contemplate
much political agency, and subjects of an alarming Lacanian lean-
ness who stay in one piece only by a persistent process of self-
misrecognition. It's hard to envisage either of them on a picket
line. Another way of phrasing the dilemma is this: that any process
of radical social transformation calls for a 'centredness' and resolute-
ness of purpose far beyond our customary dim, sporadic perception
of ourselves as effective social agents; yet that such processes of
change are also about the shattering of identities as much as the
construction of them, and blow the lid off the unconscious in ways
which tend to outrun our conscious political grasp. Revolutions are
only made by those who in some sense know who they are – yet
if they were fully aware of *that*, revolution would not be necessary
in the first place. Revolutions are about constructing the conditions
in which it would be in principle possible to discover and determine
what one might become, not just the conditions in which one might

freely express what one already is; yet how is a group or class or nation wholly bereft of a strong self-identity in the present to set about anything as formidable as that? It's in this sense that what happens to the subject in this process of social upheaval is quite literally unthinkable in terms of either the broad paradigms currently on offer: the centred, unified, self-authoring subject on the one hand, or the fissured, dishevelled, imaginary function of a structure on the other. (It is ironic, incidentally, that those who most euphorically disseminated the latter paradigm in the 1970s were also enraptured briefly by the most brutally voluntaristic brand of Marxism of all: Maoism.)

In aesthetic production, Nietzsche claims, it is futile to try to discriminate the more determined from the more voluntarist moment: each subsists, unthinkably, in terms of the other. This seems to me true of political transformation too: such change needs a conscious collective author, more than usually confident in its identity, yet any such process which is authentic will always be marked by a certain *necessity*. This is not to invoke the supposed iron laws of history, it is simply to re-emphasise that we have all learned from the modern-day interpreters of Antonio Gramsci to be suitably pessimistic about the suppleness and resilience of the hegemonies under which we languish. As long as the condition of being subjugated yields people even minimal gratification, then the understandable terrors and insecurities of an alternative will tend to bind them masochistically to that power. It would be simply irrational for women and men to revolt against a hegemony which is still in some sense tolerable, which can still yield them marginal satisfactions, for the risks and displeasures of an uncertain political future. We are all familiar with that side of the narrative, but we too often hesitate to draw its logical corollary. Once one hegemonic power is unable to afford that margin of gratification, or to exploit the masochism of its subjects, then it follows as surely as night follows day that those subjects will revolt. Once there is no longer enough in it for them to be oppressed, they would be acting irrationally to remain in that condition, and history suggests that men and women are moderately rational in this respect. This is the kind of necessity I have in mind, which can never be properly distinguished from the most conscious, clear-eyed organisation, and which can never be thought within the framework of the supremely centred subject, any more than it can be in terms of the ecstatically ungrounded one.

Reference

Nietzsche, F., *Beyond good and evil, basic writings of Nietzsche*, ed. W. Kaufman (New York: Vintage Books, 1968).

PART II

The responsibility of the critic

3

Authority, history and the question of postmodernism

Thomas Docherty

An important duality lies at the very heart of the concept of authority. The OED offers the definition: 'the power or right to enforce obedience'. For authority to exist, therefore, there must be two poles: on one hand, there is the force to be obeyed, and, on the other, the obeyer of the force. This makes it clear that authority is always 'in history', in that it does not depend upon one transcendent individual, but is necessarily articulated in a social and historical situation. Even if the term is given a metaphysical resonance, implying a divine law, then still the effects of authority – and hence its very existence as event, fact or even concept – depend upon an act of recognition, in history, by others who are prepared to subject themselves to such a law. *It is in history that authority authorises itself as such.*

Yet my contention here is that the Modernist conception of authority, which has dominated most thinking on the matter since broadly 1500, implies a resistance to precisely this historical situating. In Modernist culture, authority is aligned with an ideology of individualism which is ultimately dependent upon a theology or an idealist and positivist conception of authority. Most commonly, theorists have considered the issue in terms of a theme of 'influence' between individuals (most powerfully in the work of Harold Bloom).[1] On the one hand, authority is commonly represented as a more or less amorphous power to which the individual is subjected and whose laws he or she corroborates through repetition. (That power may be a government, a dictator, an artist, etc., but the crucial factor here is that it can always be *identified*, even if only vacuously as, say, an 'ideology'.) On the other hand, authority is considered in terms of the individual's ability to circumvent such subjection and to inaugurate a rival set of 'authoritative' or authorised laws. This framework (close to Edward Said's formulations in *Beginnings*) is drastically limited.[2] It constrains us to think of authority as something experienced in the first instance always 'privately', divorced from history as such, as an element in what Althusser would have called the ISA, whereas in practice authority is predominantly an effect of the RSA.[3]

There are three sections to my argument. In the first, I indicate how Modernist thinking is idealist on the issue of authority, and how it therefore constitutes a resistance to history both in authority itself and in critical thinking about it. Secondly, I explore authority as a mode of transgression, which is implicitly or explicitly the model with which most contemporary theory works; and I shall show that in fact there is a resistance to transgression within this model as it stands, and hence a resistance to authority within authority. This is important for the simple fact that the 'transgressive' authority is that which we tend to think of as the 'critical' authority; hence what is at issue here is not only the very possibility of criticism, but also the possibility of historical agency on the part of the intellectual subject. Finally, I offer a model of postmodernism which will release the historicity of authority and avoid these tendencies to idealism and complicity with a dominant – uncritical, unreflective – ideology.

Modernism: the nomad under arrest

At an early point in *Orientalism*, Said indicates that:

> There is nothing mysterious or natural about authority. It is formed, irradiated, disseminated; it is instrumental, it is persuasive; it has status, it establishes canons of taste and value; it is virtually indistinguishable from certain ideas it dignifies as true, and from traditions, perceptions and judgments it forms, transmits, reproduces. Above all, authority can, indeed must, be analyzed. (pp. 19–20)

In one sense, all that this says is that authority is ideological, institutionalised, and available for critique or for ideological unmasking. But Said's terms are instructive. One vital component to which I will return is that of authority establishing 'canons of taste and value', alongside its relation to acts of judgement and criticism. But what is immediately apparent is Said's denial of mystery to authority: in common with his work elsewhere, Said wants here to establish the secular credentials of authority. In *Beginnings*, this takes the form of the distinction between 'origins' (which are sacred) and (secular) 'beginnings'. Said's suggestions are important in a context in which theory has approached authority in an idealist manner, frequently ignoring the specificities of authorities in their distinct historical situations.

The distinction I am stressing for authority, a distinction between heterogeneous specificity and the homogeneity of generalisation, has occurred before in theory. Bakhtin attacked the Formalists in similar terms. In order to authorise *ostranenie* and *literaturnost* as guiding principles, the Formalists had to construct a model of 'ordinary language' against which the autonomy of the aesthetic function could be asserted. This was fine, apart from the fact, as Bakhtin indicated, that their view of ordinary language was a fictional – even false – constructed hypothesis which bore no relation to the real specific conditions of how language worked in historical fact. These conditions, of course, involved what Bakhtin called 'speech tact', a tact which acknowledges the real conditions of acts of communication in their specificity:

> Speech tact has a practical importance for practical language communication. The formative and organizing force of speech tact is very great. It gives form to everyday utterances, determining the genre and style of speech performances. Here tact (*taktichnost'*) should be understood in a broad sense, with politeness as only one of its aspects. Tact may have various directions, moving between the two poles of compliment and curse. Speech tact is determined by the aggregate of all the social relationships of the speakers, their ideological horizons, and, finally, the concrete situation of the conversation. Tact, whatever its form under the given conditions, determines all of our utterances. No word lacks tact.[4]

Hence the historical dialogicity of all language and all communication. Authority has too often been analysed in the 'Formalist' mode, as some pure effect of the 'who is speaking':[5] that is, it has always been seen from the idealist position of the speaker/writer in monological isolation, and as a result, authority has been idealised as an effect of an individual. This would obviously be the case in the kind of intentionalist theory of literary criticism advocated by Hirsch; but it is also the case in many modes of reader-response criticism (as in Fish, Jauss or, most extremely, Bleich). What makes both such positions (intentionalist and reader-centred) idealist is, finally, the *identification* of authority: authority is located in a single proper name, distinguished from all other interfering historical factors. We work with that version of the word which Vico derived from the authority of etymology when he suggested that authority had to do with property, and by extension with the individual (*The new science*, p. 109).

Authority, however, like speech, never happens in a void. It is always inherently 'tactful', 'tactical': dialogical. It is thoroughly determined by a socio-historical situation which far exceeds the capacity of any individual consciousness (writer's or reader's; law-giver's or law-obeyer's) for intentionality or substance. It is thus a mistake to adopt an intentionalist position which ascribes a specific name to a specific authority. Authority is not a matter of individual intention, but is rather an effect of the interplay of various intentionalities.

Hartman proposed something close to this in *The fate of reading*, where he contemplated authority in terms of the issue of the 'exemplary text':

> ... it is hard to conceive of a literary reader who is not immersed in the search for an exemplary text: a text to be used against the wastefulness of living without concentration, or a text to support by one's life, given the need. So at the end of Ray Bradbury's *Fahrenheit 451* (as filmed by Truffaut) each exile from the book-burning state adopts the name of a text he has learnt by heart and which he represents: one person is now called *David Copperfield*, another *Emile*, or even *Paradise Lost*. ... The extinction in this symbolic situation or the personal names of *both* author and reader shows what ideally happens in the act of reading: if there is a sacrifice to the exemplary, it involves the aggrandizement neither of author nor of reader but leads into the recognition that something worthy of perpetuation has occurred.[6]

This drive to the extinction of the proper name acknowledges the real relations between those who exert authority and those subjected to it. What is at stake is a transpersonal articulation of a play of forces which we call 'authoritative'. For Hartman, the transpersonal authority ('this thing that's bigger than both of us', as it were) is the authority of the text. Yet this is still not counter-idealist enough, for in the case of Hartman, the intension of the text, *its* intentionality, becomes a determining *and originary* authority. Given that authority is an effect of history, that is, authority is produced as a result of the socio-historical relations between two or more forces which are *a posteriori* assigned positions as 'author' and 'reader' (or, in wider terms, authority and its subjects), it follows that there can be no originary moment of authority which simply subtends or effects a historical situation in the way that Hartman and other latently idealist critics require. In every case, authority is made into a 'property' which can be assigned (to) a proper name. It is this manoeuvre, the construction and identification of a single authorising source or intention, which constitutes the fabrication deployed to maintain an implicitly idealist version of authority, an authority of origins rather than beginnings, an authority which bears no relation to the real state of historical affairs in which authority is produced.

Given the status of the text as a dialogical formation, the authority inscribed in it is intrinsically multiple and self-transforming; it is subject to modification or even substantial change depending upon the different socio-historical situations in which the text is articulated, enacted, produced or – more simply – understood. That is a truism, of course. But it is this undecidability of the text, its 'nomadicity' as it wanders towards the occupation of a temporary stability (called understanding), which the ascription of a proper name as its guiding authority arrests. The manoeuvre by which the nomadic text is arrested also serves the function, then, of making the text seemingly available for understanding. At least temporarily, it offers a *point de repère* from which a reader can identify him- or herself in an act of intellectual apprehension, and thus as an authoritative subject of consciousness even in the very instant in which he or she is subjected to the authority of the text. In short, the manoeuvre is one which repeats the ideological interpellation of the subject as delineated by Althusser (in 'Ideology and the ideological state apparatuses'); any such reading, critical or unreflective, is caught in ideology and idealism precisely at the moment when it thinks it is free, 'authoritative'.

The fact that we attribute a proper name or other designation of identity to an authority is indication enough that authority becomes a marker of 'distinction'. As Bourdieu has shown, acts of distinction such as this are not innocent. Bourdieu traces the way in which 'the definition of art, and through it the art of living, is an object of struggle among the classes' (*Distinction*, p. 48). It is, of course, the authority given to such art that is at issue here. For Bourdieu, as for Lyotard, there is a close relation of analogy between the aesthetic and political dispositions, and acts of distinction are important in both. Here is where Said's idea of authority as something instrumental in the formation of 'canons of taste' has a greater purchase. Bourdieu argues that taste is affirmed through negation, through the refusal of other competing tastes as 'disgusting'. He writes:

> The most intolerable thing for those who regard themselves as the possessors of legitimate culture is the sacrilegious reuniting of tastes which taste dictates shall be separated. This means that the games of artists and aesthetes and their struggles for the monopoly of artistic legitimacy are less innocent than they seem. At stake in every struggle over art there is also the imposition of an art of living, that is, the transmutation of an arbitrary way of living into the legitimate way of life which casts every other way of living into arbitrariness. (*Distinction*, pp. 56–7)

Taste, the act of distinction which identifies an authority, is no mere aesthetic practice, but one which involves the formulation of class distinctions. Further, the activity we call 'understanding' (and which is actually, as I have argued, merely ideological interpellation) lies behind the strategies which enable such 'taste' to become institutionalised and thus vested with a weight of authority which far exceeds the capacity of the individual bearer of taste. For in this case, individuals are aligned with a class or with an institution which validates their activity and grants them authority as its representative.

This is nowhere more the case than in the incidence of what I will call 'parasitic citation', an appeal to some prior authority, the function of which is to invest the present speaker with the weight of the prior authority and also with the status of an authority in her own right, as she becomes the representative not of herself as an individual but rather of the *institutionally agreed* force of taste and, *ipso facto*, correctness. In this mode of citation, the present speaker identifies himself closely with the prior author, appropriating her words: 'I think it was Schiller who once remarked that...', etc. When citations are attributed, we have the same situation. To demonstrate the point, I shall do it myself and cite Bourdieu:

> A practical mastery of social significance, based on functional and structural homology, underlies and facilitates everyday reading of the 'classics', and, even more, since it is a practical use, literary quotation, a quite special use of discourse which is a sort of summons to appear as advocate and witness, addressed to a past author on the basis of a social solidarity disguised as intellectual solidarity. The practical sense of meaning, which stops short of objectifying the social affinity which makes it possible – since that would nullify the desired effect, by relativizing both the reading and the text – provides simultaneously a social use and a denial of the social basis of that use. (*Distinction*, p. 73)

Institutional authority, it follows from this, depends upon a self-contradictory notion of distinction. To be an author, one must distinguish oneself from those who merely obey some already existing authority: one must be 'nonconformist'. Yet this distinction also involves an affiliation – more importantly, an identification – of the self with a class or institutional force; hence the extreme delimitation of distinction at the same time. In social terms, at least as these relate to questions of general cultural practice, this formulation of authority, vested in the names of certain authors, depends most immediately upon the class affiliations of those involved in acts of canon-formation, which is, of course, nothing more or less than parasitic citation writ large.

In the formulation of authority which comes in canon-formation we have an exemplification of the very essentialism of authority which circumvents history. Those involved in such an institution-alisation of authority pretend to be involved in a critical under-standing of certain texts. In fact, of course, what happens is slightly different. A group shares certain class values, and then pretends that according to their understanding of specific texts those values are validated by the texts which are deemed to 'contain' those values. Their understanding, of course, is one which depends upon the ideological interpellation by which they recognise themselves and their values not in the texts as such but in what they call their understanding of the texts' real meaning and value. The texts are thus vested with authority as the bearers of such values. Axiomatically, of course, the group defines its own understanding of the texts as valid and legitimate, rejecting competing possible understandings as tasteless, disgusting misreadings, which simply show not the fallibility of their own judgement but rather the lack of proper understanding and acknowledgement of authority on the part of other tasteless readers. This, the examination system which dominates education, is the manifestation of the aristocracy of culture, as Bourdieu calls it, an aristocracy which is profoundly essentialist:

> the holders of titles of cultural nobility – like the titular members of an aristocracy, whose 'being', defined by their fidelity to a lineage, an estate, a race, a past, a fatherland or a tradition, is irreducible to any 'doing', to any know-how or function – only have to be what they are, because all their practices derive their value from their authors, being the affirmation and perpetuation of the essence by virtue of which they are performed ... Aristocracies are essentialist ... The essence in which they see themselves refuses to be contained in any definition. Escaping petty rules and regulations, it is, by nature, freedom. (*Distinction*, pp. 23–4)

This 'aristocracy', then, in its essentialism, is precisely the police who arrest the nomads. By this, I mean to suggest that it is the very institutionalisation of authority, constitutive of an aristocracy of culture, which serves to fix and identify authority automatically (though ideologically), and to lead to an idealist and anti-historical construction of authority. Those who would be 'free' under this (modernist) system of thought must subscribe to such authority; but this, of course, in its essentialism, is precisely the counter to any more genuinely emancipatory deployment or articulation of authority on behalf of the subject who would be critical. The parasitic aristocracy looks both ways: back to prior authors whom they claim as their 'legislators' (and whom they edit, pretending to know them better than they knew themselves); and forward to those who will be subject to their legislation, the other 'disgusting' classes whose taste requires correction or, as we more frequently call it, education. Such education, of course, is nothing more or less than the policing of a thought which might otherwise threaten to proceed beyond the bounds controlled by the aristocracy of culture. The aristocracy, then, identify themselves firmly with and as the legislators of taste, value, legitimate cultural and political authority. The essentialism of this aristocracy – its closed nature, and the fact that it is unanswerable to anything outside its own ideological formation and values – is instrumental in the denial of history, a denial of the possibility of historical change. Certain institutions of learning acquire part of their authority from tradition, that is, from the fact that they are five hundred or so years old; but some universities have *always* been, and always will be, 'five hundred years old': their authority is vested in tradition or heritage, but not in history.

Understanding: authority as transgression

Understanding – as we understand it – is fundamentally an act of intellectual appropriation. There is a phenomenological situation in which a Subject of consciousness comes to inhabit a position from which the text makes sense, and thus he or she gains an 'authoritative' understanding of the text. 'Under-standing' is, of course, in these terms, 'over-coming', mastering a text. In it, the Subject identifies itself, as a Subject of consciousness, with the immediate (unmediated) substance of its thought; it thus *recognises* itself in a moment which is called free apprehension but which is actually ideological interpellation. More generally, to understand an enigma, one goes through certain moves. Firstly, one recognises it as an enigma because the language in which it is formulated does not immediately conform to the language in which we 'ordinarily' think. Secondly, one effects a translation so that the language in which the enigma is articulated is translated into something already known and recognisable within the rules and tenets of the language in which we formulate ourselves as authoritative Subjects of consciousness. In this way, the alterity of the world is reduced to identity: consciousness expands to grasp that which was foreign or alien. Alterity is reduced to homogeneity: the world is not unknown, it is simply the forgotten or repressed. The world becomes the unconscious of the Subject whose act of understanding involves a colonisation of the space of alterity and the collapsing of that complex and three-dimensional space into the narrow but reassuring confines of the two-dimensional and stereotypical mirror. It is in these terms, of course, that we 'understand' literary and other texts. We translate Chaucer into modern English; we translate the problems presented by that text called 'Shakespeare' into terms, values, categories – even dress – which we can at least recognisably comprehend. As Said has indicated, we 'understand' the plurality of the Arab world by collapsing it into a myth in which we see the undesired face of the American Subject, and so on.[7]

In every case of such understanding, there is an exercise in cartography. An alien terrain is redrawn as part of an extended 'home' terrain. 'Understanding' a text, then, implies the drawing of a strictly policed boundary within which we can either agree or disagree with the 'author' of the text under discussion. But the crucial point is that the *parameters* of agreement and discord have already been fixed through the imperialism which we call understanding. Such 'understanding' is an act complicit with the aristocracy of culture and its falsifications and idealist non-historical tendencies.

Yet this is what modernity calls 'reason'; and the aristocracy of culture professes itself reasonable. As part of Enlightenment (Habermas' 'project of modernity'[8]), we ascribe authority to reason itself. But there is, clearly, an aristocracy of reason which formulates itself in precisely the same 'distinctive' way as the aristocracy of culture. Such neo-Cartesian, 'self-evident' reason is one which arrests intellection, and which becomes fundamentally essentialist and class-based; and, as Baudrillard has it, 'les masses font masse' (*In the shadow of the silent majorities*, p. 1). Class reason provides the brake upon the authority of reason even as it formulates itself. Once more, this 'free' exercise of reason is not at all free but is rather predetermined and constrained in advance by class (as well as other) interests. This mode of reasoning is what Kant was to call 'determining judgement', a mode of thought which would have its basis in 'theory' as we would now call it. Its claims to a free objectivity are, however, contradicted by its inherent dependence upon a will which is introduced into reason and which perverts its free operation. There is, in short, a resistance to reason within the very Enlightenment reason that explains and underpins our 'understandings'.[9]

This mode of rationality, then, whose inherent imperialism of understanding renders alterity available for comprehension in terms which produce only the dialectic of mastery and slavery such that knowledge is always necessarily imbricated with power, might be countered by a different order of reason. A modernist rationality, contaminated by the introduction of the will into reason, leads only to a comforting imperialism of understanding, in which the Subject knows him- or herself to be axiomatically (or, we might now say, 'aristocratically') correct and tasteful in his or her judgements, both aesthetic and political. The counter to this would be an order of reason which eschews the world as Imaginary, and which prefers a Levinasian concern for the maintenance of alterity as alterity. Bachelard argued in quasi-Nietzschean fashion that 'One must return to human rationality its function as a force for turbulence and aggression. In this way surrationalism will be established, and this will multiply the occasions for thought.'[10] So instead of there being a will to conformity in reason, a will which reduces the world to the known but merely forgotten part of the Subject's identity and self-presence, we might have a contrary movement wherein lies the possibility of a mode of authority based upon a specific kind of transgression: a transgression against the very identity of the Subject him- or herself. This would entail a situation which would transgress against 'understanding'. The Subject of consciousness and thought itself would here be separated such that it would be possible to think without mastery, to know without power.

But Modernist authority is already, as I remarked, founded in transgression. Authority is linked in modernity to novelty, to what Said thinks as a 'heresy' or proposal of alternative beginnings to the narratives we live by. In order to be an author in modernity, one must do something avowedly 'new'; in order to be new, it must be in contradistinction to prevailing norms. Three things follow. Firstly, authority depends upon distinction. Secondly, to be an author one must hypothesise a prior system of law in the area in which one wants authority. Thirdly, once this hypothetical system

RIDING HOUSE STREET LIBRARY
...SITY OF WESTMINSTER
... Riding House St., W1P 7PT

is in place, one must intervene with some violation or transgression of its norms or laws. I set this out as if it were diachronic, but it is in fact synchronic: the three moves occur simultaneously, and their effect is the production of authority, of a position in which a Subject claims the mastery of understanding/overcoming.

The synchronicity of this is important. The authority or law against which one will transgress is actually produced coterminously with one's own intervention. Both the new and the prevailing authorities are effected at once. But this means that the prior law is a hypothetical construction whose formation is deployed in the interests of a particular set of present requirements. When, for instance, one attacks 'the entire history of Western philosophy' in the name of something called, say, deconstruction or feminism, it is important to realise that this 'entire history of Western philosophy' does not exist as such until deconstruction or feminism has formulated and characterised it in the particular way which will enable Derrida or Irigaray[11] to distinguish themselves from it.

Two questions now propose themselves. In the first place, the hypothetical law against which I will transgress in becoming an author itself determines and constructs the possibility of this transgression, which is thus drastically limited: the 'new' authority is predetermined and thus not very new at all. Secondly, something else now appears as a more primary determinant of the authoritative act, for it appears that my hypothetical prior law is constructed according to the requirements of a particular programme which states that if I want to perform a particular action, then I shall have to construct an authority-model whose transgression will inexorably demand or at least enable that action to take place in a valid and legitimate manner. I shall deal with these two issues separately.

To be an author, I must consciously transgress against a prevailing law.[12] But this means that I must already understand that law. 'My' authority sets up the law against which I transgress; and it is *according to those laws* that my action is deemed to be transgressive. Thus it is a transgression which, far from denying or refusing that law, serves simply to corroborate it as a law, norm or authority; and, by extension, to place me in the position of the renegade, the outlaw, the unconventional, the eccentric – or the critic. But it is now apparent that this 'criticism' is hardly a differential serious or radical kind of criticism, if it implicitly serves to consolidate the very laws it aims to attack.

In the case of the second problem, that of there being some more primary drive to authority in my actions, we have a slightly different issue. If it is the case that my transgressive act is itself predetermined, then one has to ask from where does the decision to transgress come in the first place? What is it that wants to perform the particular action which my authoritative intervention enables? Here, we find the crux of the modernist problem of authority. For if I suggest anything to fill in this blank originary space (be it instinct, ethics, social demand, ideology, neurosis, biology or whatever), then all I do is to repeat the first problem in a slightly different place, for I would then be forced to hypothesise a model of the authority of instinct, ideology or whatever fills my originary space. It is this very demand for the location *and identification* of a source for authority that is the problem: it is a theological (or at least idealist) impetus which remains within so-called secular modernist or enlightened thinking. In Said's terms, it is the demand for an origin rather than for a beginning. We should, therefore, simply scrap the problem. After Wittgenstein, it should be clear that I do not know what I mean until I have said it: my actions are necessarily undirected, experimental, 'avant-garde' in the sense of being 'untimely'. Their meaning, as they say, is not present to themselves. To pretend otherwise is to remain within the falsification and self-contradiction of modernity, whose secularism is thoroughly contaminated by idealism.

A modernist version of authority, which is determined to make meaning present-to-something, usually a proper name (of text or writer) is, in fact, a therapeutic inoculation against the seizure of authority and against the genuinely revolutionary historical act. It is an inoculation against the historicity of meaning with its drives towards deterritorialisation, anonymity and a revolutionary kind of avant-garde. Modernist authority is, to borrow Baudrillard's terms, a 'scenario of deterrence' (*Simulations*, p. 36), and what it wishes to deter – like capital and its aristocracies of culture – is the very possibility of history, mutability, and the concomitant threats posed to a social formation and a philosophy in which this aristocracy remains in explicit control and in which 'criticism' is locked away in that space reserved for dissidents: the institution of the academy. In this respect, authority – which appears to involve a specifically historical intervention on the part of an author – is precisely the scandal which preserves laws, norms and a principle of reality which is presented as fundamentally idealist and essentialist. If one task of Marxism was to get history started, we might add that one task of the postmodern is to get historical criticism started.

The question of postmodernism

Fredric Jameson writes of the 'effacement' in postmodernism of some 'key boundaries or separations, most notably the erosion of the older distinction between high culture and so-called mass or popular culture'. He goes on, in terms which should be placed alongside Bourdieu, to suggest that:

> This is perhaps the most distressing development of all from an academic standpoint, which has traditionally had a vested interest in preserving a realm of high or elite culture against the surrounding environment of philistinism, of schlock and kitsch, of TV series and *Reader's Digest* culture, and in transmitting difficult and complex skills of reading, listening and seeing to its initiates. But many of the newer postmodernisms have been fascinated precisely by that whole landscape of advertising and motels, of the Las Vegas strip, of the late show and Grade-B Hollywood film, of so-called paraliterature with its airport paperback categories of the gothic and the romance, the popular biography, the murder mystery and the sciencefiction or fantasy novel. They no longer 'quote' such 'texts' as Joyce might have done, or a Mahler: they incorporate them, to the point where the line between high art and commercial forms seems increasingly difficult to draw. ('Postmodernism and consumer society', p. 112)

This, to rephrase it in Bourdieu's terms, is precisely that taste which reveals itself as 'bad taste' because it mingles tastes to the point of indistinction. It is also the taste which thereby threatens socio-political 'identity', the class-identities which depend upon the formation of an aristocracy of culture and of a 'proletariat', those excluded from such an aristocracy.

If we begin from Jameson, we can see how postmodernism might help reinstate historicity to authority.[13] The melange of tastes, the eclecticism, of postmodernism leads to an inherent drive in the postmodern work to deterritorialisation and immaterialisation. For perhaps the first time, aligning oneself with a taste for the post-modern is not the articulation of a clearly defined class position. On the contrary, it implies a refusal of any such clear, stable iden-tification. There is no stable terrain from which or into which a colonising act of imperialist understanding can take place; nor is there any 'essential' work to be understood. In a particular sense, *the postmodern is not available for understanding*, at least in so far as understanding is actually the drive to mastery, to 'overcoming'.[14]

Kroker and Cook, in *The postmodern scene*, describe post-modernity as 'the quantum age', one in which a Virilian 'hyper-speed' problematises what we think of as normal epistemology:

> If the Newtonian law of gravity could postulate a *real* body whose ob-jectivity is established by its mass, the (quantum) law of postmodernity eclipses this body by flipping suddenly from mass to energy. (p. *v*)[15]

This description of a slippage from mass to energy is a recurring figure in many descriptions which strive to explain the elusiveness, the svelte lissom nature of the postmodern. Lyotard thinks it in terms of the growing 'immaterialisation' of culture; Virilio thinks it in terms of the effect of speed in technology; Deleuze in terms of a Bergsonian interior temporality or historicity of what appears superficially to be a stable mass; Baudrillard in terms of the questioning and problematisation of the entire principle of reality through the parodic simulacrum. A formulation of the same effect in specifically literary matters might be the suggestion of McHale that postmodernist fiction is a fiction which prioritises ontology over epistemology, in a reversal of the modernist priorities.[16]

There is something to all this. Lyotard describes the postmodern (seemingly paradoxically) as that which comes before the modern, as the founding condition of the possibility of the modern. The classic formulation of this is in terms of a future anteriority which is deemed the proper tense of the postmodern:

> A postmodern artist or writer is in the position of a philosopher: the text he writes, the work he produces are not in principle governed by

preestablished rules, and they cannot be judged according to a determining judgment, by applying familiar categories to the text or to the work.
Those rules and categories are what the work of art itself is looking
for. The artist and the writer, then, are working without rules in order
to formulate the rules of what *will have been done*. Hence the fact that
work and text have the characters of an *event*; hence also, they always
come too late for their author, or, what amounts to the same thing,
their being put into work, their realization (*mise en oeuvre*) always
begins too soon. *Post modern* would have to be understood according
to the paradox of the future (*post*) anterior (*modo*) ('Answering the
question', p. 81)

This can be briefly explained. The postmodern is the exercise of a
Kantian 'reflective judgement', as opposed to a 'determining judgement' in which the Subject of consciousness has merely to conform
with some overarching theory or set of prescriptions which will
tell him or her how to judge correctly in a particular case. The
postmodern is working without rules or theory, experimentally:
it is energetic, undirected, unprogrammed – and hence it lacks
any *identifiable* authority. The Modern is the moment in which
this radical energy reifies in a work/object, which can then become
a commodity, available for analysis and imitation. The 'event'
that is the postmodern becomes the 'work' that is Modern: the
historicity inscribed in postmodernity is drained, as the event is
given a location in space and time which can be identified and
referred to, and, ultimately, made available for knowledge, under-
standing/overcoming and the 'authority' that comes with it. The
fundamental opposition, thus, is between what I'll call the 'even-
tual' (which is postmodern, full of historicity) and the 'punctual'
(which is Modern, and is an identifiable location which literally
'roots' the postmodern, enables it to form an earth).

This postmodern is 'avant-garde' in the sense that it provokes
an 'untimeliness'; in its eventuality, it refuses punctuation, refuses
a 'proper' moment. Most importantly, it refuses a collocation *or
identification* between the Subject of consciousness and the
substance of his or her thought: it opens up a temporal *décalage*
between the Subject of consciousness and the substance of that
thought. It is this temporal *décalage* which is properly called
criticism.[17] In this postmodern, texts, writers and readers are all
fundamentally 'displaced'. As a result, authority is also displaced,

its interior energy released in 'lines of flight' or quanta. But this displacement is two-fold. Firstly, there is a displacement from the individual named authors to a socio-political formation – the historical events – which make the formulation of a specific work possible; secondly, there is the displacement of those authors in history as well, in their own 'untimeliness' with respect to the substance of their thought. Like Lacanian subjects, authors are always thinking just precisely where they are not and they are not where they think; hence they are always historically out of step with themselves.

The task of a criticism which would be historical is to reveal these displaced authorities which enable the constitution of specific individuals at specific moments as 'authors'. It is only in this way that knowledge will cease to be merely 'punctual' and that it will be released as an event, a historical eventuality. That is, knowledge will become inherently historical and *material*, and will produce an authority which is divorced from the totalising pretensions of a modernist knowledge with its drive to power and mastery, a mastery which requires slavery and which requires one individual to be recognised and identified as an essentially aristocratic master, an 'author'.

Notes

1 See, for example, H. Bloom, *The anxiety of influence* (New York: Oxford University Press, 1973); *A map of misreading* (New York: Oxford University Press, 1975); *Poetry and repression* (New Haven: Yale University Press, 1976); and *Agon* (New York: Oxford University Press, 1982). Prior to Bloom, the most succinct theoretical statement concerning the issue of such influence is W. Jackson Bate, *The burden of the past and the English poet* (London: Chatto & Windus, 1971).

2 See E. Said, *Beginnings* (New York: Basic Books, 1975) and 'On repetition', in *The world, the text, and the critic* (London: Faber & Faber, 1984). For some recent work on repetition, see G. Deleuze, *Différence et répétition* (Paris: PUF, 1968); J. Mehlman, *Revolution and repetition* (Berkeley and Los Angeles: University of California Press, 1977); and J. Hillis Miller, *Fiction and repetition* (Oxford: Basil Blackwell, 1982).

3. L. Althusser, 'Ideology and the ideological state apparatuses', in *Essays on ideology* (London: Verso, 1984). This Althusserian distinction between the realms of operation of the ISA and RSA corresponds, to some extent, with Gramsci's distinctions between civil and political society; and Gramsci's articulation of such different orders may, in fact, be more appropriate here.

4 M. Bakhtin and P.N. Medvedev, *The formal method in literary scholarship*, trans A.J. Wehrle (London: Harvard University Press, 1985), 95. By analogy with this argument, of course, one might veer towards the kinds of propositions advanced by the later Jean Baudrillard, that Marxism authorises capital. See, in this regard, J. Baudrillard, *Simulations*, trans. P. Foss, P. Patton and P. Beitchman (New York: Semiotext, 1983), 36–7; and cf. my comments on this in T. Docherty, *After theory* (London: Routledge, 1990), chapter 9.

5 This, of course, finds its most sophisticated version in Roland Barthes' question: 'Who is speaking thus?' in his 'The death of the author', in *Image-music-text*, trans. S. Heath (Glasgow: Fontana/Collins, 1977), 142.

6 G. Hartman, *The fate of reading* (Chicago: University of Chicago Press, 1975), 255; cf. Flaubert's famous comment that 'Madame Bovary, c'est moi'.

7 See E. Said, *Orientalism* (London: Routledge & Kegan Paul, 1978) and *Covering Islam* (London: Routledge & Kegan Paul, 1985). Said explicated this point further in direct relation to American foreign policy on the Iraqi Gulf crisis which began on 2 August 1990 in discussion with Michael Ignatieff on BBC2's edition of 'The late show', 6 September 1990.

8 See J. Habermas, 'Modernity – an incomplete project', in H. Foster, ed., *Postmodern culture* (London: Pluto Press, 1985) and, for a fuller argument, J. Habermas, *The philosophical discourse of modernity*, trans. F.G. Lawrence (Oxford: Polity Press, 1987).

9 See J.-F. Lyotard, 'Svelte appendix to the postmodern question', trans. T. Docherty, in R. Kearney, ed., *Across the frontiers* (Dublin: Wolfhound Press, 1988), 263–7. Where he indicates that what is at issue in the postmodern debate with Habermas is not so much reason itself as the introduction of the will into reason, an introduction which is there in Enlightenment thought.

10 G. Bachelard, as cited in Said, *Beginnings*, 40. See also S. hand, ed., *The Levinas reader* (Oxford: Basil Blackwell, 1989), passim.

11 See, for examples, J. Derrida, *Writing and difference*, trans. A. Bass (London: Routledge & Kegan Paul, 1981); *Of grammatology*, trans. G.C. Spivak (Baltimore and London: Johns Hopkins University Press, 1976); *Margins: of philosophy*, trans. A. Bass (Brighton: Harvester Press, 1982); *Dissemination*, trans. B. Johnson (Chicago: University of Chicago Press, 1981); and L. Irigaray, *Speculum* (Paris: Minuit, 1974).

12 Strictly speaking, the unconscious is not really admissible here. The entire issue is complicated by the reception of a transgression, itself of course to be transgressed if it is to become the source of an authority. Relevant examples would include the effects to which Nietzsche's writings were put by later agents, such as the Nazis, or the Heidegger and de Man controversies of recent years. To what extent are the authors 'responsible' for events which are not and cannot be in their consciousness?

13 But see Jameson's comments on the 'weakening of historicity' in a later version of the 'Postmodernism and consumer society' article, the much-quoted 'Postmodernism; or, the cultural logic of late capitalism', *New Left Review*, 146 (1984), 58.

14 For a more detailed elaboration of this argument, see my *After theory* (London: Routledge, 1990). On understanding as mastery and the complications proposed by this, see B. Johnson, 'The frame of reference', in her *The critical difference* (Baltimore and London: Johns Hopkins University Press, 1980).

15 A. Kroker and D. Cook, *The postmodern scene* (London: Macmillan, 1988).

16 See, for examples, B. McHale, *Postmodernist fiction* (New York: Methuen, 1987); P. Virilio, *L'horizon négatif* (Paris: Galilee, 1984); Deleuze, *Différence et répétition*, etc.; and the works of Lyotard and Baudrillard.

17 A fuller version of this argument is to be found in my article 'Anti-mimesis: the historicity of representations', *Forum for Modern Language Studies*, 26 (1990), 272–81, and in my study *After theory*.

4

Distant voices, real lives: authorship, criticism, responsibility

Graham McCann

> We read that the traveller asked the boy if the swamp before him had a solid bottom. The boy replied that it had. But presently the traveller's horse sank in up to the girths, and he observed to the boy, 'I thought you said that this bog had a hard bottom'. 'So it has', answered the latter, 'but you have not got halfway to it yet.' So it is with the bogs and quicksands of society; but he is an old boy that knows it.
> (Thoreau, *Walden*, p. 378)

When one believes in the idea of an author, one makes a choice, one commits oneself to a certain way of thinking. This discussion concerns itself with the possible reasons for making such a commitment. I wish to argue that the critical enterprise is founded in hope, and that a great deal of what currently passes as criticism cannot accommodate such hope. Criticism is oriented toward the future: the critic must believe that the conduct of other people can conform more closely to a moral standard than it now does, or that their self-understanding can be greater than it now is, or that their institutions can be more justly organised than they now are. Such belief is now under threat. Many influential voices inform us that the 'author' is dead (or at least, for practical purposes, in an advanced stage of mortification), and that the biographical analysis of an artist or thinker is either irrelevant or not fully serious. Roland Barthes argued, in his highly influential article, 'The death of the author', that 'To assign an author to a text is to impose a brake on it, to furnish it with a final signified, to close the writing' (p. 53). What may have been in 1968 a polemical overstatement is now entrenched academic dogma.

In the hands of its most gifted practitioners, poststructuralism has yielded a brilliance of critical analysis that only the intellectually prejudiced can discount, and has generated an appeal that only the professionally indifferent can deny. However, much poststructural criticism tends to carry what has sometimes been called the 'hermeneutics of scepticism' to the point of converting disbelief into the only operative intellectual category, and playful cynicism into the only viable critical stance. What Steiner has aptly termed 'corner-of-the-mouth criticism' is commonly heard. Too often deconstructive procedures (like analytical procedures) seem readily used to bring theory a false peace, which may well present itself in the form of bustling activity. Professional theory has always been a somewhat armoured (not to say combative) activity in which distance, sobriety, impersonality and methodology have been the favoured positions – in many seminar rooms as well as in most critical and scholarly books and journals. There are obvious reasons for this, and obvious benefits have come from it. However, the losses have also been great, for the very adoption of such postures wards off many gifts that theory offers and blunts many of its powers, perverting its best intentions. Not only its power to move, excite and trouble its readers, but also its offering of certain kinds of truths – those truths that come into being only when armour and distance are removed or when both author and audience permit themselves to concentrate as nearly as possible with what Coleridge called the whole of one's soul.

Traditionally, text and author have been regarded as in some sense linked: texts result from the activities of authors, authors are responsible for the existence of texts. The word 'textuality' is introduced to question this entire attitude; instead of depending so much upon an author, a text has an independence, a 'textuality' in its own right. This argument moves in a different direction from that of the older argument concerning the 'intentional fallacy' (which notes that people may not always see the significance of their own actions, and thus they may need someone else, working from a different, broader, perspective, to go further). The concept of textuality, however, is a far more radical idea: in cutting the tie with the author, the implication is that we cut the tie with *any* idea of a statable meaning. The text now has a life of its own and an endless series of possible meanings, which are no longer subject to control either by the author's actions, decisions, and intentions, or by the rules and conventions of language. Textuality replaces the author with the reader. Now the critic's task is to enter into the infinite play of meanings without ever coming under their sway. The trick is to keep from being 'taken in', and this requires an almost superhuman critical vigilance. In this radically sceptical hermeneutics, the motive force behind all interpretive activity is not to understand the integrity of other minds but to resist their domination, and criticism is reduced in whole (rather than, as surely it is, in part) to a science of the semantics and semiotics of discourse, which not only delimit but essentially control all forms of expressive interchange.

The idea that signs play infinitely and indiscriminately against each other is one that is asserted without any real supporting argument, and it is inherently an impossible one to justify. To postulate a sign that simply played indefinitely and infinitely against other signs is to imagine one with no distinct character at all, one not recognisable as having any shape or function of its own. This produces not more and richer meanings (as advocates of this position like to suggest), but no meaning at all. Vagueness in signs introduces diminution, not augmentation, of meaning. If one believes that previous criticism has been superficial and incomplete in its account of what a text signifies, one must offer a more inclusive and complex view of its meaning. This does not necessitate any novel theory of signification. The critic shows something *particular*; it is self-delusion to believe one has shown something indeterminate and indiscriminate.

One of the most important errors of the thinking commonly associated with the concept of textuality lies in the failure to recognise that there are *two* steps, not one, involved in the notion that a text must be liberated from its author to mean whatever it is taken to mean. First, there is liberation from the author; second, there is liberation from the rules and conventions of the language it is written in. In effect, the textuality argument operates with just two alternatives: either a text means what its author meant, or we have free play. The assumption that to liberate a text from its author is to liberate it from all constraints is a primitive one; it leaps from one extreme to another – total constraint or no constraint whatsoever. Even ambiguity requires specificity for it to work; textuality would destroy it, along with all other meaning in a text, by making that text too indeterminate even for ambiguity to be visible. Indeed, the idea of fidelity to the text in translation (trying to 'listen' to what the text says) is lost in such an approach. One closes one's ears to the call (and the plight) of the other.

When Stanley Fish tells us that if two readers disagree there is no way of appealing to the text to decide the issue between them (p. 340), he leaves us with two people and two opinions that never come into contact with each other; they remain what they are, never meet, therefore never modify. This is an insultingly fanciful supposition; in the real world, progress in all spheres of life occurs through the clash of conflicting opinions. In that clash, views do not simply persevere unaltered; on the contrary, the development of knowledge is dialectical, it is a *social* process, and appeal to the text under discussion is a vital part of that process. The issue is not necessarily what one *meant* to say but *what one can reasonably be held to have said.* What such writers as Stanley Fish inscribe is the naming of a wish (and the possibility of someone wishing) to strip oneself of the responsibility involved in meaning (or in failing to mean) one thing, or one way, rather than another. I would contend that this view of criticism speaks to an emotional attitude that has long been widespread among critics. Textuality is only a particularly egregious formulation of the traditional *laissez-faire* attitude of that strain of criticism that has always wanted above all else to be free to do and say whatever it wished, without being held accountable or required to justify its comments and their consequences. If the metaphysica of presence has been undermined by the critical philosophy of the last three hundred years, the fact remains that these 'newest' critics of culture can no more do without its assumption of an ontological centre *somewhere* (of what Thoreau once called 'a hard bottom and rocks in place' (p. 142)) than can the most intransigent Platonist or neo-Aristotelian. Adopting a theory means living with its consequences. The theory in question leaves us no one to live with, and nothing to live for.

Such is the volume of printed material that no one could hope to read more than a small fraction of all that is published. We are compelled to make choices to read this rather than that; how are we to decide and take seriously (and sometimes even act upon)

this rather than that piece of criticism? The inability to monitor
the quality of criticism is a serious omission, yet textuality is
committed to such an omission as a matter of principle. Such a
theory commits us to a careless amorality: we are unable to
discriminate when faced with a number of differing interpretations,
and we are unable, and unwilling, to offer argument or support for
our own interpretation.

When a theory has such embarrassing consequences as these,
any prudent theorist will surely have the courage to admit that
the theory has gone badly wrong and must be revised. Textuality's
infinity of meanings in a text makes a paradox out of a platitude.
It is, in practice, a most pernicious doctrine; it encourages us to
stop discriminating, to stop thinking about interpretations and
their strengths and weaknesses. Deconstruction is not incorrect in
saying that the critic is creative; where it *is* disastrously wrong,
however, is in its assumption that creativity means freedom from
constraints and from standards of judgement operating on its results.
Effective perception and communication necessitate a judicious
mixture of suspicion and trust: universal scepticism and complete
credulity are equally disabling. To be creative is not to let one's
imagination run wild: it is to use one's imagination productively.
What counts as 'productive' is, of course, a matter we must debate.

In practice, many critics who advocate textuality do not fully
accept its consequences, but this critical stance has none the less
had enough influence upon the practice of criticism to cause a
considerable decline in its quality. A constructive theory exerts its
pressure on the status quo by continual examination of the basis and
rationale for the accepted activities of an area of study. Inevitably,
the results will in principle be unlike the usual deconstructionist
attitudes: they should introduce a *clarification* and a *differentiation*
of fundamentally different kinds of activities. The consequence of
such activity will generally be a pressure to rearrange priorities;
by its very nature, then, theory is indeed unsettling. Theoretical
argument must, for this very reason, proceed with extraordinary
care. There is no room in theoretical argument for individual
licence, for claims of exemption from logical scrutiny, for appeals
to an undefined unique logical status, for requests to allow obscurity
to stand unanalysed, or for freedom to do just as one wishes.

The replacement of the human by the linguistic turns out to be a self-defeating gesture in every sense. For the human subject always returns in the act of writing, and to attempt its suppression in writing is ultimately an act of self-violence. Although critics often seek to justify the importance of language as a means of eliminating the aggressive authority of the human subject and its history of misdemeanours, they cannot escape this same history, and they end by erecting the edifice of language upon the tomb of the human self. The human face, as it were, must be washed away to make way for language. Lukács' concept of reification explains how the modes of production in capitalism gradually peel away all signs of the human from our lives; modern critics have fallen prey to a form of reification in their preference for language over the human. Every day the idea of the human grows fainter and more distant even as theories of language become more fragmented. Modern theory consequently enacts a maddening gesture doomed to repeat the crimes that it despises the most: killing the concept of the self because the self may kill does not extricate one from the cycle of violence. There are luxuries of detachment one should like to afford, but cannot. 'Violence' is a term that captures the area of concern currently shared by criticism and ethics because it alone evokes the visceral reaction that provides a key to the stakes at issue. The word 'violence' evokes fear and pity, courage and compassion, exposing those emotions that define us most as human beings. This anthropological base is central to an understanding of the ethics of modern criticism because theorists today, despite all claims to the contrary, are engaged in a species of argument that has startling implications for the way in which we relate to and define the human world.

Violence exists whenever human beings harm other human beings. Such violence takes many forms, arising in physical attacks or words and actions that deprive human beings of their humanity. Violence is a human problem. It is never an infernal machine without a maker; it is never without a victim. Criticism would seem far removed from such matters. Its isolation in the seminar room and the scholarly journal makes it a tame occupation, and many of the dangers now associated with criticism by those in search of a vicarious thrill would be laughable, given the state of terrorism and brutality in the world, if they were not so misguided. Yet language is one instrument of human violence, and in that respect critics have a responsibility not only to supervise their own unjust practices as critics but also to think about the ways in which language carries on the work of human prejudice, racism, sexism and nationalism.

The reaction of critics to violence needs to be interpreted, first and foremost, as an ethical gesture performed within a human context, and in this context literary and ethical problems cannot be separated, no matter how zealous the claim for the autonomy of the text. The substitution of language for the self produces its own distinct moral dilemma because it has created a view of human consciousness in which ethical reflection is always destined to fail. The character of language promoted by theory today makes extremely difficult the type of consciousness necessary to moral reflection. The consequence of most modern criticism is, at best, a politics of indifference and reaction, at worst, a politics of anarchy and hedonism. It certainly does not make for a serviceable account of human life. Even when the verbal play of the performance, instead of being 'serious', is at its most whimsical and promiscuous, where it turns against itself and contemplates the absurdity of its own predicament, something about the exercise, if not disturbingly logocentric, is disconcertingly egocentric. If only because of the radical energy of mind and imagination required by its intellectual procedures, one is compelled to say that the discourse tends to focus an inordinate amount of attention directly upon itself. Thus, while the language of the discourse is successfully subverting everything within it, the 'voice' of the discourse is effectively subordinating everything outside it. In short, the discourse is always tending to become a monologue.

A moral defensiveness pervades the definition of the critic's character in almost every major thinker on the current scene. Each tries to capture an aura of innocence and moral disinterestedness by cultivating personal marginality. Lévi-Strauss uses the idea of *dépaysement* to characterise the anthropologist. Foucault allies himself with the outcasts of history. Derrida appropriates Rousseau's rhetoric of marginality to develop a theory of linguistic difference that enacts a kind of morality play dependent on

Rousseau's ideas of human equality and difference. Only some instances of feminist criticism have foreseen the dangers of turning marginality and suffering into a commodity or privileged claim to critical insight. A marginal position may be converted into a sensational claim for literature and the critic, but its value is highly suspicious. It sometimes cloaks itself in mystical language to achieve a distance from the real issues of living and hoping and caring and choosing in the world.

Criticism requires critical distance, but it is not at all clear how *much* distance critical distance involves. Collingwood noted the problem at the end of his autobiography when he acknowledged how the political events of the day had 'impinged upon myself and broke up my pose of a detached professional thinker' (p. 167). The conventional view is that critics must be intellectually and emotionally detached, disinterested and dispassionate. However, in spite of the 'heroic' difficulty of finding a properly detached position, the conventional critic is more than compensated for by the ease of criticism once one is settled there. Such a notion has become conventional in part because of a confusion between detachment and marginality. Marginality is not a condition that makes for disinterest, dispassion or objectivity. The difficulties experienced by marginal figures are not the difficulties of detachment but rather of ambiguous connection: liberate them from those difficulties, and they may well lose the reasons they have for embracing the critical enterprise.

A truly constructive and compassionate critic, on the contrary, is someone who earns authority, or fails to do so, by arguing with his or her fellow citizens – someone who, angrily and insistently, sometimes at considerable risk (of professional censure, physical and verbal abuse, and public mockery) objects, protests, persuades and remonstrates. Criticism that goes beyond crass negation involves the taking of risks, and the possibility of being taken. One risks getting things wrong, being deceived, and even, sometimes, being astonished. As Steiner has observed:

> We have come into a time which is not, as Auden said, the age of anxiety, but the age of embarrassment. The blackmail of embarrassment is absolutely upon us: about the major experiences – death, love,

self-sacrifice, madness. *We're embarrassed by just about everything*. The great phrase 'come off it' could have made Beethoven stop the Ninth Symphony, and Michelangelo the Sistine ceiling. Creation by a great artist is one hell of an enigma. ('Interview')

Criticism is one of the more important by-products of a larger activity – the activity of cultural elaboration and affirmation, the work of story-tellers and sages, poets and teachers. The resources necessary for criticism of some sort, and more than a minimalist sort, are always available, because of what a moral world is, because of what we do when we construct it. These are urgent concerns: they derive from the persistent cares and desires of people who think, write, read and live together. They are *human* concerns, focused on the eminence of society and the forms of violence that threaten community, and they represent the only space from which people cannot free themselves and still exist. The human space is often heavy with the stale grandeur of annihilation. More often it is simply mundane, as it should be, sounding of human language, conversation and noise. Both aspects constitute the world not as seen from above, but as seen by human beings, a world of ethics and aesthetics, life and literature, and human beings cannot escape.

The New Criticism and its various descendants rescued texts, and continue to do so, from certain kinds of distortion and emasculation by insisting on their autonomy and examining them carefully and closely. However, by viewing them essentially as sets of internal relations or as objects in a network of other cultural objects, such criticism also in some fundamental way dehumanises them. To cut a work off from its source is to cut it off from life (a real life, no matter how distant). What kind of critic would (or *could*) do such a thing? Coleridge described such critics (with a passion one misses today) as 'truants and deserters from their own hearts' ('A prefatory observation on modern biography', p. 59). When we remove an account, whether explicitly or implicitly, from the context of author and reader, we obscure the fact that whatever the theoretical rationales and whatever the layers of static or disguise, these works are forms of communication, often quite wonderful ones, between human authors and human readers. We are clever enough to play games at the borderline between sense and nonsense and to dance at the edge of the abyss. We have become clever enough, in fact, to deconstruct the planet, but why do we have to go on proving it? If we deny to words and theories their power to move and motivate us; if all that lies before us is a landscape of 'texts' to decode, what an empty prospect, what a frightening thought. These are anxious times for all of us; our own anxiety is not irrelevant to our work. Just as one's choice of work must not be due to mere convenience, chance or expediency, but should directly reflect how one reaches for self-realisation in the modern world, so the realisation of one's work, besides being objectively purposeful, should also reflect one's own purpose in life.

The critic must guard against intolerance and insensitivity as well as indulgence and infatuation; when we are too little attentive to each other's presence, each other's wonder, each other's human plight, we are unworthy of our subject. One cannot say that all suffering is caused by the hard-hearted or by those who sit too comfortably within their critical armour or look down from too great a distance, but such complacencies do much to compel the roar and to define the shape of the cross. Primo Levi once wrote: 'The aims of life are the best defence against death' (p. 120). In order to highlight these aims and encourage their pursuit, we, as academics, need to spend more time demonstrating the links between the compassion that moves us and the knowledge that makes and masks us. Theory must do more than reflect on catastrophe; it must help us to survive it and prevent its reoccurrence. The primary aim of theory is not more theory, but rather to improve the ways in which we live. The terrible fragility of a human life is something that should inform the ways in which we teach and act.

No amount of academic abstraction can erase the sufferings of those people we study, and we have no right dispassionately to 'use' their tragedies for our theoretical work. If we are to be of help to others, we must be responsible for what we write (and how we write it). There must be a movement away from the repressive extremes of critical distance and dispassionateness, a movement whereby academics neither muffle their own voices nor use them to despoil, but rather seek to make audible their personal stakes in the work that engages them. Only after despair and equally only after hope can we discover what it is on which our existence depends. As Thoreau says in *Walden*, 'You may sit as many risks as you run' (p. 199): you need not look for moral adventure, it will find you if you are serious.

References

Barthes, R., *The rustle of language* (Oxford: Basil Blackwell, 1986).
Coleridge, S. T., 'A prefatory observation on modern biography' (1810), rpt. in J. Clifford, ed., *Biography as art* (London: Oxford University Press, 1962).
Collingwood, R. G., *An autobiography* (Oxford: Clarendon, 1978).
Fish, S., *Is there a text in this class?* (Cambridge, Mass.: Harvard University Press, 1980).
Levi, P., *The drowned and the saved* (London: Michael Joseph, 1988).
Steiner, G., 'Interview', on *Third Ear*, BBC Radio 3, 21 May 1989.
Steiner, G., *Real presences* (London: Faber, 1989).
Thoreau, H. D., *Walden* (Harmondsworth: Penguin, 1983).

PART III

The Rushdie affair: responses

5

Authorship and the supplement of promotion

Andrew Wernick

> But the supplement supplements. It adds only to replace. It intervenes
> or insinuates itself *in the place of*; if it fills, it is as if one fills a void.
> If it represents and makes an image, it is by the anterior default of a
> presence. Compensatory (*suppleant*) and vicarious, the supplement is
> an adjunct, a subaltern instance which *takes-(the)-place* [*tient-lieu*] ...
> the sign is always the supplement of the thing itself. (Jacques Derrida,
> *Of Grammatology*[1])
>
> Are you genuine? or only an actor? A representative? or that which is
> itself represented? – Finally you are no more than the imitation of an
> actor ... (Friedrich Nietzsche, *Twilight of the Idols*[2])

Advertising/writing

An opening move of late 1960s poststructuralism was Derrida's
critique of the primacy in Western thought of speech over writing.[3]
Far from writing being a mere, and yet (following Rousseau)
'dangerous' derivative from the spoken word, the *phone* itself is
within language and thus subject to the play of substitutions which
define both writing and its danger. In that play, the subject and
object of signification are always absent, and meaning is endlessly
dispersed in the 'seminal adventure of the trace'. Writing, then,
becomes the key for understanding speech, in an understanding
which undoes the very rationality on which the distinction is based.

Derrida's manoeuvre cut several ways. In the first instance it
was philosophical: an attempt, in line with the projects of Husserl
and Heidegger, to close the book on the Western tradition by having
done, in one last meditative spasm, with its circular metaphysics
of being and presence. It was also a move within literary theory,

wherein 'deconstruction' has both provided a new (and prodigiously productive[4]) interpretative method, and, in its pan-textualism, given renewed impetus to literary theory itself. Derrida's critique of phonocentrism, finally, has an ideological aspect. It undoes the authority of every *auctor*. Moreover, if it is the signifying, authorial, subject whose ontic and explanatory status is most immediately laid waste, the discredit extends to the whole notion of the individual as the rational agent of practice and history, and thus to what has evidently been a cornerstone of liberal capitalist discourse. And not only that, for the category of the collective subject (as producer of history, etc.) likewise falls to the ground.[5]

These issues have been debated endlessly. But what has tended to disappear from view is that Derrida's depreciation of the oral undermines not only the West's traditional forms of metaphysics, hermeneutics and politics, but also all those currents of critique, whether naturalist, organicist or neo-Hellenic, for whom the (face-to-face, auratic, etc.) values of oral culture have served as a culturological vantage-point from which to dissect industrial and post-industrial society at the level of its communicative (in)authenticity. Perhaps the clearest versions of this position are to be found in the work of the culture-and-technology thinkers who gathered in mid-century Toronto. The school's founders were Eric Havelock and Harold Innis, its most recent representative was Walter Ong, and its most influential figure (though he ambiguously embraced TV as a return of the oral) was McLuhan.[6]

I mention the Toronto school's largely forgotten project of developing a humanist historiography of communications in the belief that, while the deconstructive damage certainly obliges us to rethink their phonocentric theory of media, it is worth preserving at least the sense of cultural unease to which it was linked. It is in that spirit, at least, that the following remarks are offered on an aspect of contemporary writing (and of what media students sometimes call 'superwriting') which Derridian concepts can powerfully illuminate, but which his own more philosophical preoccupations led him to gloss over. (I should immediately add that my borrowing is analogical, and I shall leave to one side the question of how the unease from which I want to speak can itself be cogently conceived if the phonic subject loses its originary place.)

The theme I want to bring to the surface is not easy to introduce, for it concerns the most banal, grubby and self-interested side of the writing process. So let me begin obliquely by recalling the familiar poststructural dictum about the birth of the reader and the death of the author, and then note a paradox. This is that what springs to mind, even as we hear these phrases, is the famous authors (Barthes, Foucault, Derrida ...) with whom they are associated. It will be objected that two different senses of 'author', not to mention of mortality, are here being confused. On the one hand is the concrete-historical individual whom we have learned *not* to think of as the expressive subject of 'his' or 'her' text. On the other is a name, an identification tag, which circulates independently of the phantom individual, and which functions at once as the signatured assertion of a property right, and as a vehicle for whatever significance, reputation, or myth (including, generically, the myth of the author-creator itself) that name has come to acquire. To be sure, as person and label, they differ. The Julia Kristeva or Elmore Leonard who 'wrote' the original manuscript of this or the other published book is not the same entity as the name that appears on its front cover, and whose lustre induces us, often sight unseen, to buy them. At the same time, these different manifestations of the signifying subject evidently interconnect. Subjectively, indeed, the tie can be so intimate as to be confusing. With due regard for the participation of others, the author authors the 'author', even as he or she writes.

In effect, it is a matter of confronting the Barthian formula about the death of the author with another from Harold Innis. In his *Idea File* Innis noted that with the industrialisation of print the profession of writing was not only encroached upon by advertising (with its demand for copy-writers and the like), but that published writing became, in itself, a 'device for advertising advertising'.[7] In the first instance Innis was thinking about the conjoint rise of journalism, department stores, and an advertiser-sponsored mass press. But he also had in mind the impact on even serious, and autonomous, writing of the publishing industry's own marketing needs, including those of writers themselves.

What I want to foreground, then, is the relation that the market economy institutes between the communicative aspect of writing and (an increasingly salient aspect of) its performative aspect: that is, between what texts 'say', and what they help circulate. The word I use for the force/function engaged in the latter is *promotion*, which I will define as *any act or process of communication that serves to stimulate the circulation of something in the context of its competitive exchange*. With that understanding I shall propose: first, that the author, even the most exalted and the least immediately commercial in motivation, is doubly implicated in promotion, both as the operator of a (self-)promotional practice and (via the imaging and publicising of a name) as its object, as a produced promotional sign; secondly, that this implication registers the supplemental effects of the commodity, effects that feed back into every aspect of the production and dissemination of the commodifed sign; and thirdly, that this state of affairs, which affects all media, creates problems for the intellectual and artistic producer which exceed those usually ascribed to commercialism. And for cultural consumers too: if the well of authenticity is poisoned at source, it is hard to know where, or how, to drink.

The name of the author

Consider the following newspaper extract. It is taken from a piece by Amit Roy, entitled 'A year of living dangerously', which appeared on the front page of the *Sunday Times* review section on 14 January 1990. The top half of the page is dominated by a grim-faced picture of the endangered man himself. This is flanked by two smaller ones: a gesticulating Ayatollah, and a group of placard-waving British Muslims ('Free speech is the privilege of the powerful'). No prizes for guessing the identity of their target. Reports Roy:

> Since there is cachet in getting copy from a writer in captivity, the *New York Times* book review section today leads with Rushdie's review of *Vineland* by Thomas Pynchon, a mysterious American author who leads the life of a recluse. Adopting California beach slang, Rushdie remarks wryly: 'The secrecy surrounding this book ... has been, let's face it, ridiculous. I mean, really. So he wants a private life and no photographs and nobody to know his home address. I can dig it, I can relate to that (but like, he should try it when it's compulsory instead of a free-choice option).'

I will pass over the irony that is admitted to concentrate on a second which is not. This is that the reluctantly constituted publicity value of both literary names becomes the occasion for a further round of publicity in which the drawing power of each serves to promote the books and reputations of the other. The way this works is straightforward enough. But as we move back and forth from Roy's own piece to the one he cites, and through the many promotional levels both contain, we see that there is a complexity to this interplay which is worth pondering.

Let us start with the Rushdie piece to which Roy refers. At the most immediate level, Rushdie's review in the *New York Times* amounts to a boost for Pynchon's book. From this angle it is almost irrelevant what Rushdie's judgements actually are. Even a pan would do. The very fact of the review, the notice it provides, the implicit judgement that the book is significant, and so worth reviewing, are positive publicity in themselves. As too, of course, is the signature attached to it. For in this little scene, Rushdie is not just the writer of the ad. He is inside its frame, in a promotional operation wherein the name of one master of the postmodern novel (his own) is being invoked to sell the most recent work of another.

But through that same gesture, the favour is returned. For what is signified by the fact that Rushdie was asked to do the review, and by the way in which, through it, Rushdie's name is associated with Pynchon's, is the implication that there is a rough parity between them. You do not invite a midget to pass public judgement on a giant. The linkage to Pynchon, moreover, not only reinforces Rushdie's professional status – pointing towards his own admission into the company of Great Contemporary Writers. By inserting Rushdie into a schema of recluse/fugitive, paranoid/persecuted, that same linkage also has an imaging effect: it gives nuance, and sharpness, to what 'Rushdie' means.

Besides the fee, then, what Rushdie the writer gets for his authorial labour is a small but actual boost to the sign-exchange value of his name. But there is more. From the *New York Times*'s own point of view, Rushdie's selection as a reviewer was not an idle choice. He was approached, we may suppose, not just as an appropriately qualified writer, but also because his signed authorship ensured that the piece would be noticed; indeed, that the whole review section in which it appeared would be noticed. Through Roy's citation, this particular issue was even brought to the attention of a million and a half *Sunday Times* readers in Britain. Evidently, then, hooking readers through Rushdie helps promote not only Pynchon, but the *New York Times* itself. Nor is such self-generating publicity incidental to the kind of publication the *New York Times* is. However intelligent or worthy its contents, the book review section of America's number one 'quality' paper is no less commercially conceived than any of its other parts. By addressing the 'educated reader' with matters of current literary interest it not only helps sell books: it draws towards itself those who are the paper's primary target market. As such, the *NYT* book review section is only a special and complicated case of a wider phenomenon: the way that consumer reportage on one or another branch of the culture industry has itself been commodified. Here, with Rushdie splashed across its front cover, and as one of more than a dozen theme fold-outs, the review is sold as part of a larger package. The magazine world offers a plethora of examples where this kind of material has been turned into a commodity in itself. But in every case, from upscale qualities to downmarket tabloids, from *People Magazine* to the *New York Review of Books*, the use made of big name cultural producers and performers is the same. They are promotional signs, serving to advertise not only the books, films, records, etc., with which these personalities are 'creatively' associated; but also the publications which have them on their covers, or feature them prominently within.

Let us now turn to Amit Roy's own piece. One year after the *fatweh* drove him underground, it similarly headlines Rushdie in the lead article of the review section of a quality Sunday newspaper. Indeed, it replicates exactly the promotional structure of the review from which it quotes. Of course, the elements are transposed. In the *Sunday Times*, it is not Rushdie who ratifies and enhances his prestige by being the named commentators, but (in smaller print, as is fitting) Amit Roy. And the main focus of attention is not on Pynchon (though he gets a plug too), but on Rushdie himself. Both articles, in fact, are part of the media splash through which Rushdie's books, especially the notorious one, are promoted by the very movement that has tried to ban it.

Even this is not the end. On the same page as Roy's piece on Rushdie are a number of straightforwardly commercial notices. They range from ones for the Midland Bank and Pilgrim Payne Upholsterers ('by appointment to Her Majesty the Queen') to an ad for an anonymous car sale company which just invites us to 'call this number'. The *Sunday Times*, like the *New York Times*, is not just a saleable product. It carries paid advertising for other products as well. Because of advertising revenue, its production costs are subsidised. (The *Sunday Times* charges 60p a copy, but reportedly makes a net unit surplus of just over a pound.) The business of newspapers, in fact, is not so much to sell newspapers as to sell advertising space. Indeed, considering that the price of the latter depends on the size and composition of the paper's readership, its real business is organising and selling that readership itself.

The fact that newspapers, and other media, should have come to play this role is not surprising. The public provision of information and entertainment (in modern media, these merge) are, precisely, *public* activities, sites therefore for publicising not just themselves but everything. Over the past hundred years these sites have proliferated, and new technologies have made possible a vastly expanded audience reach. Today we still have billboards on city streets, but the highways of print and electricity have replaced physical ones as the most important place for displaying promotional messages. The advantages have been mutual: on the one side, an ever-expanding culture industry, financed in large measure through marketing costs passed on to the general consumer; on the other, for product and service manufacturers, marketing access to the enormous and variegated audiences that mass media attract.

But financial dependency carries a price. Whatever its ostensible and first order content, the function of the material disseminated through ad-carrying media is – and has to be – to draw audiences towards the commercials that punctuate the flow.[8] From *The Cosby Show* to literary chit-chat about Pynchon and Rushdie, it is all a 'device for advertising advertising'. Moreover, the commercial need to attract a saleable audience feeds back into every detail of the way newspapers, or the programmes of network TV, are conceived, presented, and produced. Thus the Roy piece on Rushdie, like Rushdie's review of Pynchon, not only helps publicise the review section it heads up, and, through this, the newspaper to which the section belongs. Its function is also to attract, and maintain, the particular kind of readership (affluent ABs) that the paper's advertisers seek. Conjuring with the names of Rushdie and Pynchon is a submarket tactic within the wider circulation of cultural and other commodities. If we consider how reportage can promote, how ads themselves continually quote from non-ad culture, and how famous names can become outright product sponsors, there is a further corollary. The brand-name promotion of cultural goods and the brand-name promotion of non-cultural goods intersect, indeed condense, within the same mass-communicated textual space.

From example to schema

On the basis of this sketchily analysed example, I would like to suggest a more general schema: four (logico-historical) moments in the promotional constitution of the authorial name.

In the first moment, the name of the author, as with the name of anyone in the public domain (and who, ultimately, is not?) is a site around which cluster various perceptions of who and what they are. Whence, mediated by all the vicissitudes of reception, comes an overall sense of an author's reputation on the local – or global – literary stage. There is something organic in the development of this 'name'. Even today, canon formation is not completely reducible to the vagaries of market-driven fads and fashions. But there is also something ambiguous about it. Reputation is a composite of identity and standing; and the latter involves a competition for status which is both invidious and conducive to hierarchy. Of course, the biggest stakes are beyond the grave. But even if History is to be the final judge, the contest for *fama* can leak back into the writing process, and the author's ego can get involved. 'I have completed', boasts Horace at the end of Book Three of the *Odes*, 'a monument more lasting than bronze'.[9] Just by being individually (as)signed, then, the name of the author is at least nascently caught up in a process of (self)-promotion – and this even without the calculated appearances, and masked instrumentalisation of discourse, which characterise promotion in a more fully developed sense.

This fuller development comes with the second moment: the entry of writing into relations of exchange; into a situation, that is, where publishing is a business, where authorship is a specialised profession, and where inter-individual competition for money and status is the acknowledged basis of social life. Under these conditions the authorial name undergoes a double transformation. First, in so far as that name can be cashed in on, via mutual favours, publishing contracts, and sales, it becomes directly implicated in exchange. Secondly, the authorial name becomes subject to a process of artificial imaging. At this stage, its connotative value emerges not only from a spontaneous, if mediated, process of reception, but also from the interventions of a distinct kind of practice. Besides the promotional calculations involved in the writing process itself – what to publish, under what title, and (if there is choice) with whom – this practice may involve direct advertising, as well as signings and speaking tours, interviews and newspaper reviews, and even the media full-out provoked (wittingly, or unwittingly) by a *succès de scandale*.

From the point of view of the author's career (itself a compound of professional/popular standing and income-earning capacity) and authorial name is *promotional capital*. From that of the commodified literary product (behind which stands the publishing industry, as well as, in the role of petty commodity producers, writers themselves) it is a *promotional sign*. That is: a sign with associative value (Agatha Christie, the next novel by Rushdie, an anthology on authorship which uses 'name' contributors) which gives differential identity and appeal to a purchasable literary product.

There is a clear analogy between the author, as a kind of sign, and ordinary brand-names. Brand-names developed out of patents, at first as a way to lay title (against stealers and forgers) to the personal ownership of the formula, invention or design embodied in a product. But, from the start, they also doubled as an element of publicity, serving at once to identify that product, and to guarantee its quality to the prospective buyer. This latter role has evidently been enhanced. Through advertising and related promotional arts, the brand-name has served as a site on to which additional qualities, of a more symbolic kind, can be semiotically transferred. In this same role, moreover, the brand-name and its image multiply their effects. For they assist the differential appeal not only of individual commodities, but of a whole stream. The brand-name is a patronymic. What it bears, or pretends to bear, is the family name of an entire producing company. To attach this, generically, to whatever that company sells, enables the promotional capital invested in old products to be used in the marketing of new ones. This is reflected, on the consumer side, by the way we shop. When we enter a store, whether for clothes, diskettes, bath oil or newspapers, we look, inter alia, at the tags they bear. In writing, the enhanced importance of the author's name similarly began as an assertion of intellectual property rights which similarly assured the quality of whatever was identified as flowing from a named quality pen. In writing, too, this second function has become more pronounced; and the authorial name has similarly become the site of an artificially induced process of imagistic enhancement.

With the evolution of capitalism has come yet a further change. The brand-name of products has been progressively detatched from that of their actual producer/owner. This corresponds to the depersonalisation of capital, a movement in which individual entrepeneurship was replaced by family capital, family capital by the corporation, and the latter, finally, by a magma of conglomerates and financial pools in which hallmarks are traded like bubble-gum cards and the autonomy and identity of producing units has itself become just a promotional fiction. At the limit, the brand-name becomes a wholly arbitrary sign – Pepsi Cola – which can even transfer its name back from the product itself to the enterprise that makes it. More importantly, this attenuated brand-name becomes a screen on which anonymous capital can be repersonalised (and reauthorised) through the projection on to it of human attributes. Trailing old myths of the artisan, and new ones of the soulful corporation, these attributes are usually warm and parental (MacDonalds' 'We do it all for you'). They can even be mock-divine. Against a soaring skyscape, a Hilton Hotel ad of the late 1970s proclaimed 'Marriages are made in heaven. Leave the reception to us.'

In the most industrialised forms of writing (the newspaper press, or romance), as well as in collaborative media like film (Steven Spielberg presents ...), a similar process can be seen. In such cases, too, authoriality is artifically reinscribed within a domain from which, practically speaking, it has been drained. Even in forms of writing where an individual writer can, in the commonsensical sense, still be said to exist, a parallel disjuncture has opened up. As poststructuralists have noted, behind the inflation of authorship (and we might add, of titles) lurks an ideology of (equally integral) creators and works. The fact that this dichotomy persists in every field of commercial expression – writers and books, hits and stars, famous plays and famous players – need not be explained, though, by the mere tenacity of an old myth. Promotion requires 'authors' through whom to address consumers from the heart of the product, even where the craft mode it implies is wholly absent.

In a third moment, the promotionalised name of the author becomes completely detachable from its related literary product. Free to circulate on its own, that name is able to serve as a promotional sign not only for the career and writings of the writer it designates, but also for others. We have seen this in Rushdie's tango with Pynchon. But it can go further. Names with a star value can be rented out as endorsements for all manner of products and services. Income generated this way can form the basis of a career. Such a system is well established in spectator sport; and, through the commercial endorsements of pop music, soap opera and comedy stars, it has diffused generally into the economics of the popular performing arts. Of course, even if they wanted it, none but the tiniest minority of writers have enough publicity-value to be able to negotiate such deals. And even then, since indiscriminate or bathetic associations would undermine the promotional value of their name to themselves, it is not in the interests of serious writers to do what Michael Jackson did for Pepsi. For writers, then, such activities are generally confined to the literary or intellectual scene itself, and, at that, to such relatively low-key and virtue-preserving ventures as doing critical reviews in the *New York Sunday Times*.

However, the imaged authorial name is not wholly controllable by its owner. Once in circulation, and subject only to such diminishing restrictions as are imposed by the laws of libel, it is free just to go on circulating. In part, this happens simply through the process (not, in itself, necessarily commercial) through which names and texts get absorbed into the general cultural fabric.[10] But the wider circulation of the authorial name also has a promotional meaning for the media through which this occurs. Celebrities are news. They can be appropriated as infotainment. So it is that pictures of, and references to, those who have become well known are constantly being used for their power to attract audiences, and all without permission or fee.

Through these various publicity channels, the imaged name of the author enters into general promotional circulation where, in a fourth moment, it becomes absorbed into the vast discourse constituted by promotion as a whole – a discourse that virtually covers mass mediated culture, and which also extends far beyond. If it is proper, against 'an ideology of the Book', to think of literature as an intertext, that term is even more appropriate here. For, besides its intertextuality at the symbolic level – amplified by the way in which ads quote from every branch of culture and, increasingly, vice versa – every item in the wider discourse of promotion is always advertising something else. Programmes, press stories, sports events, are ads for other ads; and, compounding the effect, commodities themselves, whether 'material' or 'immaterial', are packaged and designed so as to double as a kind of advertising.

The whole interweaving complex of what Innis called 'commercial writing' has a vertiginously hollow feel. Every point on its fascinating surface is not only promotional but multiply so. There is a temporal dimension to this feeling of emptiness too. Between what is actually and symbolically proferred there is always a gap. This is not just a matter of false promises, nor just of the difference between wants and needs. In promotion, the commodity being promoted is only present through a surrogate, through a representation – even in the special case where that commodity is itself (another can of Budweiser, another package of Persil) a perfect clone of the good being summoned to mind. The act of consumption is always in the future, the consumed object always somewhere else. This continually reproduced absence, capitalism's originary lack, is the fundamental dynamic of a circulation whose end, moving the merchandise, is absolutely pre-given – as external to the culture it ransacks and shapes as it is essential, in a fully commodified world, to the maintenance of material life.

We may find here a reason why postmodernism (especially as characterised by Jameson[11]) has become, if not *the* 'cultural dominant' of late capitalism, at least for many artists and intellectuals, a salient and preoccupying theme. Through being implicated, willy-nilly and at many levels, in the practices and discourses of promotion, the contemporary writer, and not only because of the fragmentation, relativisation, and multiplex character of current sensibility, is placed within a vortex – coil upon coil of promotional traces, of pleasures continually deferred – where referentiality, meaning, and any sense of *telos* other than narcissistic or material self-interest, threaten constantly to disappear.

Promotion as supplement

The rise of promotion has evidently been bound up with that of modern capitalism as a whole. But an account of this, from street cries and petty commodity production to Madison Avenue and transnational capital, would remain wholly empirical if it failed to note that it potentiates something which is absolutely intrinsic to competitive exchange. To realise their exchange value, commodities must circulate, for which there must also be a process of communication linking both ends of the producer/consumer chain. Sellers must know from buyers what they want, and buyers must find out from sellers what is available. In the pure, primitive case – the Marshallian model of perfect competition – this exchange of information can be thought of as a reciprocity. But even in Marshall's fish market, where every aspect of a sale is subject to negotiation, it is the buyer's voice that fills the air and the buyer who has the informational advantage. It is, at any rate, from this side of the informational transaction, from the side of the competitively mediated messages that pass from seller to buyer, that modern promotion has developed. With the development of modern capitalism what has happened, in effect, is that exchange relations, *and therefore promotion*, have spread into more and more aspects of social life; and that because of the mass marketing requirements of capital intensive mass production, the sphere of circulation has, both economically and culturally, come to power.

Ernst Haug[12] is the only theorist (I know of) to treat promotion in this way, by grounding an historical account of its growth in an enquiry into its essence. For him, though, the generic feature of the commodity which has so spectacularly grown is *commodity aesthetics*; by which he means the myriad ways in which commodities are dressed up to enhance their appeal. Thus he conceives of promotion as ornamentation, embellishment, with Marx's figure of the pander as his guiding metaphor. To be sure, this enables him to illuminate some of consumer capitalism's deeper psycho-cultural effects. But in the end it is to reduce advertising to a trick of appearances; a trick which falsifies the 'real' use-value of the commodity in play. His ideal is a world without such falsification: the hyped commodity unmasked, and the world put back on its feet. Behind which lurks not only a dubious distinction between real and artifical needs, but a utopia of transparency whose best known expression today is the Habermasian ideal of undistorted communication.

For all its critical edge, this view (which is in fact the commonest way of looking at the matter, and at its weakest amounts to an appeal for Truth in Advertising) inhibits a fuller understanding of what promotion in its modern form actually is.

There is, in the first place, no such thing as a non-symbolic item of human use. Whatever their pragmatics, artefacts (and, indeed, contractual services) have always been endowed with a cultural meaning, a meaning which not only has a context and a history, even an element of the ineffable, but may also be expressed (think of classical pottery) in physical form. In this respect, the imagistic marketing of commodities does not add a dimension to the commodity – the symbolic – which was not already there. What it does, rather, is to change that symbolic dimension's mode of instantiation. With the industrial production of consumer goods, the organic relationship of artefacts to symbolic culture is severed and, on the wings of fashion as well as invention, new products are turned over at an increasingly giddy rate. On the marketing side, correspondingly, inscribed significance becomes a matter of deliberate calculation. It becomes threaded through with an effort to draw attention. Furthermore, it feeds back, as design, into production itself. Hence, on the one hand, *artificial semiosis*; on the other, a *commodity-sign* serving, both through associated ideas and through material inscription, as a promotional sign of itself.[13]

To promote something, then, is not just to clothe its nakedness in order to increase its appeal. What is imagistically promoted is, by that very fact, transformed. There is something strange, too, about the entity that results. The promoted *circuland* (if the term be permitted) is certainly more than just a minor variant on the amalgamated disjunct of use-value and exchange-value known to Classical Economy. For here, the element of use not only has a symbolic side (this was always the case), but this same element is also tangled up in the element of exchange. And this in an active sense: for the manufactured meaning of a commodity is both integral to its consumable being and also designed, through all the phases of its circulation, to make it sell. To call the outcome a manufactured sign understates what it is. It is also a performative speech act – a circulatory force – whose instantiation as a sign is irreducible to its purely signifying form.

It is likewise misleading to think of promotion as simply a kind of (seductive, duplicitous, etc.) communication about an object. For this implies that it can be grasped as a series of isolatable communicative acts. Promotion is, rather, processual and dynamic. Its every element is hooked into a wider, circulatory, motion, and the same character extends to the promoted commodity itself. With the development of modern promotion, both its unity and its discreteness dissolve: its unity, because the imaged commodity doubles as a promotional sign; its discreteness, because imaged commodities are caught in a web of promotional discourse in which what is advertised itself advertises something else, and so on endlessly. As a cultural development, therefore, the rise of promotion has meant not only the quantitative spread of advertising and related imagistic discourses. It has also established a culturo-economic regime of objects and signs which defies comprehension in terms of the rational/representational vocabulary in which the market's consumerist rationale (delivery of the goods; material abundance; an objectified world confronting an autonomous subject) has always been expressed.

Overall, then, promotion is something which at once completes what the commodity is (as part of its conditions of existence) and (through the ascendancy of circulation) changes it: so radically, indeed, that the traditional critique of the market finally dissipates into nostalgia for its lost object; while that object itself – the commodity as a priced item of use – volatilises as an intelligible category. What promotion exemplifies, in short, is what Derrida called the logic of the supplement. The fate of contemporary writing (and of other commercial and quasi-commercial forms of mediatised expression) is to be doubly caught up in this supplementality. First, by being commodified in itself, whence: writing as self-advertising; the name as a promotional sign; and the crucial place of the series. All of which intermixes with the promotional needs (and editorial discipline imposed) by the publisher. Secondly, by being incorporated into an economic sector (Adorno's 'culture industry') which itself serves as a promotional vehicle for the general circulation of commodities.

On neither of these levels is the promotional aspect of writing to be grasped as just a matter of motives (acknowledged/unacknowledged; manipulative/non-manipulative). This is not to deny, at the same time, that the inextricability of writing from sales talk – for itself and others – has profound implications for the subjectivity of the living authorial subject. For what is sales talk? At root, a species of persuasion, a form of rhetoric. It is so, moreover, in precisely Plato's sense: not only as a kind of discourse in which the tricks of form prevail over an indifferent content; but as a discourse constructed in strict fidelity to an instrumentality – persuading potential buyers to buy. (In the *Phaedrus* it may be noted, Socrates' enquiry into rhetoric actually begins with a promotional example: in a story about a man who sells a donkey to another by passing the animal off as a horse.[14])

This instrumentality must be carefully considered. As in all cases of instrumental reason, its ends are pre-established. But what grounds them here? Certainly not (as in Heidegger's Technology) a Cartesian dualism powered by a survival-driven or patriarchally-driven will to dominate the Being of the Other. An intentionalist account of any sort, in fact, should be especially inappropriate in this context. Considered systemically, the human motives behind promotion – the maximisation of value through competitive exchange – are not so much supplied as demanded. They are the derived imperatives of a game which we did not decree and which, to one degree or another, we are all obliged to play.

It may be said that this instrumentality nevertheless accords with the author's self-interest. And so it does, but even in the immediate case of self-promotion not in a way that is autonomously given. The need to promote imposes itself as a logic and a power. This is evident in the marketing questionnaire which publishing companies require writers to fill out. The promotional effect of a communicative act can also be quite unintended since, whether willed or not, every public gesture in the creative or intellectual process has a promotional implication for the person making it. We can see, for example, how illusory it was for the Dadaists – not to mention their pop and punk epigones – to think that the commodification of art could be combated by destroying the fetishised object. However shattered the object and its mystique, the defetishing gesture is itself a publicisable occurrence that instantly enters into the wider publicity process; and all this over and above the uncontrollable way that the names of authors and their works become available aids in the publicity for others the moment they enter the public domain.

It is a commonplace to observe that commercialism undermines standards, privileges the sensate, and leads to media monopolies which fabricate a 'speech without response'.[15] But we can now see that the problem posed by the late capitalist cultural economy for the production and interchange of ideas, expressions and visions is at an even deeper level: through the way in which, throughout the length and breadth of its practice, the supplement of promotion breaches *ab initio* the actual and constructed authenticity of the speaking/writing subject. In an exchange economy, where whatever is publicly inscribed necessarily participates in heteronomous processes of circulatory competition, there is no way for an author to avoid this problem. There is no *hors-promotion*. The well-founded suspicion, moreover, that behind every public act of communication someone is trying to sell us something, multiplies its effects by rebounding from the reader on to the writer: a cynicism which at once sows self-suspicion, and confronts the writer with a resistance to writing that writing itself must find a way to overcome.

Under such conditions, a clear conscience in the author is a sign of bad faith: a self-deceiving dissimulation which testifies not (*pace* Plato or Rousseau) to the fallen condition of writing as such, but to the impossibility, in any commodified medium, of being able completely to avoid the rhetoric of 'bad writing'. Barthes' formula, then, can be rephrased. The birth of the author, as an imaged Name for the 'originator' of a text, has meant the death of authorship as an authentic activity. Whether in the field of philosophy, poetics or cultural critique, that is to say, the birth of the author as a promotional subject – and as a promotional site – has made impossible that self-possessed command over authoring which has provided an ideological cover for the transformed relation of authorship to the market that itself brought the modern elevation of authorship about.

Notes

1 J. Derrida, *Of grammatology*, trans. G. Spivak (Baltimore: Johns Hopkins Press, 1976), 145.

2 F. Nietzsche, *Twilight of the idols/the antichrist*, trans. R.J. Hollingdale (London: Penguin, 1990), 36–7.

3 The most straightforward articulation of these themes is in *Of grammatology* whose second part hinges on a commentary on Rousseau's *Essay on the origin of languages* and related texts in *Pleiades* and *The confessions*.

4 'At its worst', Dana Polan remarks (thinking for example of the way in which a mechanical application of the post-structuralist 'paradigm' just breathes spirit into the flagging body of New Criticism), 'postmodernist discourse frequently functions to allow entrenched academics a new way of doing the same old work'. 'Postmodernism and cultural analysis today', in *Postmodernism and its discontents*, ed. A. Kaplan (London/New York: Verso, 1988).

5 The allergic reaction of social activists to the postmodern turn – and the polemical construction of a stereotyped 'postmodernism' – is no surprise. Movements of individual and collective self-empowerment, whether gender, race or class-based, can hardly be thought (let alone expressed) outside the category of reflexive subjectivity. Derrida himself, in an early (and leftish) essay, excoriated the humanised Marxist appropriation of phenomenology through Sartre. See J. Derrida, 'The ends of philosophy', in *Margins of philosophy*, trans. A. Bass (Brighton: Harvester, 1982). More recently, through the writings of Richard Rorty, Derrida's name has been invoked to support a postmodernist recomposition of liberalism itself.

6 Besides the familiar works of McLuhan, key texts in the Toronto School include: E. Havelock, *Preface to Plato* (Cambridge: Harvard University Press, 1963); W. Ong, *Orality and literacy: the technologising of the word* (London: Methuen,

1982); H. Innis, *The bias of communication* (Toronto: University of Toronto Press, 1953); G. Grant, *Technology of empire: perspectives on North America* (Toronto: House of Anansi, 1969). Two interesting and wide ranging commentaries are D. Theall, *The medium is the rear-view mirror: understanding McLuhan* (Montreal/London: McGill-Queens Press, 1971) and A. Kroker, *Innis/McLuhan/Grant: technology and the Canadian mind* (Montreal: New World Perspectives, 1984). See also A. Wernick, 'The post-Innisian significance of Innis', *Canadian Journal of Political and Social Theory*, 10: 1–2 (1986), 128–50.

7 The note reads in full: 'Pervasive influence of advertising – writers of one media (sic) place articles in another media and secure advertising for the former as well as the latter – writing becomes a device for advertising advertising.' W. Christian (ed.), *The idea file of Harold Adams Innis* (Toronto: University of Toronto Press, 1980), 125.

8 In analogy with the nuts and pretzels regularly provided as courtesy fare in North American bars, Ben Bagdakian (in *media Monopoly* (Boston: Beacon, 1984) coined the term 'free lunch' to describe the subsidised (or 'free') information and entertainment content provided by ad-carrying media. Dallas Smythe refined the idea in *Dependency road: communications, capitalism, consciousness and Canada* (New Jersey: Ablex, 1981).

9 The first line of Carmen XXX in Book Three of Horace's *Odes*. The Latin reads: '*Exegi monumentum aere perennius*' and continues '*regalique situ pyramidum altius*' ('and more lofty than the pyramids placed by kings' – my translation).

10 The mediating significance of an exchangist cultural economy for the circulation of ideas in academia has been explored by Pierre Bourdieu in *Homo academicus*, trans. P. Collier (Stanford: Stanford University Press, 1988).

11 See F. Jameson, 'Postmodernism, or the cultural logic of capital', *New Left Review*, 146 (1984), 55–7.

12 W. Haug, *Critique of commodity aesthetics: appearance, sexuality and advertising* (Cambridge: Polity, 1986).

13 For a more extended discussion of these terms, see A. Wernick, *Promotional culture: advertising, ideology, and symbolic expression* (London: Sage, 1991), 12–16.

14 Plato, *Phaedrus*, trans. W. Hamilton (London: Penguin, 1973), 72.

15 See especially J. Baudrillard, 'Requiem for the media', in *Towards a critique of the political economy of the sign*, trans. C. Levin and A. Younger (St Louis: Telos Press, 1981).

6

Reading *The Satanic Verses*[1]

Gayatri C. Spivak

In post-coloniality, every metropolitan definition is dislodged. The general mode for the post-colonial is citation, reinscription, re-routeing the historical. *The satanic verses*[2] cannot be placed within the European avant-garde, but the successes and failures of the European avant-garde are available to it.

Peter Bürger pointed out to Jürgen Habermas some time ago that all deliberate attempts at integrating the aesthetic sphere with the *Lebenswelt* must take into account their profound and continued separation.[3] But, in post-coloniality, all metropolitan accounts are set askew. The case of the *The satanic verses* is a case of the global *Lebenswelt* – the praxis and politics of life – intercepting an aesthetic object so that a mere reading of it has become impossible.

The case of Mr Fukuyama, fully 'assimilated' Asian-American, who, put off as a graduate student by the nihilism of Derrida and Barthes, has written an article on Hegel's 'end of history as USA today', bored but in charge, indolently defending freedom of expression against terrorism, is not outside of this contemporary fact of life. The United States is not outside the post-colonial globe.[4]

Here is a metropolitan aphorism: 'The birth of the reader must be at the cost of the death of the Author.'[5] Faced with the case of Salman Rushdie, how are we to read this sentence? I have often said that the (tragic) theatre of the (sometimes farcically self-indulgent) script of post-structuralism is 'the other side'.[6] The aphorism above is a case in point. Let us read slowly, word for word.

Barthes is writing here not of the death of the writer (although he *is* writing, quite copiously, of writing) or of the subject, or yet of the agent, but of the *Author*. The author, who is not only taken to be the authority for the meaning of a text, but also, when possessed of authority, possessed *by that fact* of 'moral or legal supremacy, the power to influence the conduct or action of others'; and, when authorising, 'giving legal force to, making legally valid' (*OED*). Thus, even on the most 'literal' level of the dictionary, 'the birth of the reader must be at the cost of the death of the Author' takes on a different resonance.

Barthes is speaking of the birth not of the critic, who, apart from the academically certified authority of the meaning of a text is, also, in the strictest sense, a judge. It is not of such a being that Barthes announces the birth. He announces the birth of the reader who 'is simply that *someone* who holds together in a single field all the traces by which the written text is constituted'.[7] It is the birth of this someone that is conditional upon the death of the Author. The writer is, in this robust sense, a reader at the performance of writing. Or, as Barthes writes, '*writing* can no longer designate an operation of recording …, rather, it designates exactly what linguists, referring to Oxford philosophy, call a performative … in which the enunciation has no other content … than the act by which it is uttered'.[8] When Barthes writes, further, that 'the reader is without history, biography, psychology', I believe he means there is no specific set of history, biography, psychology, belonging to the writer-as-privileged-reader or the ideal reader implied in the text, that gives us the Reader as such. When the writer and reader are born again and again together, the Author(ity)-function is dead, the critic is not mentioned. There is the pleasure of the text.

In the next decade and a half, Roland Barthes will tone down the binaries that seem entailed by these pronouncements. But the words 'the Death of the Author' have become a slogan, both proving and disproving the Authority of the Author. And Foucault's question 'What is an Author?' has been construed by most readers as a rhetorical question to be answered in the negative.[9] I reckon with these signs of the times by turning, as usual, toward Derrida.

Derrida usually comes at these things from the other end. He is not an overthrower of myths but rather is interested in seeing how a myth works both as medicine and poison. For him the Author is present in excess. I have not yet read *The critical difference*, but I believe I will agree with Barbara Johnson's distinction between Barthes the anti-constructionist and Derrida's de-construction.[10]

Moving with Derrida, I can say, that when Barthes and Foucault are monumentalised as marks for the death and nothingness of the Author, everything happens as if the sign 'Author' has no history, no linguistic or cultural limits. I turn back to the dictionary, where I began, and I see that, in the Rushdie affair, it is the late Ayatollah who can be seen as filling the Author-function, and Salman Rushdie, himself, caught in a different cultural logic, is no more than the writer-as-performer. I will say more about this in the body of my paper. Let me now turn to another aspect of the excessive presence of the author in Derrida's reading habits: what he calls 'the politics of the proper name'.[11]

In order to read the politics of the proper name, Derrida pays close attention to the staging of the author *as* author by the author. 'We would,' he writes, 'be mistaken if we understood it as a simple presentation of identity. (Me, such and such, male or female, individual or collective subject.)'[12] I believe the author of *The satanic verses* is 'staged' rather than 'simply presented' in the vestigial rememoration of a face and a proper name in the poem published in *Granta* last autumn.[13] Because the Author function dies hard, that poem has no free Readership. It is not only outside of technological reproducibility, *hors de reproduction*, but also, and strictly speaking, an artwork, an *hors d'oeuvre*, an exergue or a flysheet, whose topos, like (its) temporality, strangely dislocates what we, without tranquil assurance, would like to understand as the time of life and the time of life's *recit*, or the writing of life by the living.[14]

As I will go on to propose, *in* the novel, Rushdie's staging of the author is more recognisably 'modernist' (not what Barthes, or indeed French critics as a rule would call 'modern'), not decentred but fragmented by dramatic irony, the question of authorship repeatedly and visibly suspended by foregrounding. But the violence of the *fatwa* continuing the signature after *its* author's death, has jolted modernist playfulness into a Nietzschean *Ecce Homo* in Rushdie's irreproducible poem.

In the first part of my paper, I will attempt the impossible: a reading of *The satanic verses* as if nothing has happened since late 1988. The second part will try to distinguish the cultural politics of what has happened, by assembling a dossier of responses from various subject-positions in contemporary political geography. In the third part, I will try to make parts I and II come together in

the element of an intellectual history. And perhaps this will allow
me a conclusion.

I

First, then, the reading: *The satanic verses*, in spite of all its
plurality, has rather an aggressive central theme: the post-colonial
divided between two identities: migrant and national.

As migrant, the post-colonial may attempt to become the metropolitan: this is Saladin Chamcha in his first British phase: 'I am
a man to whom certain things are of importance: rigour, self-
discipline, reason, the pursuit of what is noble without recourse
to that old crutch, God. The ideal of beauty, the possibility of
exaltation, the mind' (*SV* 135–6). This self-definition of the migrant
as metropolitan is obviously not the book's preferred definition.

The post-colonial may, also, keep himself completely separated
from the metropolis *in* the metropolis as the fanatic exile. This is
represented in the least conclusive section of the book, the place
of dark foreboding, the subcontinental Imam ('desh' is a north
Indian word which signifies his country), who must destroy the
woman touched by the West. This is also not preferred: 'Exile is a
soulless country' (*SV* 208).

What we see in process in the greater part of *The satanic verses* is
the many fragmented national representations coming together in
serious and comic – serious *when* comic and vice versa – figures
of resistance. In the hospital, a highly paid male model based in
Bombay,

> now changed into a 'manticore' ... [with] an entirely human body, but
> [the] head of a ferocious tiger, with three rows of teeth ... whisper[s]
> solemnly ... [while] break[ing] wind continually ... They describe us ...
> They have the power of description, and we succumb to the pictures
> they construct. (*SV* 167–8)

These monsters organise a 'great escape', and 'take ... the low roads
to London town ... going their separate ways, without hope, but
also without shame' (*SV* 170–1).

On another register, and two-hundred odd pages later, 'a minute
woman in her middle seventies' gives us a related but more upbeat
message:

We are here to change things ... African, Caribbean, Indian, Pakistani,
Bangladeshi, Cypriot, Chinese, we are other than what we would have
been if we had not crossed the oceans ... We have been made again:
but I say we shall also be the ones to remake this society, to shape it
from the bottom to the top. (*SV* 413–14)

There is framing and dramatic irony everywhere, but never all
the way. For example, it is at this meeting that Saladin encounters

a young woman [who gives] his [conservative British] attire an amused
once-over ... She was wearing a lenticular badge ... At some angles it
read, *Uhuru for the Simba*; at others, *Freedom for the Lion*. 'It's on
account of the meaning of his chosen name,' she explained redundantly.
'In African.' Which language? ... she shrugged ... It was African: born,
by the sound of her in Lewisham, or Deptford, or New Cross, that was
all she needed to know ... As if all causes were the same, all histories
interchangeable. (*SV* 413, 415)

Most strongly in the hospital section of the book, aptly called
'Ellowen Deeowen', the effect of fragmentation, citation, fast-
shifting perspectives is sustained through echoes from British
literature. This embedding in the history of the literature of England
and Ireland – the echoes from *The portrait of the artist as a young
man* are a text for interpretation in themselves – may prove the
most seductive for metropolitan readers.

But the book will not let us forget that the metropolitan reader
is among 'the describers'. The post-colonial is not only a migrant
but also the citizen of a 'new' nation for which the colonial experience is firmly in the past, a past somewhat theatrically symbolised
in Gibreel Farishta's dream of Mirza Sayeed Akhtar's house *Peristan*,
'built seven generations ago', perhaps 'a mere contraction of
Perownestan', after 'an English architect much favoured by the
colonial authorities, whose only style was that of the neo-classical
English country house' (*SV* 230).

Mirza Akhtar is a *zamindar* – member of a landowning class,
collecting land-revenue for the British, created at the end of the
eighteenth century. He and his wife thus mark modern Indian elite
post-colonial public culture in rather an obvious way:

In the city [they] were known as one of the most 'modern' and 'go-go'
couples on the scene; they collected contemporary art and threw wild
parties and invited friends round for fumbles in the dark on sofas while
watching soft-porno VCRs. (*SV* 227)

Because the migrant as paradigm is a dominant theme in theorisations of post-coloniality, it is easy to overlook Rushdie's resolute
effort to represent contemporary India. Whereas the topical
caricature of the Bombay urban worlds of the popular film industry,
of rhapsodic 'left' politics, of Muslim high society, of the general
atmosphere of communalism, carries an idiomatic conviction, it is
at least this reader's sense that so-called 'magical realism' becomes
an alibi in the fabrication of Titlipur-Chatnapatna, the village
and the country town. But then, these might be the constitutive
asymmetries of the imagination – itself a fabricated word – that
is given the name 'migrant'.

(And perhaps it is only in this sense that the drifting migrant
imagination is paradigmatic, of the 'imagination' as such, not only
of the historical case of post-coloniality. Here migrancy is the name
of the institution that inhabits the indifferent anonymity of space
and dockets climate and soil-type and the inscription of the earth's
body. In this general sense, 'migrancy' is not derived.)

But since this general sense is never not imbricated with the
narrow sense, – our contemporary predicament – the trick or
turn is not to assume either the metropolitan or the national as
the standard and *judge* some bit of this plural landscape in terms
of it. In learning to practise the turn, if only to sense it slip away,
we can guess that the deliberate oppositional stance of the European
avant-garde is itself part of an instituted metropolitan reversal,
among the 'describers' – again.

Thus every canvas will have a spot that is less 'real' than others.
Excusing it away as an entailment of migrancy in general is no less
dubious a gesture than accusing it as a historical or sociological
transgression. I do therefore note that, within the protocols of *The
satanic verses*, it is contemporary rural India that clings to magical
realism as an alibi and thus provides a clue to the politics of the
writing subject, the scribe. This would lead us to a deconstructive
gesture toward the claim of magical realism as a privileged
taxonomic description, and a consideration of alternative styles
and systems of the representation of rural India.[15]

Within the labyrinth of such gestures, we must acknowledge
that, writing as a migrant, Rushdie still militates against privileging the migrant or the exilic voice narrowly conceived, even as

he fails in that very effort. A *mise-en-abyme*, perhaps, the eternal site of the migrant's desire, but also a persistent critique of metropolitan migrancy, his own slot in the scheme of things. The message and the medium of his book are marked by this conflict.

In other words, I do not think the 'cosmopolitan *challenge* to national culture' is perceived by Rushdie as only a challenge.[16] Perhaps it is even an aporia for him, an impossible decision between two opposed decidables with two mutually cancelling sets of consequences, a decision which gets made, none the less, for one set, since life must operate as a passive or active difference of death, as we know from our most familiar experiences: 'I wanted to write about a thing I find difficult to admit even to myself, which is the fact that I left home'.[17]

The Indian world of the books is Muslim-based. India's Islamic culture, high and low, is too easily ignored by contemporary hegemonic constructions of national identity as well as international benevolence. Islamic India is another theme of migrancy, unconnected with the recent colonial past. For Islam as such has its head turned away from the subcontinent, across the Arabian Sea, perpetually emigrant toward Mecca. Within this turned-away-ness, Rushdie plants the migrant's other desire, the search for roots as far down as they'll go. The name of this radical rootedness is, most often, religion. Thus in the section called Mahound, Rushdie reopens the institution of Revelation, the origin of the Koran. It is paradoxical that the protection against desacralisation, writing in the name of the false prophet, Mahound rather than Mohammed, has been read, quite legitimately, by the Law where Religion is the 'real' (there can be no other Law), as blasphemy.

The question is not if the book is blasphemous. The question is not even the profound belief of heretics and blasphemers. The question is rather: how is blasphemy to be punished? Can it be punished? What is the distinction between punishment and nourishment? And further, in the name of what do we judge the punishers? We will look at these questions in the two following sections.

The story of Mahound in *The satanic verses* is a story of negotiation in the name of woman. As so often, woman becomes the touchstone of blasphemy.

One of the most interesting features about much of Rushdie's

work is his anxiety to write woman into the narrative of history.
Here again we have to record a failure.[18] (But I am more interested
in failed texts. What is the use of a 'successful' text? What happens
to the recorder of failed texts? As a post-colonial migrant, 'a tall,
thin Bengali woman with cropped hair' (*SV* 536), like Swatilekha –
the 'real' name of the woman playing the lead character in Ray's
film version of Tagore's *The home and the world* – an 'actress'
acting out the script of female Anglicisation – read emancipation –
by male planning in the colonial dispensation, I am part of Rushdie's
text, after all.) In *Shame*, the women seem powerful only as
monsters, of one sort or another. *The satanic verses* must end
with Salahuddin Chamchawalla's reconciliation with *father* and
nationality, even if the last sentence records sexual difference in
the idiom of casual urban fucking: ' "My place", Zeeny offered.
"Let's get the hell out of here." "I'm coming", he answered her,
and turned away from the view' (*SV* 547).

All through, the text is written on the register of male bonding
and unbonding, the most important being, of course, the double
subject of migrancy. Gibreel Farishta and Saladin Chamcha. The
two are tortured by obsession with women, go through them, even
destroy them, within a gender code that is never opened up, never
questioned, in this book where so much is called into question,
so much is reinscribed.

Gibreel is named after the archangel Gabriel by his mother.
But his patronymic, Ismail Najmuddin, is 'Ismail after the child
involved in the sacrifice of Ibrahim, and Najmuddin, *star of the
faith*; he'd given up quite a name when he took the angel's' (*SV*
17). And that name, Ismail, comes in handy in an echo of *Moby
Dick*, to orchestrate the greatest act of male bonding in the book
as an inversion of the angel of death, when Gibreel saves Saladin's
life in the blazing Shaandaar Cafe: 'The adversary: there he blows!
Silhouetted against the backdrop of the ignited Shaandaar Cafe, see,
that's the very fellow! Azraeel leaps unbidden into Farishta's hand'
(*SV* 463). The allusion in the otherwise puzzling 'there he blows'
is the white whale, of course.

Yet it must be acknowledged that in Mahound, we hear the
satanic verses inspired by possible *female* gods. Gibreel's dream
of Mahound's wrestling with himself, acting out an old script,

restores the proper version, without the female angels, man to man. By the rules of fiction in the narrow sense, you cannot assign burden of responsibility here; although by the law of Religion, in the strict sense, the harm was already done. Rushdie invoked those rules against these Laws, and it was an unequal contest. We will not enter the lists, but quietly mark the *text*'s assignment of value. The 'reality' of the wrestling, the feel of the voice speaking through one, is high on the register or validity, if not verifiability. By contrast, in 'Return to Jahilia', prostitution is mere play. Ayesha, the female prophet ('historically' one of his wives), lacks the existential depth of 'the businessman' prophet. To her the archangel sings in popular Hindi film songs. Her traffic with him is reported speech.

If post-colonial plurality is one aggressive central theme of *The satanic verses*, the artist's identity is another. Rushdie's tactic is boldly old-fashioned here, and the tone reminds one of, say, George Meredith's 'Authorial voice' in *The egoist*. Everything is taken care of by this overt comic self-undermining miming manipulation of 'dramatic irony' on so many levels. The multiple dreams, carried to absurdity, support as they take away the power of this planning genius. Here is the entire shift from Religion's God to Art's Imagination – a high European theme – played out in the staging of Author. Ostentatiously appearing as God or Devil (*upparwala* or *nichaywala* – the one above or the one below), he clearly produces error in Gibreel, who has a delusion of angelic grandeur and nearly gets run over by a motor car as a result. Almost a hundred pages later, the authorial voice reveals that it had been the authorial voice posing as the Almighty, capable of 'mobiliz[ing] the traditional apparatus of divine rage ... [making] wind and thunder [shake] the room' (*SV* 319), and looking like photographs of Salman Rushdie 'medium height, fairly heavily built, with salt-and-pepper beard cropped close to the line of the jaw ... balding, ... suffer[ing] from dandruff and [wearing] glasses'. Does this make the author less reliable or more? Does this make the voice less real or more? Does this make the dream more true than truth? Is this a serious use of Romantic Irony in a contemporary comic format or a caricature of Romantic Irony? In an era of industriously decentred subjects and radicalised citationality, these questions are disarmingly cosy. Are we obliged to repeat the argument that, as metropolitan writing is trying to get rid of a subject that has too long been the dominant, the post-colonial writer must still foreground his traffic with the subject-position?[19] Too easy, I think. Not because the migrant must still consider the question of identity, plurality, roots. But because fabricating decentred subjects as the sign of the times is not necessarily these times decentring the subject. There is the wake of the European avant-garde, is also a confusion of the narrow and general senses of the relationship between subject and centre. The trick or turn is not to assume the representation of decentring to *be* decentring, and/or judge styles of conjunctures.

All precautions taken, there is no risk in admitting that Rushdie's book reads more like a self-ironic yet self-based modernism ('a myopic scrivener' setting two gentlemen a-dreaming) than an object-coded or subject-decentred avant-garde. Although he does broaden out to other Empires – notably Argentina through the Rosa Diamond sequence which also stages the Norman Conquest as immigration, once you have finished the phantasmagoric book, the global slowly settles into the peculiar locale of migrancy.

What are these dreams, these phantasmagoria, these shape-changes that convince not only the shape-changers themselves but the inhabitants of the world of the book as well? Like the taxonomy of migrancy, Rushdie provides what may be called an oneiric multiplicity, the dream as legitimising matrix. The story begins in a miracle, a series of supernatural events tamely accommodated into the reasonableness of the everyday. Vintage 'magical realism' – Asturias or Marquez – has taught us to expect a more intricate mosaic. Alleluia Cone's 'visions' can be validated by her personality and experience. Gibreel's fantasies have a firm diagnostic label: paranoid schizophrenia. But what about the peculiar authority of the many times repeated 'Gibreel dreamed' ... and then a noun of event or space? What is the relationship between this and the chain of 'and then ...' 'and then ...' that Deleuze and Guattari assure us is the mode of narrativisation of the schizo?[20]

And what about the metamorphosis of the migrants in the hospital where Saladin is brought after the embarrassment of the discovery that he is a British citizen? What about his physical trans-formation into the Devil, setting a trend in the fashion world of

'Black Britain', only to be cancelled when he learns to hate Farishta? Saladin is never 'diagnosed', he is the side-kick that negotiates the book from beginning to end. And isn't that story about eating kippers at public school supposed to be a bit from Rushdie's own life-story? Is this a clue? Is Rushdie graphing his bio here as President Schreber, British-citizen-escaping-the-angel-of-god-by-demoniac-metamorphosis-and-returning-home-for-a-wished-for-entry into the real?[21]

In *Capitalism and schizophrenia*, Deleuze and Guattari have suggested that the schizo as a general psychic description entailed by capitalism stands as a critique of the Oedipal recuperation of the great branching-out of social – and desiring – production inscribing the unproduced. I should like to think that *The satanic verses* presents a portrait of the author as schizo under the desiring/social production of migrancy and post-coloniality, a displacement of the Oedipal project of Imperialism as bringing into Law of the 'favourite son'.

Farishta finds *The marriage of heaven and hell* in Alleluia Cone's house. But the genius of this book is more the paranoid Schreber than the visionary Blake. This is no 'Prophet Against Empire', to quote the title of a well-known book on Blake.[22] The confident breaching of the boundaries between dream and waking in the *text* – not merely in the characters – and, indeed, in a text that sets store by the paradox of the so-called 'creative imagination' – can earn for *The satanic verses* a critic's subtitle: 'Imperialism and schizophrenia'. Not because empire, like capital, is abstract, but because empire messes with identity.

Good and Evil, set up with such pomp and circumstance, have therefore no moral substance in the persons of the protagonists. They are no more than visual markers, inscribed on the body like special effects – a halo, a pair of horns. I am uncomfortable with this, of course, but then ask myself if this is not the peculiar felicity of post-coloniality, good and evil as reactive simulation, overturning the assurance of 'a performative utterance will be *in a peculiar way* hollow or void if said by an actor on the stage, or if introduced in a poem'.[23]

I can anticipate critics suggesting that I give resistance no speaking part here. But the point is that a book such as this might at least be inviting us to consider the following question: who am I, or my critics, or indeed Salman Rushdie, to *give* resistance a speaking part? To 'state the problem' is not bad politics. In fact, it might be poor judgement to consider academy or novel as straight blueprint for action on the street. Chamcha gives himself the assurance that if a ' "chimeran graft" ... were possible', as shown on TV, 'then so was he; he, too, could cohere, send down roots, survive. Amid all the televisual images of hybrid tragedies ... he was given this one gift' (*SV* 406). In that very section, Rushdie's 'authorial voice' puts it in the first person singular in the classic tones of the psychotic as savant:

> But, it had to be conceded, and this was his [Chamcha's] original point, that the circumstances of the age required no diabolic explanation. I[authorial voice]'m saying nothing. Don't ask me to clear things up one way or the other; the time of revelations is long gone. (*SV* 408)

It is after this that we come to the only real act of intended, gratuitous, cunning cruelty and persecution represented in the book: the destruction of Farishta and Alleluia through the anonymous telephoned messages, in the pluralised ventriloquilism of the radio-waves, of sexual innuendo couched in childish doggerel. No conceivable high allegorical connection with the great narrative of post-coloniality can be found in this important nexus of the book's narrative energy: this is rather the absurd discontinuity of the hyper-real. *Etre-pour-la-mort* is *etre-au-telephone*.

(A word about the 'tall, thin Bengali woman with cropped hair', whom I cannot really leave behind. Rukmini Bhaya Nair gives her some importance:

> Narration in Rushdie's novels is shaped as gossip, an undervalued form of everyday talk that is now creatively empowered to reclaim the metaphors of an elite history. In S[atanic] V[erses], Rushdie, tongue very much in cheek, presents the following case through one of his minor characters, an intellectual Bengali woman. [']Society was orchestrated by what she called *grand narratives*; history, economics, ethics. In India, the development of a corrupt and closed state apparatus had "excluded the masses of people from the ethical project." As a result, they sought ethical satisfactions in the oldest of the grand narratives, that is, religious faith['].[24]

Ms Nair goes on to make a persuasive case for *The satanic verses* as 'satirical gossip'.[25]

The case that I have made for religious faith as a counter-narrative with a generalised subject focused on the moment when, *within the colonial rather than post-colonial context*, religious discursivity changed to militancy, gossip changed to rumour as vehicle of sub-altern insurgency.[26] In the present essay, my opening point is that, in *post*-coloniality, the praxis and politics of life (the *Lebenswelt*) intercept aesthetic objects away from their destined ends. Thus, if the project of the *novel* is gossip, the post-colonial *Lebenswelt* wrenched it into rumour, criticism by hearsay, a text, taken as evidence, as talked about rather than read.[27] Upon the wings of that rumour, the metropolitan migrant subaltern (rather different from the colonial subaltern in the colony, though we tend to forget this) forged a collectivity which they could stage as a strike *for* the Imam *against* the West. The narrative of the state and the narrative of religion overdetermined the rumoured book into a general mobilising signifier for crisis.

II

I come now to the cultural politics of the specific (mis)reading of the book as disposable container of blasphemy, signifier of cultural difference, rather than the field of the migrant's desiring/social production. As Aziz Al-Azmeh comments:

> The enracinations, deracinations, alienations, comforts, discomforts and mutations which constitute the novel are kept entirely out of view by Rushdie's islamist critics, and his putative treatment of Muhammed and Abraham brought into view.[28]

Literature is transactional. The point is not necessarily and exclusively the correct description of a book, but the construction of readerships. 'The birth of the reader must be at the cost of the death of the Author.'

A great deal has been written and said about the Rushdie affair in the last half-year. I will concentrate on a spectrum of historically constructed readerships here and assemble a highly selective dossier.[29] My main argument attempts to lay out the full impli-cations of the statement made by Gita Sahgal, a member of the Southall Black Sisters, based in Britain: 'It is in this crisis where

our own orthodoxies have collapsed that the doubters and transgressors must once more create a space for themselves'.[30]

India banned the book first: on 5 October 1988. Of the twenty-
one deaths associated with *The satanic verses* to date, nineteen
took place on the subcontinent. Of these, twelve were Muslim
anti-Rushdie demonstrators, shot in Rushdie's home town, Bombay,
on 24 February 1989. Ayatollah Khomeini called for Rushdie's
death on 14 February.

Why did India ban the book? In the name of the rights of a
religious minority in a secular state, Syed Shahabuddin, an opposition Muslim MP, launched a campaign against the book. 'Doubters
and transgressors must create a space for themselves' by taking a
distance from mere rational abstraction, and here is the first one:
'rights of a religious minority in a secular democratic-socialist
state'. Rational abstractions can be staunch allies, but *they can
always also be used as alibis*. Gita Sahgal's *'this crisis'* is *always*
implicit in the principle of reason. Her 'once more' is the activist's
shorthand for what must be *persistent*.

In India it was not an islamist decision, but a decision related to
the functioning of the rational abstractions claimed catachrestically
by the post-colonial state.[31] Artists and intellectuals were immediately vociferous against the decision, but, from personal accounts
that I have heard, the logic of the protests was extremely hard to
manipulate, still in the realm of rational abstractions.

In addition, perhaps precisely because the rational abstractions
of democracy are claimed catachrestically and therefore critically
by the secularist in the post-colonial state, there was a voice raised
in India against the West's right to claim freedom of expression.
The best succinct statement of this may be found in a letter to
The Economic and Political Weekly signed by, among others,
Asghar Ali Engineer, one of the strongest analysts and critics of
'communalism' (religious sectarianism) in India: 'We do not for
a moment belittle [the] Ayatollah's threat ... But we also see
the danger of "freedom of expression" being fetishized and the
embattled context in which a writer finds her/himself over-
simplified.'[32]

Wole Soyinka, travelling in India in December, wrote as a native
of Nigeria:

a nation which is, in the estimation of many, roughly equally divided amongst Muslims and Christians and animists, with the former two constituting a floating adherent population of the 'animist' in addition to being what they publicly proclaim ... I caught some flak from sections of the artistic and intellectual community for commenting that I quite understood the action of the Indian government in banning Salman Rushdie's book, ... I stated that, given India's harrowing situation of religious unrest, I probably would have done the same if I were the Prime Minister. I did not condone the ban; I merely tried to understand the horrible dilemma in which the government of India was placed.[33]

A dilemma, a crisis, an aporia, peculiar to democracy as checks and balances, rights and duties computed on the normative grid of rational abstractions inherited from the culture of imperialism. Bhikhu Parekh, a British-Indian political theorist has asked: 'Is there a release from this highly claustrophobic post-Enlightenment world view?'[34]

Rushdie's own reaction was straightforward:

The right to freedom of expression is at the foundation of any democratic society ... My view is that of a secular man for whom Islamic culture has been of central importance all his life ... You know, as I know that [the Muslim parliamentarians] and their allies don't really care about my novel. The real issue is the Muslim vote.[35]

Still within 'the claustrophobic post-Enlightenment world-view', let us step back and ask, what exacerbated the situation of the Muslim vote so dramatically? It is of course idle to assign a single efficient cause to such trends but, for strategic reasons that I hope will be evident to at least a section of my readership, I choose the successful censoring of a woman, contained within national boundaries, a national *cause célèbre* for a time, but nothing about which it can be said 'Islam today has displayed its enormous mobilizing power.' I refer, of course, to the Shahbano case. I quote a few passages from 'Shahbano' by Rajeswari Sunder Rajan and Zakia Pathak:

In April 1985, the Supreme Court of India ... passed a judgment in favor of Shahbano in the case of Mohammed Ahmed Khan, appellant, versus Shahbano and others, respondents. The judgment created a furor unequalled, according to one journal, since 'the great upheaval of 1857 [the so-called Indian Mutiny]' ... awarding Shahbano, a divorced Muslim woman, maintenance of Rs. 179.20 (approximately $14) per month

from her husband ... and dismissed the husband's appeal against the
award of maintenance under section 125 of the 1973 Code of Criminal
Procedure ... When some by-elections fell due in December 1985, the
sizeable Muslim vote turned against the ruling party (the Congress-I)
partly because it supported the judgment ... When Hindu fundamen-
talists offered to 'protect' her from Muslim men, her religious identity
won ... In an open letter, she denounced the Supreme Court judgment
'which is apparently in my favour; but since this judgment is contrary
to the Quran and the *hadith* and is an open interference in Muslim
personal law, I, Shahbano, being a Muslim, reject it and dissociate
myself from every judgment which is contrary to the Islamic Shariat.' ...
When the battle was carried to Parliament and the government of India
passed the bill that threw her on the mercy of the male relatives of
her natal family, her gender status was again activated. She became a
Muslim woman pursuing the case for the return of her *mehr* (dower)
under the provisions of the new act.[36]

Sunder Rajan and Pathak are quite right in saying that what is
at issue here is not 'whether this spacing, temporalizing self is a
deferral of the unified freely choosing *subject* or whether the latter
is itself only a metaphysic'.[37] What we are concerned with here is
the question of *agency*, even *national* agency within the effect of
the nation in the real – just as Rushdie's novel is concerned with
the *migrant* agency represented in a magical but none the less
serious layout. 'Agent' and 'subject' are different codings of something we call 'being'. Shahbano, as citizen of the same post-colonial
nation invoked by Rushdie in his letter to Rajiv Gandhi, has her
agency censored by the script of religion and gendering. In this
context, to bring up the question of the staging of free will in the
subject has a hidden ethico-political agenda that may give support
to the very forces that recode her as gendered and therefore make
her dependent upon the institution of heterosexual difference.
This has something like a relationship with what militants in
the Rushdie case have pointed out: that arguments from cultural
relativism are profoundly complicit, when invoked at certain
moments, with racist absolutism. It is quite correct to point out
the immense mobilisation of national resistance – the provisional
fabrication of a collective agency on the occasion of Shahbano.
But woman *as* woman (unavailable to class agency in the particular
context) is still only an occasion here. The question of free will
should not be inscribed within arguments from subject-production;

it is rather to be seen in connection with the presupposition of individual agency in collectivities. It is here that Shahbano stands censored. Within this frame, there is no real polarisation between self-censoring and other-censoring (conversion and coercion); that is the opposition we must learn to undo. In the sphere of the production of political value, the mute as articulate in the service of 'orthodoxy' (to borrow Gita Sahgal's word) – a discontinuous naming of collective agency in the name of the 'sacred' rather than the 'profane' (in the other coding called 'secular', 'national') – is more spectacularly muted because so abundantly audible. And, in the context of the international collectivisation brought about by way of Rushdie's book, of which she is among the first efficient causes, she has dropped out, become invisible. How can she *become* one of 'the doubters and transgressors' before she can participate in their 'clearing a space for themselves'? By counter-coercion through the orthodoxy of reason? *This* is the genuine dilemma, the aporia, the double bind of the question of agency. The condition of (im)possibility of rational collectivities must be seen, not as instrument, but as last instance.[38]

> By being categorized as a vagrant – the destitute woman – widow, divorcee, or abandoned wife – ... fulfills her (anti-)social role. The psychological damage of potential vagrant status is partially minimized by the depersonalizing effects of legal action. Section 125 offers women 'negative' subjectivity: the new act responds by reinserting the divorcee within the family, this time as dependent on her natal family and sons.[39]

As impersonal instrument, rational abstractions can operate as *pharmakoi*, a poison that can be a healing drug.[40] It is thus that one must turn to the extraordinary and (ex)orbitant category of 'legal vagrant'. In the subordinate, gendered, decolonised *national* space, the category of *female* 'vagrant' as 'access to public space' (section 125 of the Uniform Civil Code) must be recognised beside the category of 'migrant' within ex-colonial metropolitan space, where, as the migrant feminist group 'Women Against Fundamentalism' have pointed out 'women's voices have been largely silent' – and, I repeat, audible as muted ventriloquists – 'in the debate where battle lines have been drawn between liberalism and fundamentalism'.[41] Paradoxically, categorisation as vagrant is 'psycho-

logically damaging' only if the religious coding of gendered hetero-
sexuality is implicitly accepted by way of a foundational concept
of subject-formation. The freeing pain of a violent rejection from
a system of self-representation (a mode of value-coding) is not
confined to the franchised or disenfranchised.

This would take me into the arena where the reversal empire-
nation is displaced, about which I have written elsewhere.[42] Here
we are obliged to go forward to the most visible agent, the late
Ayatollah Khomeini.

Who punishes? How was the Ayatollah produced?

Although we cannot afford to forget, as Alberto Memmi writes in
the context of the Rushdie case, that 'monotheism, philosophically
and pragmatically speaking, is totalitarian', we must of course also
see that the stake in Khomeini's agency (in every sense) is not Islam,
but islamism.[43] And, at first glance, islamism in the regulation
of diaspora/migrancy. In the words of Farzaneh Asari, a pseudo-
nymous and exiled Iranian writer, 'it is the Muslims of America,
Britain, India, Lebanon and so on whom the Islamic Republic
wants to persuade of its continued hold on the Iranian people'.[44]
'It is important to underline that virtually all the pronouncements
from Teheran on *The Satanic Verses* begin and end with the
denunciations of *imperialism* and *colonialism*, accusing Rushdie
of complicity in a crusade aimed at Islam', writes Mehmet Ali
Dikerdem.[45]

But who punishes? How was the Ayatollah produced? These are
still merely the question of stakes. In answer to this question,
Asari offers an account of Khomeini's biography, that concept-
metaphor whose importance I have learned from Derrida:

> He ... chose his 'transcendent' self, the one that had been made into
> an almost Gandhian leader, over his 'real' theocratic self – what by
> temperament and belief he was and has remained. Khomeini's [political
> appointments] ... following the victory of the revolution to testify to
> the primacy of this 'transcendent' self in the crucial pre-revolutionary
> period.

Asari relates 'his gradual loss of popular support' as due to the
overcoming by the 'real' of the 'transcendent'.

> This loss has been more than made up for by the reconstruction and
> vast extension of the Shah's repressive apparatus ... (though the social

base of the present Iranian regime is still ... much broader and deeper
than that of the Shah ...)

Here is a rather convincingly proposed doubling, then, of the man
playing the monolith.[46] To sacrifice the heretic in a defence of the
faith is a ruse to 'recover lost territory', to cover over the political
and military defeat in the war with Iraq.

This monolithic face, defending an unchanging word, this 'construct' – with the piercing eyes under the iconic turban – 'at the
center of attention, [desperately attempting to] mak[e] ... reading,
writing, and meaning seem to be very close to the same thing' is
a product of complicity between Khomeini's 'direct interest in
presenting Iran as a static monolith defined by the steadfast devotion
of its people to a "fundamentalist" brand of Islam' and a sanctioned
ignorance, 'the accepted wisdom which makes ... ignorant lines
eminently reasonable' (Asari).[47] 'Reason' and 'religion' are thus
clandestine co-operators. Asari describes the conflation of 'the
estimated five million that celebrated Khomeini's return in the
streets of Teheran in February, to the fewer than three thousand
that greeted his call for Rushdie's murder ... in the same city in
February 1989'. It is not certain that the corporeal textuality of
Khomeini's body, levitated by helicopter, will do anything to rip
apart this conflation. For this conflation of collectivities in fact
projects a 'central image' of the 'omnipresent if often physically
absent Ayatollah ... when a crowd is large enough to fill the small
screen, how is the viewer to know the number of people involved
or the significance of such a number?'

Once again I emphasise the implausible connection-by-reversal –
the simulated Khomeini as Author and the dissimulated Shahbano
marking the place of the effaced trace at the origin: an invocation
of collective support projecting a singular agent filled with divine
intention; an invocation of collective resistance displacing a
censored patient as cross-hatched by discursivities. If we yield
ground and grounding by deliberately 'writing otherwise', analysing
a Shahbano by subject-formation rather than agency-deformation,
the forces of the Author claiming as Author to write 'the same'
come forward to occupy the space cleared. The case of *The satanic
verses*, a realist reading of magical realism, makes visible the violent
consequences.

Deliberate cultural relativism is a seemingly benevolent rational abstraction that shows its insidious credentials here. Al-Azmeh calls it 'apartheid – expressed in culturalist and religious tones'. Mehmet Ali Dikerdem calls it 'inflecting ... into ... ethnic pathology'; Gita Sahgal insists that

> fundamentalism has been the main beneficiary of the adoption of relativist multi-cultural norms by large sections of the political estab-lishment ... Anti-racist rhetoric ... sees only that a black religion feels powerless in a racist society. Any debate within the community – among Muslims, between believers and non-believers, men and women – is irrelevant from this viewpoint.

Asari again:

> Clearly the explanation for [BBC's documentary *Inside the Ayatollah's Iran* (14 February 1989)] *Panorama's* account lies in the basic assumption of the radical otherness of 'the Ayatollah's Iran'. But Iran does not consist entirely of Ayatollahs.

The radically other is a warning to the power of reason, not a featured face blocking out accessible heterogeneity. Those of us who have been troubled by the fetishisation of Levinas into a prophet of marginality feel comforted by Asari's enviably sober tones:[48]

> Cultural relativism and the recognition of the limitations of Euro-centrism have been important achievements of the radical consciousness and cultural anthropology that have developed in this century and whose wisdom must be preserved. But in the current climate these insights are being used or abused in unexpected ways.

I must, of course, insist that the 'use *and* abuse' are both entailed by institutionalised relativism, even as use and abuse are entailed by 'the principle of reason' that generates 'the post-Enlightenment claustrophobia' that such a relativism would contest. The answer is not the 'preservation' of the positive and perennial and the 'elimination' of the negative and contextual. It is not even to attempt to sublate – preserve and destroy. My peculiar theme is always *persistent* critique – and, I must emphasise, an *asym-metrical* persistent critique, focusing on different elements in the incessant process of recoding that shifts the balance of the *pharmakon's* effect from medicine to poison; while insisting on the necessity of the broad grounding position. Admittedly this brings practice to a breaking point in its acknowledgement of the everyday, but what else is new? I cannot develop this here, for, in this brief compass, I think it is more urgent to dramatise a diversity within the dossier that I have been presenting, in order to close this section by reminding ourselves first of an often unacknowledged desire and, secondly, of the United States, for we migrants in the US are parked in a spot claimed by some to be united by democratic reason.

Gita Sahgal speaks as a migrant fighting for racial equality in a metropolitan space, and sexual justice within the migrant community. Soyinka speaks as a national in a space where speaking of a *minority* religion would involve recasting dominance in the inaccurate language of numbers. Asghar Ali Engineer speaks as a national of a *religious* minority in a *secular* state. And Farzaneh Asari, speaking necessarily in a false name, speaks as an exile from Iran, *one* nation united under God. Standing in the United States, and accepting the responsibility for that highly dangerous positioning we must ask the question that Homi Bhabha has recently brought to our attention: 'what do these people want?' These people: migrant, national in an equally-divided-religion state, national in a majority-religion state, exile from a theocratic state.

Seen as collectivities (and that is not the only way to see them) they all want an access to generality *and* difference through the mediation of access to national agency. The migrant wants to redefine the nation, the post-colonial wants to identify the nation, the exile wants to explain and restore the nation and be an agent in terms of its normative and privative discourse. Rushdie's novel is not only a novel of migrancy, but also a novel of return. Thus Al Azmeh hears religion as the cry of the oppressed heart living in ghettos in a land of false dreams, 'impervious to the logic of cultural relativism and multi-culturalism but not to the logic of capitalism'. Soyinka wants to ban 'everything which is Iran ... as long as Ayatollah Khomeini remains accepted as a leader in Iran, everything except the voices of Iran's political and cultural dissidents and the protests of her repressed womanhood'. But to the Muslims in Bradford, where it all began, who wanted to conserve and establish Islamic education in Britain, the Ayatollah showed the fantasmatic vision of a nation, not a religion but a theocratic state. And Sahgal puts it this way:

> When [we] went to Bradford to make a documentary on *The Satanic Verses* ... it emerged that their main problem was to maintain faith in a secular society. What would future generations of Muslim children believe in, one asked rhetorically, if the book remained in circulation and was seen to be sanctified by society?

Yet the desire of these British Muslims is not to abdicate from the nation, but to insert Islamic education into the state. To participate in the nation in general, and yet to remain an enclave. And in the statement of the collective to which Sahgal belongs, it is the word 'nationality' that carries this contradiction: 'We will take up the right to determine our own destinies, not limited by religion, culture or nationality.'[49]

It is only if we acknowledge the heterogeneous desire for that great rational abstraction, agency in a nation, that we post-colonials will be able to take a distance from it. It is here that the transgressor must persistently critique that transgressed space, which she cannot not want to inhabit, even if coded another way. We can sometimes be released from the claustrophobia of the post-Enlightenment bunker if we acknowledge that we also want to be snug in it. What is punishment is also nourishment. It is only then that we can sense that the spectacular promise of democracy – those rational abstractions coded as Human Rights – is desirable precisely because those abstractions can be used as alibis to deflect critique. In fact, it is only then that we can begin to suspect that the ethical, without which any hope for civil society or social justice must crumble, and which must therefore remain eminently desirable, bases itself upon what might be the lowest common denominator of being-human, objectivity and the universal, and yet *must* code itself as the highest.[50] *Neither* radical alterity *nor* universal ipseity is an unquestionable value.

The United States is the dream of post-Enlightenment Europe. It is here that the bunker is a *trompe-l'oeil* of the wide-open spaces. It is here that the rational abstractions of formal democracy are most resolutely trotted out on behalf of cultural relativism, sanctioned ignorance, idiot goodwill, as well as racism and classism. As Rushdie himself said in a less harried time, American liberals just can't shake the habit of wanting to take care of the world. By the logic of this coding, communism and capitalism have of course already been recoded as state censorship versus free choice.[51] And

the Rushdie affair has been coded as freedom of speech versus terrorism and even as 'a triumph of the written word'. It has been domesti-
cated into a possible 'Western' (why?) 'martyrship' for literature,
or rather for the book trade! – 'to the cause that we [as an industry]
supposedly espouse!' (Emily Prager in *The village voice*).[52]

It is only if we recognise that we cannot not want freedom of
expression as well as those other normative and privative rational
abstractions that we on the other side can see how they work as
alibis. It is only then that we can recode the conflict as racism
versus fundamentalism.[53]

In the name of what do we judge the punisher? In the name of
right reason, of course, but from what does it detract our attention?
It hides, and I quote Mehmet Ali Dikerdem again:

> one of the most elemental fears and phobias of European cultural
> consciousness which regarded this new faith as the incarnation of the
> 'anti-Christ' ... Islam and Christianity confronted one another for a
> millennium in possibly the longest and bitterest 'superpower struggle'
> of all time ... Islam is thus the opposite of the accumulated values and
> institutions of the evolution from Renaissance and Reformation to the
> Industrial Revolution via the American and French Revolution.[54]

Dikerdem relates this adroitly to the political history of the
Middle East since the Second World War. This therefore is the
appropriate moment to record a response particularly to my dossier,
from Alia Arasooghly, a diasporic Palestinian. Earlier in this piece,
I remarked that, at first glance, it seemed that the stake in
Khomeini's agency was islamism in the regulation of migrancy.
Arasooghly points out persuasively how the production of the
Ayatollah Khomeini as the punisher was also a *mise-en-scène* of
the claiming of proper agency in Islam's own house, 'as though
God's death were but a play'.[55] This is, paradoxically, not a realist
reading of magical realism, but the reverse move: here scripture,
the ground of the Real, is performed as representation, a script.
Arasooghly cites a counter-claim by the Iraqi film *al-Qadissiya* ...

> which recreates the early Arab/Muslim battle and defeat of the Persian/
> Zoroastrian at Qadissiyah which opened Persia to Islam and to the
> Arab Empire (at the time of the Ummayad dynasty/defeaters of the
> Shiites!), a most significant and crucial battle for the Arabs, against
> claims to leave the Persians alone.

By her reading,

> the main audience the Iranian Islamic Republic has addressed itself to
> since its inception, after its own people has been the 'real Muslims' –
> the Arabs. *Khomeini could not speak in the name of Islam if he did
> not also speak for the Arabs.* The Quran [and the Prophet were sent to
> the Arabs] in Arabic, other Muslims either have to learn Arabic, or have
> access to a second hand interpretation via a translation ... the largest ...
> Islamic Empire/State was during Arab rule. Ottoman rule brought
> stagnation and decay. Islam's three Holy cities, Mecca, Medina, and
> Jerusalem are in Arab lands.

The *mise-en-scène*, 'the main audience', and now the substance
of the performance: 'the Ayatollah declared/showed Muslims how
to be powerful against the Great Satan, the U.S.A. and denounced
its client satan, Israel'.

An interesting conclusion arises from Arasooghly's reading.
Khomeini's 'anti-democratic, anti-Enlightenment' behaviour was
not only not direct and unmediated evidence of the immutable
essence of Islam, but it was a deliberate cultural-political self-
representation as an unmediated testifier for the immutable essence
of Islam. Thus Arasooghly suggests that 'Khomeini as Salahdin',
the counter-crusader, 'baffled the "international" sensibility [by]
not playing by the rules put out by Europe': the hostage syndrome,
the death threat against Salman Rushdie.

III

I promised in the final section to provide an element of intellectual
history. I will make no more than a few cryptic suggestions, remaining within the story of what Michel de Certeau has defined as a
shift in the *Lebenswelt* – the formal praxis of life – 'from religious
systems to the ethics of the Enlightenment'.[56] De Certeau must be
read against the grain because, like most European intellectuals
writing on the history of European consciousness, he does not take
imperialism into account.

In section 4 of *The writing of history*, de Certeau lays out a story
that is not altogether unknown, although in the telling of it, a
Derrida would emphasise Kant and Hegel, an Abrams the poets.[57]
With his brilliant historian's eye, de Certeau tells us how 'the

practical organization of Christianity is "socialized" in being stripped of its beliefs' (C 179), how in the seventeenth and eighteenth centuries Christianity is recoded, laundered and sublated into philosophy and ethics.

> *De-Christianization reveals in its formality the Christian practice*, but hereafter that practice is thrown out of the orbit of the *Logos* which had verified it ... It 'betrays' Christianity in both senses of the term: it abandons it, and it unveils it. A social reinterpretation of Christianity is thus inaugurated, which will flow back over Christian milieus: in them it will develop missionary practices turned toward the 'other' ... in them it will later provoke the reproduction of the ethics of progress in the form of a theology of history ... (C 179)

Such a sublation/graduation of a monotheism into secularism as such at the end of the seventeenth and eighteenth centuries in a certain place has something like a relationship with the ideological requirements of the release of the abstractions of monopoly capitalist (rather than pre-capitalist) imperialism. To repeat that move with the other great monotheism, Islam, is not possible again precisely because the seventeenth and eighteenth centuries have taken place. The ethical has to entail the universal, although it must always also be accessible to a singular or a collective case. The attempt to fashion an ethical universal out of a religious base, which is subsequently not called Christian but simply secular, then goes out of joint with the conjuncture, especially with a (national) subject not of the monopoly-capitalist dominant. 'Conjuncture' is a word that would give its antonym in plain English as being 'out of joint'.

Thus it is futile (if not reactionary) to look for parallels between the seventeenth and eighteenth century Euro-Atlantic and contemporary West Asia/North Africa/South Asia. One glimpses asymmetrical reflections, as in a cracked mirror, only to put them aside:

> these movements are symptoms of *an order that is being undone* ... religious structures begin to 'turn' quite differently, as if they were taken up en masse into the political element ... Traditional 'heresy,' a social form modeled on a theological truth, becomes less and less possible. The orthodoxy in terms of which this form was determined will now be more of a civil than religious nature ... The choice between Christianities is effected in terms of practices. (C 154, 158, 168, 162)

The residual appearances are not 'atheism, sorcery, mysticism'. Paradoxically, because the effort at globalising Islam is wounded and incapacitated by the detritus of an imperialist formation already in place, we have to locate them on a much larger scale: the Khilafat movement, dismantled by Kamal Ataturk's modernisation of Turkey; the Muslim contingency in the making of the Indian Constitution; and varieties of 'fundamentalism', a repetition and a rupture, and a reaction to the US–Israel combination.

'One of the tasks of history consists of measuring the distance or the relations between the formality of practices and their representations' (C 158). There is indeed a distance between the formality of historians' practices and their self-representation in the matter of imperialism. The invocation of 'missionary practices' cannot cover the distance altogether. And, where the descriptions are almost on target, the fact that colonialism/imperialism remains conspicuous by its absence makes the distance intractable: 'State policy already turns the country into a mercantilist and capitalist enterprise', for example, or, worse, 'a dominant *political* ethics is born of the enormous effort that allowed the eighteenth century to create nations and pass from Christianity to modern Europe' (C 155, 176).

Given that the story of Christianity to secularism is the only story around, we tend to feel quite justified when we claim, in praise or dispraise of reason, that reason is European. The peculiarity of historical narratives such as the one I have loosely put together in this section is that it is made up of contingencies which can also be read as Laws of Motion. I would like to suggest that it is the reading of one of those contingencies – the fit between monopoly capitalist imperialism and monotheist Christianity-into-secularism – as a Law of Motion that makes us presuppose that Reason itself is European. It might be better to recode the gift of contingency rather than construct a fantasmatic present or future in the name of that presupposition. In aid of what? A competition about mono-theisms? How about polytheisms or animisms? How far must discord be taken? Rather than lament reason, put it in a useful place, precisely to avoid these contingencies. Accept the limits of the contingency of history.

In place of mere secularism, the Southall Black Sisters might propose an instrumental universalism, always under the fire of doubt and transgression.[58]

IV

In this essay, I have first offered a literary critical plot summary of the book because I think one must be a schoolteacher in the classroom when it becomes impossible. I have done it almost as an act of disciplinary piety towards what is, after all, a novel. Next I have presented a dossier trying to focus on what people who are diversely connected to this event are saying. I have paused for a moment upon the uses to which the spectacular rational abstractions of democracy can sometimes be put. I have gone on to sketch the possibility of questioning what we often take as given, that the idea of reason – since I see reason itself as a *pharmakon*, rather than an unquestioned good or an unquestioned evil – is *necessarily* Eurocentric.

Finally, then, an exhortation: whenever they bring out the Ayatollah, remember the face that does not come together on the screen, remember Shahbano. She is quite discontinuous with Salman Rushdie's fate as it is being organised on many levels. The Rani of Sirmur emerged in the East India Company records only when she was needed to make 'History' march.[59] Shahbano's emergence is structurally comparable. When the very well-known face is brought out, remember the face that you have not seen, the face that has disappeared from view, remember Shahbano.

Notes

1 Reprinted with permission of *Third Text* journal. An earlier version of this essay appeared in *Public Culture*, 2.i (Fall 1989).

2 S. Rushdie, *The Satanic Verses* (New York: Viking, 1989). Page references have been included in the text, after the initial letters SV.

3 P. Bürger, *Theory of the avant-garde*, trans. M. Shaw (Minneapolis: University of Minnesota Press, c. 1984), 25–7.

4 J. Atlas, 'What is Fukuyama saying (Francis Fukuyama on the end of history)', *New York Times Magazine*, 22 Oct. 1989.

5 R. Barthes, 'The death of the author', in *Image-music-text*, trans. S. Heath (New York: Hill and Wang, 1977), 148.

6 See 'Foucault/Derrida/Mahasweta', forthcoming in collection edited by Thomas Wartenberg.

7 Barthes, 'Death of the author', 148.

8 *Ibid.*, 145–6.

9 M. Foucault, 'What is an author', in *Language, counter-memory, practice: selected essays and interviews*, trans. D.F. Bouchard and S. Simon (Ithaca: Cornell University Press, 1977).

10 B. Johnson, *The critical difference: essays in the contemporary rhetoric of reading* (Baltimore: The Johns Hopkins University Press, 1981).

11 J. Derrida, 'Otobiographies: the teaching of Nietzsche and the politics of the proper name', in *The bar of the other: texts and discussions with Jacques Derrida*, trans. P. Kamuf (New York: Schocken Books, 1985).

12 *Ibid.*, 10.

13 S. Rushdie, '...', *Granta*, 28, Birthday issue (Autumn 1989), 29. For reasons of security, I presume, this poem is irreproducible.

14 Derrida, 'Otobiographies', 11.

15 For the suggestion that 'magical realism' is a style that cannot narrativise decolonisation, see Spivak, 'Post-structuralism, post-coloniality, marginality, and value', in P. Collier and H. Ryan, eds, *Literary theory today* (Cambridge: Polity Press, forthcoming). For a somewhat tendentious but intriguing genealogy of 'magical realism', see J. Hart, *Reactionary modernism: technology, culture, and politics in Weimar and the Third Reich* (Cambridge: Cambridge University Press, 1984).

16 Brennan, *Salman Rushdie and the third world: myths of the nation* (London: Macmillan, 1989). Perhaps because of his clear-cut position on the nation, Mr Brennan is weak in the presentation of the place of the novel in the Indian literary traditions (pp.) 18, 79–80). Incidentally, Arjuna and Bhima are completely human characters in an epic, not 'figures in the Hindu pantheon' (p. 109). Rushdie's use of Hindu material gives us a sense of the non-sanctimonious 'secularism' which is a fact of the subcontinental everyday. It does matter in that context that we distinguish between Achilles and Zeus, and not call both gods. Mr Brennan's sense that *Midnight's children* put 'the Indo-English imagination on the map' (p. 80) is a step ahead of Alan Yentob's inspired polarisation of India/ Pakistan and the West as 'oral tradition' and the 'modern novel'! (L. Appignanesi and S. Maitland, eds, *The Rushdie file* (London: Fourth Estate, 1989), 197). In Macaulay's day, Arabic and Sanskrit writing at least filled a school library shelf. With friends like these!

17 Rushdie, 'Interview with Sean Franch', in Appignanesi and Maitland, *File*, 9.

18 I feel solidarity with men who let women in but cannot see this gesture as the performance of feminism. On this particular point, I must take exception even from my friend Srinivas Aravamudan's outstanding essay, a full-dress scholarly treatment of the novel. To create women as 'strong characters' is not necessarily to 'pursue ... [t]he issue of *feminism* and Islam' ('Being God's postman is no fun, Yaar: Salman Rushdie's *The satanic verses*', *Diacritics*, 19 ii, summer 1989, 13; emphasis mine). And it is here that I must also split from Rukmini Bhaya Nair's impressive 'Text and pre-text: history as gossip in Rushdie's novels': 'The Prophet's own intellectual, moral and practical dilemmas are brought closer to us through his wives, Khadijah and Ayesha, who implicitly believed in him, and the (un)common whores of Jahilia who imitated every move of the women proximate to the Prophet. Through the gossip of women, we come

to a truer understanding of the "sinuous complexities of history". Public facts alone are insufficient und unconvincing' (*Economic and Political Weekly*, 24, xviii, 6 May 1989, 997). That private–public divide is old gender-coding. We must set these things on the move.

I repeat, I support men who make the effort. And it is in that spirit that I quote here my translation of a poem, just in from Bangladesh, by Farhad Mazhar, a secularist Muslim poet, where a desire is recorded and the possibility of an alternative history is glimpsed in a counter-factual complement. I have commented at greater length on such counter-factual moves in 'Post-structuralism, post-coloniality'. I quote Mazhar's poem in full because I doubt that the present readership would otherwise have access to the work of his considerable poet-activist:

> I write these verses in Mistress Khadija's name:
> I'll not say bismillah, just take her name.
> Lord, permit me. No anger, please, just once.
> In her name I'll write my poem, Lord of Praise.
>
> Dear Prophet's name? No, his name neither, boss.
> Just'n Khadija's name – in exquisite Khadija's name
> For once I'll forget all other names on earth
> Forget you too, forget my Prophet.
>
> Only she, Lord, only in her wage work
> Was my dear Prophet ensconced, rapt with camel and trace.
> Don't show off – he was your beloved,
> But, for her, a salaried worker –
> All women know you are puny here
> But don't show it abroad for respect's sake.

19 This is the productive unease in F. Jameson, 'Third-world literature in the era of multinational capitalism', *Social Text*, 15 (1986).

20 G. Deleuze and F. Guattari, *Anti-Oedipus: capitalism and schizophrenia*, trans. R. Hurley *et al.* (Minneapolis: University of Minnesota Press, 1983), 5, 36. See also p. 12.

21 For the notion of biography – the staging of the author is part of this – see Derrida, 'Otobiographies'. For Schreber, see S. Freud, 'Psycho-analytic notes on an autobiographical account of a case of paranoia (*dementia paranoides*)', in J. Strachey *et al.*, trans., *The standard edition of the complete psychological works* (London: Hogarth Press, 1958), vol. 12.

22 D. Erdman, *Blake, prophet against empire: a poet's interpretation of the history of his own times* (Princeton: Princeton University Press, 1977, 3rd ed.).

23 J. L. Austin, *How to do things with words* (Oxford: Oxford University Press, 1965), 21–2; quoted in J. Derrida, 'Signature event context', in G. Graff, ed., *Limited Inc.* (Evanston: Northwestern University Press, 1986), 16.

24 Nair, 'Text and pretext', 995.

25 *Ibid.*, 1000.

26 Spivak, 'Subaltern studies: deconstructing historiography', in R. Guha, ed., *Subaltern studies: writings on south Asian history and society* (Delhi: Oxford University Press, 1985), 351–6.

27 The phrase 'criticism by hearsay', used in an academic context, comes from P. de Man, 'The resistance to theory', in *The resistance to theory* (Minneapolis: University of Minnesota Press, 1986), 15.

28 A. Al-Azmeh, 'More on "The satanic verses" ', cited in *Frontier*, 21, 25 (4 Feb. 1989), 6.

29 Appignanesi, *File*, is, of course, now a much more extensive source.

30 G. Sahgal, 'Transgression comes of age', *Interlink*, 12 (May–June 1989), 19. I am grateful to Peter Osborne and John Kraniauskas for help in assembling this dossier.

31 For post-coloniality and catachresis, see Spivak, 'Post-structuralism, post-coloniality'.

32 'Dubious defenders', *Economic and Political Weekly*, 24, xvii (29 April 1989), 894. A. A. Mazrui strikes a similar chord in 'The moral dilemma of Salman Rushdie's *Satanic verses*', in Appignanesi, *File*.

33 W. Soyinka, 'Jihad for freedom', *Index on Censorship*, 18.5 (May–June 1989), 20. All references to the *Index* are to this issue.

34 'Identities on parade: a conversation', *Marxism Today* (June 1989), 27.

35 'Open letter to Rejiv Gandhi', *The New York Tims* (19 Oct. 1988).

36 R. Sunder Rajan and Z. Pathak, ' "Shahbano" ', *Signs*, 14, iii (Spring 1989), 558–9, 572.

37 ' "Shahbano" ', 573: emphasis mine.

38 For an explanation of the '(im)' of '(im)possibility', see Spivak, *In other worlds: essays in cultural politics* (New York: Methuen, 1987), 263, 308 n. 81.

39 Sunder Rajan and Pathak, ' "Shahbano" ', 576–7.

40 For *pharmakon*, see Derrida, 'Plato's pharmacy', in B. Johnson, trans., *Disseminations* (Chicago: University of Chicago Press, 1981).

41 Sahgal, 'Transgression', 19.

42 See Spivak, 'Women in difference: Mahasweta Devi's "Douloti the bountiful" ', in *Cultural critique*, forthcoming.

43 A. Memmi, 'For secularism', *Index*, 18.

44 F. Asari, 'Iran in the British media', *Index*, 11.

45 M. A. Dikerdem, 'Rushdie, Islam and "Islam" ', *End*, 37 (June 1989), 4.

46 For another view, see A. Najmabadi, 'Gayatri Spivak interviewed', forthcoming in a condensed version in *Merip Reports* and submitted in full to *Social Text*.

47 The first quotation is from D. Haraway, 'The biopolitics of postmodern bodies: determinations of self in immune system discourse', *Differences*, I, i, 10. All quotations from Asari are from 'Iran in the British media'.

48 The most astute discussion of the inaccessibility of the absolutely other is still J. Derrida, 'Violence and metaphysics: an essay on the thought of Emmanuel Levinas', in *Writing and difference*, trans. A. Bass (Chicago: University of Chicago Press, 1978). For a powerful feminist reading, see L. Irigaray, 'Fecondite de la caress', in *Ethique de la difference sexuelle* (Paris: Minuit, 1984).

49 Sahgal, 'Transgressions', 19.

50 For an extended discussion of this, see my forthcoming study of P. Dickinson's *The poison oracle*.

51 For an astute practical account of this coding, see B. Epstein, 'The Reagan doctrine and right-wing democracy', *Socialist Review*, 19, i (January–March 1989).

52 'Rushdie judgment', *The Village Voice*, 34, x (7 March 1989), 23. The conduct of the Anglo-US publishing world is undoubtedly an important matter. But to reduce the Rushdie affair to nothing but an assessment of that conduct is typically ethnocentric.

53 As I have argued in Nazmabadi, 'Interview', the British dossier shows that in Britain, as opposed to the US, this critical recoding is strongly present. It is significant that Peter Porter can write as follows in so establishment an organ as the *Times Literary Supplement*:

... sincerity proves to be not enough ... Everything is Westernized so that the differences between the Christian and Imperial bigotry faced by Molière and Voltaire, and the underdog upsurge of today's Islamic crowd are ignored ... It cannot have been [Tony] Harrison's intention, but some of the scenes and part of the commentary [in *The blasphemer's banquet* on BBC1's *Byline*] took on a racist tone – our Christian heritage, it seemed to say, is falling to the Crescent of Islam (11–17 August 1989).

54 The classic analysis of the representation of Islam is, of course, E. W. Said, *Covering Islam: how the media and the experts determine how we see the rest of the world* (New York: Pantheon, 1981).

55 W. B. Yeats, 'Two songs from a play'. Arasooghly, who is a film-maker and teacher of Film Studies at Northeastern Univesity, gives a much more detailed account than I have been able to quote. Where I summarise, the interpretation is necessarily my own. 'The fatwa' section of Appignanesi, ed., *File* supports her point of view. See especially pp. 95, 106. *The Observer*, Bombay, had this to say two days after the Bombay killings: 'It has not only helped [the Ayatollah] upstage his opponents within Iran who are harking for change, but also in realising an impossible dream – through his kill Rushdie fatwa, he has succeeded to some extent in cutting across the Shia-Sunni divide and assuming the posture of the tallest leader within the global Muslim fraternity, forcing more level-headed Islamic leaders to stand up and be counted' (p. 132). Interestingly, Iqbal Wahhab, a more 'level-headed Muslim', writing from Britain one day *before* the riot, had questioned that authority: 'A negligible proportion of the Muslim population in Britain is Shia, and the Ayatollah's call has, by and large, fallen on deaf ears in this country. To Sunnis, he has no authority to make such a threat' (p. 128). See also Engineer *et al.*, 'Dubious defence', *EPW*, 894.

56 M. de Certeau, 'The formality of practices: from religious systems to the ethics of the Enlightenment (the seventeenth and eighteenth centuries)', in *The writing of history* (New York: Columbia University Press, 1988). All passages from de Certeau are from this chapter. Page references have been included in the text following the letter C.

57 See especially J. Derrida, *Glas* (Paris: Galilee, 1974), the left hand column; and M. H. Abrams, *Natural supernaturalism* (New York: Norton, 1971).

58 For elaboration of a universalism of difference, see Spivak, 'Remembering the limits: difference, identity and practice: a transcript', in P. Osborne, ed., *Socialism and the limits of liberalism* (London: Verso, forthcoming).

59 See Spivak, 'Reading the archives: the Rani of Sirmur', in F. Barker, ed., *Europe and its others* (Colchester: University of Essex Press, 1985), vol. 1.

PART IV

Authorship and the literary tradition

7

The sirens' song: authorship, authority and citation

Simon Goldhill

But Plato was ill ... (Plato)

The epigraph to this chapter is taken from Plato's *Phaedo*. In the *Phaedo*, the account of Socrates' last day in prison is presented as a dialogue between two figures, Phaedo and Echecrates, who recall a dialogue between Socrates and others in which the author carefully enters himself as an absent figure. The others were there, 'but Plato was ill ...'. Plato authoritatively represents a master, his master, Socrates, whose characteristic mode is irony, and whose characteristic gesture is to deny mastery or authority, except, perhaps, in the assertion of uncertainty. And this master's voice is represented – suitably? – only in the recession of different and dissenting voices that the double frame of a dialogue within a dialogue instigates. This strategy of indirection has prompted an unending search for Plato's voice, the author's philosophical position, as if the polyphony of dialogues could be reduced to a proposition. How often do we read 'Plato says ...', 'Plato's position is ...'? Yet it is precisely the position of the author – from where does he speak? – that is problematised by Plato's dialogic and didactic texts; much as 'writing', 'rhetoric' and 'philosophy' themselves are subject to a relentless self-reflexive scrutiny.[1]

I have taken this Platonic self-representation as a starting-point for two reasons. The first is simply to state from the outset that to turn to the ancient world in the project of 'What is an author?' is not to approach anyone's childhood stories. We are still inevitably writing footnotes to Plato, and it is not by chance that Derrida, Foucault, Barthes, Freud, those modern masters who feature so strongly in this book, turn and return to what a recent commentator on Foucault has again called the 'tyranny of Greece'.[2] The second and most important reason is to introduce the key terms I shall be exploring here: the relation between an author and authority, the relation between an author and voice, and finally, the relation between these ideas of authority and voice and the practice of citation or quotation – appropriating another author's words. The Platonic representation of the words of Phaedo, recalling the ironic words of Socrates, and, ironically, Plato's absence from the exchange will suffice for an opening image of the difficulties I will be discussing.

Now I feel I have to start with a brief semantic and sociological excursus. The Greek term around which I shall be writing is *sophos*, traditionally translated 'wise'. Socrates knew he was most *sophos* in as much as he knew he knew nothing – or so he analysed what he had heard a friend had been told by the paradigmatically ambiguous oracle at Delphi.[3] *Sophos* implies a person who has privileged access to some authoritative knowledge and the privileged ability to express it. The term is used of a range of practitioners from the poet through the politician to the pot-maker.[4] There is, otherwise, no regular term that corresponds to 'author' in the sense of a discrete category of those who produce literature, who write. The product of the *sophos* is *sophia*, 'authoritative knowledge', or 'wisdom', which is constantly and inevitably associated with the production of poetry in ancient Greece. Indeed, *sophia* is the normal term for what poets offer to the public. It is precisely because of this claim of authoritative knowledge for poetry and for other spheres of action that Plato both coins his new term *philosophia*, 'philosophy', for what he does, and attacks so many other discursive practices, and in particular poetry.[5] The association of authoritative knowledge with poetry is, however, fundamental to any notion of authorship in ancient Greece, and I want briefly to outline some of the different ways this authority is constituted.

In archaic Greece, the close association of authoritative knowledge and the production of poetry has been extensively discussed.[6] The bard has been called the 'master of truth', and the 'teacher of the people'. The poet holds this didactic, authoritative position first in the social sense that it is the *choros* – music and dance – which forms the basis of ancient education, even in Plato's last charter for a city,[7] and it is the poet, the bard, who teaches the *choros*, who provides the words and music. The poet, however, also produces the valorised representations for culture and of culture – from Hesiod's *Theogony* through Sappho's anatomies of desire to Homer's epics of power and transgression. The contestations and claims of authority within these texts are expressed and manipulated in terms of hierarchical oppositions between on the one hand truth, memorial, praise – the outcome of divine inspiration and human excellence – and, on the other, lies, forgetfulness, blame – the outcome of human slander, envy and failure.[8] The category 'fiction', so important to modern constructions of authorship, is not articulated. The *performance* of the bard – the exchange of narrative, tale-telling – is the privileged institution for the production of poetry, and, as we will see from my first passage from the *Odyssey*, it is the scene of performance, rather than the scene of writing or, in the narrow sense, the scene of reading, that forms a fundamental aspect of the representation of poetry within poetry, which is our only access to the poetics of these archaic texts.

Fifth-century Athens – classical Athens – provides us with a highly developed scene of performance, that is, the great drama festivals of democracy, from which my second passage will come. For my present purposes, two elements of this startling age of enlightenment and conflict need to be emphasised. The first is the multiplication of institutional sites for the production of discourse in the *polis*: the lawcourt, the Assembly, the public funeral ....[9] In democracy, these open the routes to power and allow displays of status; and the new intellectuals, often called the Sophists, offer an education designed for the successful entrance into these areas of public life. The result of this is that poetry, especially in a didactic frame, is seen *both* in opposition to other claims of authoritative expertise, *and* as analogous to them. On the one hand, poetry can be the object of the sophist's *sophia* – and it is in the fifth century that poetry first becomes the object of study in such a way as to valorise the analytic technique and increase the status of the critic. On the other hand, the drama festivals become the sign and symptom of democracy's ability publicly to debate an issue, publicly to speak to the people. It is tragedy that the anecdotal material would have us believe Plato wrote before he turned to other forms of writing and to banish it from his city[10] – and the status of the tragic texts can be readily seen in their immediate dissemination throughout the Greek world and their adoption as teaching texts. Thucydides expresses this dynamic of the democratic city when he calls the Athenians (3.38) *theatai tôn logôn*, 'spectators of speech-making', a phrase designed to uncover the role of language in the city of words.

If the fifth-century *polis* multiplies the institutions of performance, so too – and this is the second element of the classical city that I wish to emphasise – the possibilities of public language multiply. In particular, the invention of prose as a medium of writing alters the status of poetry. The historians, like the philosophers, set themselves against poetry: prose begins as a radical and combative new possibility of exploring and explaining the world. Medicine, dietetics, science, political analysis, rhetorical handbooks, mathematics are the product first of the fifth century, and in particular after Aristotle's masterful contribution, it is prose that maintains a privileged position in the conflicts of *sophia*.

This is particularly important for the period and place from which my third passage comes, Hellenistic Alexandria. Under the Ptolemies, with their establishment of the great Library at Alexandria – the first attempt at an inclusive written archive – and with their establishment of the Mouseion – the first attempt at a collective, state-funded research unit attached to such an archive – the context for authorship alters irrevocably. After the great public literature of the fifth century, it is typical that Callimachus, head librarian and leading poet, now writes *sikkhainô panta ta dêmosia*, 'I loath everything to do with The People'. If politics is the frame for fifth-century literature, for the Hellenistic writers it is the exclusive circle of scientific, historical, anthropological and, above all, philological research. *Sophia* becomes a claim of intellectual and artistic sophistication, of scholarship. Indeed, we are still the heirs of the Hellenistic institutionalisation of knowledge, its demarcation of disciplines and genres, its valorisation of scholarship. Writing from within the archive fundamentally affects the alignments of poetic discourse for the Hellenistic authors.

Now, I have conducted this extremely brief tour of ancient Greek conditions of literary production by way of context to the three texts I will discuss. It is so brief a tour not only because of pressure of space and all the usual rhetorical gestures in this format, but also, first, because this bare outline of a changing sociology of authorship – from the bard to the conflict of discourses in the fifth century to the scholarly alignments of writing from within the Hellenistic archive – is well known. And I hope that despite my scanty annotation the inverted commas were visible throughout. But there is a second reason too. If you are used to Renaissance scholarship, say, and have learnt from the brilliant insights into the conditions of production offered by, for example, Greenblatt, Orgel, Tennenhouse, Berry[11] ... then to approach the Hellenistic period, say, is to be faced by a dizzying lack of contextual evidence. For the Hellenistic texts, it is simply not known who constituted an audience, what the conditions of production or circulation were; we have almost no archive for this literature written from within the archive. We cannot even provide relative datings for the major works or authors of the period. You just can't do New Historicism on Ancient History. What we have is a set of extraordinarily sophisticated texts, with the barest minimum of contextualisation. And one of the points I hope to demonstrate is how difficult it is to read the poetry's self-reflexive treatments of performance, writing and the poet within the light of the accepted sociological mapping of authorship. I have chosen for this purpose three epigonal texts from different times and places – one archaic, one classical, one Hellenistic – three works that seem to deal with the ideas and ideals of poetry, performance, literary tradition and the author.

The first is from the *Odyssey*, a work whose self-reflexive poetics has been much discussed in recent years:[12] Odysseus' encounter with the Sirens. Now, the *Odyssey* is a self-consciously epigonal text in that it is a post-Trojan war epic, in that it places itself after the *Iliad*. Characteristically, the *Odyssey* redeploys Achilles, the hero of the *Iliad*, regretting in the Underworld his Iliadic behaviour – to the hero of the *Odyssey*, the man of guile and twisted words.[13] It is an epic of such lures and ambushes. Not only is it self-consciously epigonal, but also its central drama is the fight to establish patriarchal, patrilinear inheritance, to pass on the proper name and the property. It is an epigonal epic where characters

are known, sited, by their patronymics, and recognition of the
father in the house motivates the conflicts of the narrative. It is a
narrative that is deeply concerned with the exchange of words:
the performance of bards – poets within the poem – is repeatedly
represented and discussed. Odysseus himself manipulates a series
of lying self-representations, as he returns in disguise, a series of
tales that weave and reweave versions of his journeys and that are
glossed by the narrator in a complex and suggestive phrase as 'lies
like the truth'.[14] And, perhaps most importantly for my argument
here, the epic narrative is also structured so that Odysseus tells a
large part of his travels in a retrospective first-person narration.
One of the fundamental critical issues for the *Odyssey* is trying
to put together, to *relate*, the tales of Odysseus, the tales of the
various narrators within the poem, and the narrative voice – the
famously reticent 'Homer'. To articulate, that is, authority of voice
within the narrative's play of voices.

The passage I have chosen to talk about is taken from the
retrospective narrative of Odysseus. It's a passage that revolves
around the exchange of language and its dangers – like so many
of the tales Odysseus tells his hosts in return for his passage
home. Here, the threat is the threat of destruction, to be lured by
the seduction of the Sirens' song. Indeed, this image of the hero
desperate to listen, despite the evident danger, unable to use his
authority to persuade his men to untie him, as they row on with
their ears full of wax, has enchanted writers from Euripides to
Rilke. I quote the passage in my own prosaic and inadequate
translation (12. 181–94):

> When we came within call of the shore
> In our swift flight, the Sirens became aware of our swift ship
> Bearing down on them, and they broke into liquid song:
> 'Draw near, much praised Odysseus, glory of the Achaeans;
> Anchor your ship, so that you can hear our voice.
> No man yet has passed by here in his black ship
> Without hearing the sweet-toned voice of our mouths.
> Each man takes pleasure and sails off knowing more.
> For we know everything that the Argives and Trojans
> Experienced toiling at Troy at the will of the gods.
> We know everything that is to happen on the teeming earth.'
> Thus they spoke with their beautiful voices. My heart

> Longed to hear, and I ordered my companions to free me,
> Nodding with my eyebrows. But they swung forward with their oars
>   and rowed ahead ...

The first thing to note about Odysseus' representation is that he directly quotes, he recites the alluring song for us to hear: the song whose attraction is ineluctable is displayed – in inverted commas – to his audience. The song within the tale within the epic – a recession of frames ... But one Greek verb runs throughout these tales of dangerous language, *thelgein*, which means 'enchant, bewitch, seduce'. The Sirens' song seduces Odysseus. He has been prewarned by Circe, the seductive witch who has beguiled him into staying with her for a year. Odysseus' song itself seduces his listeners who sit in silent enchantment in the hall. And Homer's poetry? How does it grab you? (Setting on one side the translation ...) Like Odysseus, like Odysseus' audience, we are to hear the Sirens, framed as they are by Circe's warnings, by Odysseus' trick of hearing but escaping, by the poet's report of Odysseus' report. But the continual danger of seduction in words is marked by the continuum of a vocabulary of beguilement that seeps through each frame, each song, each narrator. Odysseus and the figure of the poet are closely associated throughout the epic, particularly here as Odysseus narratives his Odyssey, his own adventures. Yet how does such an association between the figure of the poet and the arch-manipulator of the tales of renown affect the authoritative voice of the narrator? Does the interweaving of Odysseus' seductive narrations with the poet's tale introduce a self-aware recognition of the seductive allure at the heart of the objective third-person narrative? And what's it like for the poet's voice to allow a (self-)recognition of its dangerously seductive qualities, its beguiling?

Yet there is more than this connection of narrative and enchantment here. For, as Pietro Pucci has pointed out, one striking feature of the language of this passage is how the Sirens' song seems to reproduce the language of the *Iliad*: there are several phrases and words that occur only here in the *Odyssey* but that are regularly used in the *Iliad*.[15] It's as if when the Sirens promise Odysseus a tale of what happened at Troy, they revert to the language of the *Iliad*, that most famous poem of the Trojan War's events. The

Odyssey's hero sails past those who sing of him as an Iliadic figure. Most extraordinary of all, however, is the way that the Sirens offer Odysseus pleasure and greater knowledge because 'we know everything that the Argives and Trojans experienced toiling at Troy at the will of the gods; we know everything that is to happen on the teeming earth'. This is remarkable on the one hand because the ineluctable seduction of the Sirens is the seduction of *knowledge*, of learning everything, of the pleasure of authoritative access to what happens. It's remarkable on the other hand because this claim of authoritative knowledge mimics the terms in which the Muses, the divine inspirers of poetry, are represented particularly in the *Iliad*, where it is precisely the Muses' omniscience that authorises the bard's poetry as truth and memorial and praise.[16] As much as Odysseus, the manipulative trickster, is associated with the bard in the beguilement of tale-telling, so the Sirens, dangerous, seductive singers, are associated with the Muses, the inspirational authorisation of poetry. The framing of this narrative places the claim of authoritative knowledge in inverted commas, a sign of seductive language. What sort of self-recognition are we to read in this self-reflexive poetics, this interweaving of seduction and authority?

The model of the bard as the authoritative producer of images and narratives for a culture, a bard authorised by the divine knowledge of the Muses, is, then, problematised by the *Odyssey*'s self-awareness, its framing of the claims of authority, its association of narrative and beguilement. What happens to the authoritative voice of the third-person narrative, what happens to the figure of the poet as author, when in this play of framed voices, both omniscience and tale-telling appear as signs of seductive danger?

The second case I want to look at is from Aristophanes' play the *Frogs*, produced in democratic Athens in 405 B.C. In this drama, the god of theatre, Dionysus, goes to the Underworld to bring back the dead Euripides, since the city is in dire need of a *sophos* to advise them in the desperate situation of the Peloponnesian war and the contemporary poets cannot fulfil that role adequately. I hardly need emphasise that a play in which the god of drama is a character in search of an author has a marked element of self-reflexivity. When Dionysus reaches the underworld, however, he finds Euripides and Aeschylus locked in an argument about which of them has the right to hold the Chair of Poetry in the underworld. The last part of the play is taken up with an *agôn*, a contest, between the two playwrights specifically about *sophia*, about which of them is the true *sophos* sought by Dionysus, who is to judge the contest. Euripides' famous last play, the *Bacchae*, has a repeated choral refrain *ti to sophon*, 'What is knowing?', and here Euripides enters the comic stage to debate *sophia* with his great predecessor whose plays formed an inescapable burden of the past for Euripides' innovations in tragic writing. Both the fact that poets – *sophoi*, authors – become the leading characters in a work of literature, and that the comic writing is deeply parasitic on tragic writing are characteristic of Aristophanes' self-reflexive, carnivalesque theatre.

Both the Aristophanic Aeschylus and the Aristophanic Euripides fight dirty, parodying, insulting and riotously dismissing each other's claims to *sophia*. Both figures are also subject to the parodic representation of the comic master, whose ambivalent delight in and jokes about tragedy are a constituent element of the parody. Even the idea of a debate between poets is parodied in the famous weighing – a literal weighing – of words, to determine the weightiness of precept. This contest of parodied poets parodying each other produces some dizzying effects for the idea of a poet's voice and authority of voice. Two brief passages will serve as examples. The first is part of the debate of the prologues, where Euripides is doing a trendy critique of Aeschylean prolixity. Again, the translation is mine (1152–7):

> *Aes.* 'Prove saviour for me, and an ally as I pray.
> For I have come to this land, and returned ...'
> *Eur.* The wise Aeschylus has said the same thing twice!
> *Dio.* How twice?
> *Eur.* Look at the expression. I will expound.
> ' "For I have come" ' he says, ' "and returned" '.
> 'Have come' is the same as 'returned'.

The exchange begins with the Aristophanic Aeschylus quoting from (Aeschylus') *Oresteia* as an example of his best prologue writing: 'Prove saviour for me, and an ally as I pray. For I have come to this land and returned ...'. The Aristophanic Aeschylus correctly re-cites lines from Aeschylus' *Choephoroi*. The quotation is interrupted by the Aristophanic Euripides to announce that

Aeschylus 'the wise', 'the *sophos*' – an adjective used sarcastically, but also to stress the term being fought over – has said 'the same thing twice'. The Aeschylean re-citation contains a tautology, a doubleness, to be remarked by Dionysus, the judge. 'How twice?', asks the god. 'Look at the speech', demands the figure of Euripides – literary parody's typical self-consciousness of the material of literary production – 'I will expound'. And the Aristophanic Euripides re-quotes the Aristophanic Aeschylus' quotation of Aeschylus' *Oresteia* to show its error – of saying the same thing twice. The parodic critical discussion on lines quoted and requoted itself turns on whether two expressions are the same or different. Is 'I have come' the same as 'I have returned'? The problem of parody – can you hear the difference?' – is here the stuff of parody. It is worth noting how a critic of postmodern parody, who defines parody as 'repetition with difference', can scarcely do justice to this vertiginous self-reflexivity of *sophos* parodying *sophos* parodying *sophos* parodying ....[17]

Aeschylus' reply to Euripides' critique is devastating. He gets Euripides to recite various prologues from his plays, and simply adds to each the phrase *lêkuthion apôlesen*, 'lost his little bottle', and the insertion of this phrase as a completion of the sentence reduces Euripides to helplessness. Again, the parody depends on a brilliant variation of similarity and difference, as the Aristophanic Aeschylus makes the Aristophanic Euripides seem more and more ridiculous by completing the different prologues with the same Aristophanic comic phrase. The addition of the same phrase puts Euripides' different prologues in a different light – making them seem all the same, finally. Aeschylus' repetition of the same phrase threatens the semantic security both of Euripides' prologues – as it elides the differences between them – and of the phrase itself. The brief triviality of 'lost his little bottle' may seem pregnant with meaning or inevitably empty (in its very repetitiveness). And this loss of control in and of language has produced in critics a desperate attempt to seek for a certain and secure meaning for the 'little bottle', the container that keeps getting lost. There have been a surprising number of articles in recent years claiming to demonstrate authoritatively what the phrase really means, most amusingly by competing schools of archaeologists who produce pictures of 'little bottles' to prove that 'little bottle' must have, or, alternatively, could not possibly have a sexual connotation.[18] Aeschylus' repeated expression of loss destroys or mimes the loss of language as a container of value, significance, truth. As comedy ever demonstrates, language leaks. The poets' contest of and on words provides a paradigmatic case of comedy's archetypal practice – to explore and explode the limits of language as a signifying system and as a medium of social exchange. Here the inverted commas of citation – both of Euripides' prologues and of Aeschylus' repeated phrase – threaten the security and control of language's signifying practice, as they mime the gestures of authority, of appeal to authoritative language.

My second passage from this battleground of poetics is an example of Aeschylus' semantic hooliganism (1211–13):

Eur. 'Dionysus, who, equipped with thyrsus and skins
      Of fawns, leaps dancing down Parnassus,
      Amid the pines ...'
Aes.   Lost his little bottle.
Dio. Alas! We are struck again by that little bottle.

I have chosen this example partly because of Dionysus' reaction. Euripides starts a prologue – this time, with a touch of special pleading, about his judge, Dionysus – and, as Aeschylus once more slips in the bottle, Dionysus reacts 'Alas! We are struck again by that little bottle'. As all readers of T.S. Eliot will have immediately realised, that line parodies the off-stage cry of Agamemnon as he is murdered in Aeschylus' Oresteia.[19] Dionysus' tragic reaction to Aeschylus' attack on Euripides' prologue (on the subject of Dionysus) parodies the most famous reaction to attack in Aeschylean theatre. The tragic poet's voice is disseminated throughout the parodic contest: there are inverted commas throughout.

It is not hard to see the conflict of discourses that mark the fifth-century democratic *polis* in action as the comic playwright in the public theatre parades parodied tragedians arguing about claims of *sophia*. But the comic inversions depend on the purloining of the tragic poet's voice – on, that is, the inverted commas of parodic citation. The inverted commas of comedy are *both* an act of appropriation, a concession of authority, *and* the mark of the ever-present potential for reading otherwise — comic inversion. The comic poet speaking out to the people can never escape the condition of this double-speak. The appropriating act of citation is always both a gesture towards authority and the demonstration of reading otherwise. The wild proliferation and dissemination of voices in comic theatre displays citation as a deeply ambivalent constituent of authoritative language.

My third and final example is taken from the wonderful Hellenistic epic, the *Argonautica*, written by Apollonius of Rhodes. A little-read text these days, regrettably, but one of immense influence not least in that Virgil drew extensively on it particularly for his representation of Dido and Aeneas in the *Aeneid*. It's a remarkable work, the closest modern equivalent to which might be said — provocatively — to be Thomas Pynchon, in that the *Argonautica* is an epic narrative obsessed with interconnection and discontinuity, scientific explanation and magic realism, obscure scholarly information and the grand scheme of things. Above all, it is a text that is replete with the inverted commas of irony, quotation, pastiche: the archetypal epigonal text.

It is Homer and in particular the *Odyssey* that provides *the* classic text against which Apollonius expresses his belatedness, and a fine example of this process can be seen in the Argonauts' encounter with the Sirens. It begins as follows, again in my overly literal English version (4. 891–903):

> Immediately they saw
> A fine island, Anthemoessa, where the shrill
> Sirens, daughters of Achelous, were wont to destroy
> Whoever anchored there, by the beguilement of sweet song.
> Lovely Terpsichore, one of the Muses, bore them, when she
> Slept with Achelous. Once they tended Demeter's noble,
> Virgin daughter, and sung her choruses. At that time,
> They were partly bird, partly maiden to look at.
> They always watched out from their fine-harboured prospect,
> And often and from many had they taken away sweet homecoming,
> Consuming their victims with wasting disease. Suddenly, against the men
> They sent forth from their mouths a lily-like voice ...

Some of the differences between Homer and Apollonius have been dutifully collected by the commentators.[20] Apollonius offers a genealogy for the Sirens – one of several attested in ancient authors. The island they inhabit has a name here – there's none in Homer – a name culled from Hesiod. Apollonius links the Sirens with Persephone, Demeter's daughter (as Euripides had done). In Homer, their isolation is complete. In contrast to Homer's version, in Apollonius there is a physical description of the Sirens as half woman, half bird. Where the Sirens' victims in Homer, according to Circe, have become a pile of 'rotting bones and shrivelled flesh' (*Od.* 12. 45–6), in Apollonius the Sirens wear them down with a wasting desease, a medical condition. Apollonius has, then, first fleshed out the Sirens with an Alexandrian intellectual apparatus of genealogy, history, mythological frame, physical description – culled from the archive of past texts.

It is the encounter itself, however, that shows the point of these variations, as well as some of what makes Apollonius' writing such a complex pleasure (4.901–11):

> The Argonauts were ready to cast
> Their hawsers from the ship onto the shore –
> Had not Thracian Orpheus, son of Oeagrus,
> Strung his Bistonian lyre in his hand
> And let the forceful melody of a quick moving song ring out
> So that all at once their hearing might roar with the beat
> As he spread confusion. The lyre defeated the virgins' voice.
> The west-wind and echoing wave, rushing from the prow,
> Carried the ship on. They sang on, indistinctly.

Rather than listening to the Sirens' voices and thus being able, like Odysseus, to repeat the ineluctable seduction of their song, and rather than having their ears blocked, like Odysseus' crew, the Argonauts are saved by Orpheus' overlaying of sound. Orpheus, the ideal poet and descendent of the Muses, plays over the voices of those earlier figures of knowledge and song, who are also descendents of the Muses, specifically, Terpsichore. So that the reader too cannot hear what the Sirens sang. The verb 'ring out', *kanakhêsen*, is very rare indeed, however. It is used only once, by Homer, in the *Odyssey* (*Od.* 19.469). As the contest of voices is represented it is expressed through a unique and markedly Homeric team – a philologist's revival. It is not only Homer's voice that is sounded out, however. The description of the sailors' hearing roaring,

epibromeôntai akouai, closely echoes the most famous description
of the effects of desire in Sappho: *epirrombeisi d'akouai*, 'my hearing
whirs'. Again, it uses a term, *akouai*, in a phrasing that occurs
only in this passage in Sappho – another philologist's revival.
As the lyre defeats the maidens' voice, the confusion echoes with
the most famous female lyric poet's voice. Echoes and distorts, in
a marvellous word play. *Epibromeô*, Apollonius' verb, 'roar', just
slightly metamorphoses Sappho's verb *epirombeô*, 'whir', so that
between 'roaring' and 'whirring' the confused overlaying of sound
is performed as it is described.

The rewriting of the Siren scene, then, is replete with images
of drowned out sound and echoes of past voices. The waves, too,
'echo', and Apollonius, typically, follows this game of confused
soundings with a pointed pun (911): the voice that the Sirens send
forth is *akriton*. This adjective has two senses. On the one hand,
'unceasing', hence 'sang *on*'. But it also means 'indistinct'; hence
'sang on, *indistinctly*'. At the end of a passage where both the sense
of literary tradition and the images of confused sound are marked,
the pun's mixing of meanings 'unceasing' and 'indistinct' is acutely
self-conscious – and a neat joke.

With Apollonius' Sirens, then, we can see how the past is in all
senses *written through*. How even in the act of erasure, even in
the act of trying to drown out the authoritative poetry of tradition,
it is the past that enables, the language of the past that is (to be)
appropriated, the inevitable quotation of the past that constitutes
the relation of rupture and revival which informs poetic writing.
Writing from within history. The Sirens' enchantment can be
passed by, but not, finally, left behind. You can represent your
poet sounding out the figures of the past, but the voice of the past
still sounds out from within. Apollonius represents the bard within
the poem playing so that the voices cannot be heard, cannot be
re-cited by his travellers, but Homer and Sappho still ring out, still
roar. This is a passage which seems to put inverted commas –
marks of irony and reading otherwise – around the very process
of citation itself.

From these three authors' texts I want to draw three conclusions.
The first is just to point towards an irony in our Western tradition;
to glance forward from these epigonal texts. Despite the complexity

and self-reflexive playfulness of these ancient texts' treatments of citation and authority, particularly the authority of the past, the classics enter later culture all too often as a series of authoritative and authorising quotations: the tag, the motto. Which, I suppose, shows in germ the problem of the way (literary) tradition and authority function.

The second is a specific point about the sociology of authorship that I began this chapter by outlining. It is, I think, precisely the irony and self-reflexive twisting and turning of the poet's voice that the sociology of authorship finds hard to incorporate, to make sense of. Or: sociology can never replace textuality. It is not merely the gaps in the archive of ancient literary production that give rise to the tension between the sociological mapping of authorship and the reading of texts. As language leaks, so texts go beyond the lines of the map.

The third conclusion is the most general strain of argument. What I hope to have traced here is a way in which authorship relies on an authorising of a voice; speaking (is) from a position of authority, from a position of some authority. But the instauration of that position of authority, the establishing of voice, is never a simple process. In particular, citation, quotation and even the self-reflexive awareness of the texts of the past, become an especially problematic site for the authorised voice: inverted commas open the possibility of comic inversion, or ironic interplay between authorities, or to a display of the contests of voices in and against which an authoritative position is formulated. There is an inevitable gap between the author's voice and the voice of authority. This gap opens a space – *un écart* – in which writing as an author takes place. Or: every author has to enact the self-authorisation of a voice, in the attempt to escape the condition of its own citationality, its own always already appropriated words. Living not so much on the margins, as between quotation marks. The marks of parody, of hiding behind, of instability, as well as appropriation and authority. Finding one's voice is also finding one's quotation marks. I'll repeat that: 'Finding one's voice is finding one's quotation marks'. I'll repeat that ... "

That's the conclusion. But it is not the end. I want to finish by asking the question I would be posing if I were (only) reading this.

Something like: 'Your first conclusion about the irony of how Renaissance readers choose deeply sophisticated poetry to find rather direct mottos, makes me acutely aware of a certain paradox in what you're doing. Because, aren't you – in your classics for non-classicists mode, in your chopped up bits of texts, in your prosaic translations – just enacting, just reproducing the appropriating gestures and claims of authority you claim to find problematic and problematised.' I'd have to say 'Fair point, but the positive way to make it is to say that to pose the question "What is an Author?" cannot hope to avoid the question "What is reading?", and if you think you can show me a reading which doesn't appropriate, that doesn't, precisely, authorise, I'd be surprised.' Which is to say that there is no eluding one's implication in authority, its strategies, ruses and institutions. Least of all when discussing 'What is an author?'. All of which probably means that the final line should be something like 'What Plato shows from the first is that dialogue, a multiplicity of different and dissenting voices, is a condition we cannot hope to escape, but that does not stop an author's inevitable implication in the structures of authority: it is a tension in authorship that Plato repeatedly holds up to our gaze by inviting us to read didactic dialogues.'

Notes

This paper was delivered in Cambridge to the 'What is an author?' seminar: thanks to Maurice Biriotti and Nicola Miller for the invitation.

1 The *Phaedrus* in particular has prompted discussion of this self-reflexiveness. Apart from Derrida's famous study, 'Plato's pharmacy', in *La dissémination* (Paris: Editions du Seuil, 1972) (translated by B. Johnson as *Dissemination* (Chicago: Chicago University Press, 1981), see the fine work of G. Ferrari, *Listening to the cicadas* (Cambridge: Cambridge University Press, 1988) and *Platonic writings, Platonic readings*, ed. C. L. Griswold (New York and London: Routledge, 1988).

2 M. Poster, 'Foucault and the tyranny of Greece', in *Foucault: a critical reader*, ed. D. C. Hoy (Oxford: Blackwell, 1986). The phrase 'tyranny of Greece' was, of course, coined to describe the all-pervasive influence of Hellenism in German culture from the eighteenth century onwards by E. M. Butler, *The tyranny of Greece over Germany* (Cambridge: Cambridge University Press, 1935). For a convenient, detailed account of at least one relevant author's encounter with the ancient world, see M. Silk and J. Stern, *Nietzsche and tragedy* (Cambridge: Cambridge University Press, 1981).

3 Plato, *Apology* 20d6ff. The recession of voices in this self-defence by Socrates is less often noted than its conclusion.

4 For a more detailed discussion with bibliography of this central term see S. Goldhill, *Reading Greek tragedy* (Cambridge: Cambridge University Press, 1986), 222–43.

5 Plato's most influential attack on poetry is in *Republic* 10, but see also the *Ion*. For a good general introduction to this area, see G. Ferrari in *The Cambridge history of literary criticism*, vol. 1, ed. G. Kennedy (Cambridge: Cambridge University Press, 1989).

6 See in particular M. Detienne, *Les maîtres de vérité dans la Grèce archaique* (Paris: Librairie François Maspero, 1967); J. Svenbro, *La parole et la marbre* (Lund: Studentliteratur, 1976); C. Calame, *Les choeurs de jeunes filles en Grèce archaique*, 2 vols (Rome: Edizione del'Ateneo, 1977); G. Nagy, *Pindar's Homer* (Baltimore: Johns Hopkins University Press, 1990).

7 *Laws* 654a. See H. Marrou, *A history of Greek education*, trans. G. Lamb (New York: Sheed and Ward, 1956).

8 For a detailed exploration of these ideas and a bibliography see S. Goldhill, *The poet's voice* (Cambridge: Cambridge University Press, 1990), 1–166.

9 For introductory discussion and bibliography, see Goldhill, *Poet's voice*, 167–76.

10 For testimonia and discussion, see A. Riginos, *Platonica* (Leiden: Brill, 1976), and, with regard to Plato's writing, D. Tarrant, 'Plato as dramatist', *Journal of Hellenic Studies*, 75 (1955), 81–9.

11 S. Greenblatt, *Sir Walter Ralegh: the Renaissance man and his roles* (New Haven and London: Yale University Press, 1975); *Renaissance self-fashioning* (Chicago: Chicago University Press, 1980); S. Orgel, *The illusion of power* (Berkeley: University of California Press, 1975); L. Tennenhouse, *Power on display* (New York and London: Methuen, 1986); P. Berry, *Of chastity and power* (London: Routledge, 1989).

12 For this extensive bibliography, see Goldhill, *Poet's voice*, 57, n. 98.

13 On Achilles in the underworld, see in particular A. Edwards, *Achilles in the Odyssey* (Königsten: Anton Hain, 1985).

14 19.203. This nexus of ideas is discussed in detail in my *The Poet's voice*, 1–68.

15 P. Pucci, 'The Song of the Sirens', *Arethusa*, 12 (1979), 121–32 – a detailed demonstration that I here follow.

16 *Iliad* 2. 485–6, discussed in particular by P. Pucci, 'The language of the Muses', in W. Aycock and T. Klein, eds, *Classical mythology in twentieth-century thought and literture* (Lubbock, Texas: Texas Tech Press, 1980); C. Segal, '*Kleos* and its ironies in the *Odyssey*', *Antiquité Classique*, 52 (1983), 22–47; G. Nagy, *The best of the Achaeans* (Baltimore: Johns Hopkins University Press, 1979), 16–18.

17 L. Hutcheon, *A theory of parody* (New York and London: Methuen, 1985), 32.

18 C. Whitman, 'ΛΗΚΥΘΙΟΝ ΑΠΩΛΕΣΕΝ', *Harvard Studies in Classical Philology*, 73 (1969), 109–12; J. Griffith, 'ΛΗΚΥΘΙΟΝ ΑΠΩΛΕΣΕΝ: a postscript', *Harvard Studies in Classical Philology*, 74 (1970), 43–4; J. Hooker, 'Lekythion', *Rheinische Museum*, 113 (1970), 162–4; J. Henderson, 'The Lekythos and the *Frogs* 1200–48', *Harvard Studies in Classical Philology*, 76 (1972), 133–43; R. Penella, 'κωδάριον in Aristophanes' *Frogs*', *Mnemosyne*, 26 (1973), 337–41; J. Henderson, 'ΚΩΔΑΡΙΟΝ: a reply', *Mnemosyne*, 27 (1974), 293–5; R. Penella, 'κωδάριον: a comment', *Mnemosyne*, 27 (1974), 295–7; G. Anderson, 'ΛΗΚΥΘΙΟΝ and ΑΥΤΟΛΗΚΥΘΟΣ', *Journal of Hellenic Studies*, 101 (1981), 130–2.

19 Aristophanes: *oimoi peplêgmeth' authis hupo tês lêkuthou* ('Alas we are struck again by the little pot'); Aeschylus, *Agamemnon*, 1343 and 1345: *ômoi peplêgmai kairian plêgên esô/ômoi mal' authis deuteran peplêgmenos* ('Alas, I am struck a mortal blow within'/'Alas struck again, a second blow'). T.S. Eliot uses *Agamemnon*, 1343 as the epigraph to 'Sweeney amongst the nightingales'.

20 The following points are taken from E. Livrea, *Apollonio Rodio 4* (Florence: Edizione dell'Atenco, 1973), and F. Vian, *Apollonius de Rhodes: Argonautiques. Tome 3* (Paris: Société d'edition: Les Belles Lettres, 1981).

8

Authorship overshadowed: death, darkness and the feminisation of authority in late Renaissance writing

Philippa Berry

In recent years, a poststructuralist concern with notions of authorial 'death' has produced several brilliant expositions of the priority of voice and language in the literature of the late Renaissance. The themes of death and loss which are now seen to mark these texts' rejection of the fullness of an early Renaissance (humanist) subjectivity have been related to the increasingly complex awareness of language which characterises late sixteenth- and seventeenth-century writing, and this awareness has been described as taking priority over the more visual emphasis of an earlier, outmoded aesthetic. Thus when Jonathan Goldberg comments, in *Voice terminal echo: postmodernism and English Renaissance texts*,[1] that:

> Reinscribing loss, facing annihilation, texts lose their monumental status, and regain it − as memorial stones, implacable in their refusals as much as in their recording. (p. 7)

his opposition between 'monument' and 'memorial stone' implicitly associates a late Renaissance inscription of loss with the complete rejection of a visual aesthetic. Similarly, Joel Fineman has argued in *Shakespeare's perjured eye*[2] that:

> The sonnets show what happens to poetic subjectivity when a language of visionary presence is replaced and displaced by a language of verbal representation. As a subject of representation, as a character subjected to representation, the subject of a 'perjur'd eye' is cut off, because he speaks, from the fullness of subjective self-presence that is regularly held out as a realizable personal ideal by the tradition of the poetry of praise ... the poet in Shakespeare's sonnets is therefore puffed up with

the loss of himself to himself, a loss that is not only asserted by, but
is in fact occasioned by, the language that he speaks. (pp. 247–8)

This privileging of the *verbal*, linguistic dimension of a late
Renaissance crisis in identity can be traced back, through Derrida
and Lacan, not only to Freud, but also to the writings of Martin
Heidegger, whose use of the *echo* to figure a decentring of identity
experienced at the level of language is implicitly alluded to in
the title of Goldberg's book.[3] But in fact Heidegger's influential
account of *angst*, of a 'being-towards-death' discovered through a
traumatic encounter with a 'difference' that is primarily defined in
spatial terms, had a prominent visual as well as a verbal dimension.
He described it, for example as 'the clear night of the nothing of
anxiety', in which man suddenly becomes aware of 'his inability
to see himself'.[4] And the tomb-like space in which individual
being founders, termed by Heidegger the 'clearing' or *Lichtung*,
was further defined by him, not only as the locus of what he called
'the tolling of stillness', but also in relation to a paradoxical
experience of the 'concealment' and 'unconcealment' of light. He
asserted that this clearing 'is free for brightness and darkness' as
well as 'for resonance and echo, for sounding and diminishing of
sound'.[5]

It is of course understandable that it has been the verbal rather
than the visual character of the Renaissance crisis in subjectivity
which has preoccupied Renaissance literary critics influenced by
poststructuralism. None the less, it seems important to note that
the critique of earlier concepts of vision which characterises late
sixteenth- and early seventeenth-century English literature does not
necessarily mean that its themes of authorial death are never figured
in visual terms. Indeed, in several literary texts produced at this
time, we can identify a striking representational 'shadow', cast by
their critiques of an early Renaissance obsession with colour and
luminosity. In this essay, I shall explore some of the ways in which
this authorial crisis of the early modern era associates a crisis in the
writer's relationship to language with a new (because paradoxical,
or dark) vision, where motifs of substance as well as spirit are
improbably interwoven in the critique of authorial identity. At
the same time, I shall consider how a dark encounter with sexual

difference is integral to certain poetic reformulations of this relationship between visual and verbal loss.

But let me begin by considering a passage from a seventeenth-century text which is centrally concerned with the public performance of another text, and which, in its unique attention to that moment of reception, throws surprising light upon the importance of visual imagery to the authorial crisis of the late Renaissance. In Isaak Walton's *Life of Donne*, first published in 1640, there is a memorable description of the circumstances in which John Donne's last sermon, 'Death's duell', was delivered. Walton describes how the erstwhile poet turned preacher refused to abandon his normal practice of preaching on the first Friday of Lent, despite the entreaties of his friends, who warned him that such an effort would only cause his already serious illness to accelerate:

> And when (to the amazement of some beholders) he appeared in the Pulpit, many thought he presented himselfe, not to preach mortification by a living voice, but mortality by a decayed body, and dying face. And doubtlesse many did secretly ask that question in *Ezekiel, Doe these bones live!* Or can that soule organise that tongue to speak so long time as the sand in that glasse will move towards its center, and measure out an houre of this dying mans unspent life? Doubtlesse it cannot. Yet after some faint pauses in his zealous Prayer, his strong desires inabled his weak body to discharge his memory of his pre-conceived Meditations which were of dying; the Text being, *To God the Lord belongs the issues from death*. Many that saw his teares, and heard his hollow voice, professing they thought the Text Prophetically chosen, and that D. *Donne* had preacht his own Funerall Sermon.
>
> Being full of joy that God had inabled him to performe this desired duty, he hastned to his house, out of which he never moved, untill like S. *Stephen, He was carried by devout men to his grave.*[6]

In Walton's account, the advent of death coincidentally affirms the closest possible identity between the author and his text. Indeed, in its implicit interrelationship of pulpit and tomb, the passage accords a strange supernatural authority to Donne's last appearance as preacher. Ironically, it communicates this conviction through a striking reversal of that priority of word over image which is held to have been central to Protestant theology, for it stresses the extraordinary visual impact made by the dying man. It was this

ghostly demeanour of the preacher, apparently, which gave his last
sermon the authority of a revealed truth.

For while in this, his last sermon, Donne preached mortality 'by
a decayed body, and dying face', the paradox of his appearance also
presented his audience with a visual emblem of the Christian
doctrine of life-in-death. Donne entered the pulpit like a spectre –
'to the amazement of some beholders' – and the congregation
'heard his hollow voice'. His sermon, which anticipated Easter,
stressed the original association of death with God's creation of
man, arguing that creation alone was insufficient without the
promise of resurrection:

> Thy hands have made and fashioned me round about, saith Job, and, (as
> the originall word is) thou hast taken great paines about me, and yet,
> sayes he, thou doth destroy me.[7]

But Donne's text, which was taken from Psalm 68, asserted that
'unto God the Lord belong the issues from death'. His sermon
consequently used the figure of chiasmus to redefine the relations
between life and death, offering 'a consolation to the soule, against
the dying life, and living death of the body'. For Donne, death is
a recreation or birth (and as I shall discuss later in this essay, it
therefore has an implied maternal aspect). Later in the sermon, he
mentions the passage from Ezekiel which describes a miraculous
Old Testament prefiguration of the resurrection, where God sends
his spirit to animate 'dry bones' (37, vv. 1–14). As Walton points
out, his congregation associated Donne's own extraordinary performance with the same passage, asking: 'Doe these bones live?'
It seems clear that Donne's lively representation of death – which
also suggested the possibility of resurrection, albeit a resurrection
before death – was interpreted as a sign of the motions of the
Spirit; in other words, it convinced the beholders that the text was
'prophetically' chosen. John Calvin had asserted that:

> The testimony of the Spirit is more excellent than all reason. For as
> God alone is a fit witness of himself in his Word, so also the Word will
> not find acceptance in men's hearts before it is sealed by the inward
> testimony of the Spirit.[8]

Hence, paradoxically, his performance authorised Donne's words
by displacing him as author. As an almost ghostly preacher, he

appeared to his congregation to acquire the 'ghostly' religious authority of one vivified and inspired by the Spirit or Holy Ghost.[9]

The fact that it was the sight of Donne, not his words themselves, which accorded this exceptional authority to his last sermon raises an interesting question as to the relative importance of words and images at this mysterious moment. In an earlier sermon, Donne himself had hinted at an ambiguity in the theological conception of the 'language' attributed to the Holy Ghost:

> When the holy Ghost fell upon the waters, in the Creation, God spoke so, in his language of *Workes*, as that all men may understand them. For, in this language, the language of *workes*, the *Eye* is the *eare*, *seeing* is *hearing*. How often does the holy Ghost call upon us, in the Scriptures, *Ecce, quia os Dominum locutum, Behold, the mouth of God hath spoken it!* he calls us to *behold*, (which is the office of the *eye*) and that that we are to behold, is the *voice* of God, belonging to the *eare*; seeing is hearing, in Gods first language, the language of *works*.[10]

But what is the significance of this equation of 'seeing' with 'hearing' in that 'language of Workes' derived from the Holy Ghost? Donne points out that in biblical texts (held by Christian commentators to be inspired by the Holy Ghost) we are frequently asked to 'behold' the 'voice' or 'mouth of God'. This sacred text of especial authority consequently requires a visual as well as a verbal attention; yet strangely, it directs the reader's gaze to an authorial source – the mouth of God – which is by implication hidden.[11] The accidental circumstances of Donne's last sermon as described by Walton similarly equated a supernatural mode of 'seeing' with spiritual 'hearing', for his congregation 'saw' the spiritual meaning of his text in the decaying but living body of its author, who addressed them literally in the shadow of death, yet also as one whose individual authority was eclipsed and 'overshadowed' by the Holy Ghost.

When read alongside Donne's own words about God's 'language of workes', Walton's account of the delivery of 'Death's duell' suggests that the relationship between the visual and the verbal in late Renaissance English culture was rather more complicated than is often assumed. While critics such as Goldberg and Fineman have rightly stressed the late Renaissance rejection of any simple relationship between literary mimesis and a Platonic 'visionary presence', what they omit to emphasise is that this move actually occurs at a time when several different intellectual traditions were preoccupied by a rather different mode of vision – one which was dark or shadowy rather than bright and colourful. Renaissance neo-Platonism itself, while frequently obsessed by light, had an equal fascination with darkness. This shadow side is often over-looked, because of the element of inconsistency which it introduces into an intellectual scheme usually thought to be unambiguously dualistic. But the inspired Saturnian melancholy which fascinated Florentine neo-Platonist Marsilio Ficino was intimately associated with blackness.[12] Another neo-Platonist, Pico della Mirandola, stressed the darkness of the first principle of Jewish Cabbala, the En-Soph, by comparing it to the originary abyss of the Greek Orphics, Night or Nox.[13] And in the late sixteenth century, the neo-Platonist Giordano Bruno was likewise much preoccupied by shadows; he called his first book, published in Paris in 1582, *De umbris idearum* (Concerning the shadows of ideas). In *De gli eroici furori* (Of the heroic frenzies), published in England in 1585 and dedicated to Sir Philip Sidney, Bruno described the shadow as the sole object of philosophical speculation, for:

> ... it is impossible for anyone to see the sun, the universal Apollo and absolute light as the supreme and most excellent species; but very possible to see its shadow, its Diana, the world, the universe, the nature which is in things, the light shining through the obscurity of matter, and so resplendent in the darkness.[14]

Here, while Bruno invokes a Platonic transcendent realm – that of Apollo – he acknowledges that this luminous sphere of presence is only knowable through its apparent lack or negation: that is, in the night-time world of shadows associated with the moon goddess Diana, who was Apollo's sister in Roman mythology.

Of course, the flood of alchemical treatises published in the late sixteenth and early seventeenth centuries also stressed the creative role of darkness, in their accounts of the *nigredo*, or blackening, which figured the alchemical death which preceded the first stage of the 'Great Work'.[15] But there were other, quite orthodox religious influences which also contributed to a contemporary interest in darkness. Following Martin Luther, Protestantism stressed the necessary hiddenness of God. Luther described the soul which has been 'snatched' by the word of God as undergoing a metaphorical death which is also an entry into darkness:

> But this leading, this snatching, this cleansing torments it [the soul] wretchedly. For the way is hard and narrow, to forsake all visible things, to be stripped of all senses, to be led out of all accustomed things, indeed, this is what it means to die and descend into hell. It seems to it as if it were being destroyed down to the ground, where it is deprived of everything on which it relied, with which it had to do, to which it clung; it touches neither earth, not heaven ... Having entered into darkness and blackness I see nothing; I live by faith, hope and love alone and I am weak that is, I suffer, for when I am weak, then I am strong.[16]

In this emphasis on darkness, Luther may well have been influenced by that idea of an inspired or 'dazzling' darkness, derived from pseudo-Dionysius the Areopagite, which had figured prominently in the *via negativa* of late medieval mystics such as Meister Eckhart and Nicholas of Cusa. By the late sixteenth century, similar themes were appearing in the writings of the Counter-Reformation mystics John of the Cross and Teresa of Avila. And in the Geneva as well as the King James translation of the bible into the English, the creative associations of 'shadow' and 'shadowing' are given as much emphasis as its negative, deadly, associations of darkness. The several references to the 'shadow' of God's wings in the Psalms seem to associate this protective divine darkness specifically with the winged Spirit or Holy Ghost, which 'overshadows' Mary in the Gospel of Luke. Donne himself notes in *Devotions upon emergent occasions*:

> Even the visitation of the most blessed *Spirit*, upon the blessed *Virgin*, is called an *overshadowing*. There was the presence of the *Holy Ghost*, the fountaine of all *light*, and yet an *overshadowing*.[17]

As Nigel Smith has noted, English radical sectarians were soon to give especial emphasis to this dark and hidden aspect of God.[18]

One result of this contemporary interest in a creative darkness was a new awareness of the ironies inherent in literary representation as 'shadowing'. Anthony Gash has recently pointed out that the original Platonic associations of shadow, as an inferior copy or counterfeit, are much punned on in this literature.[19] But Gash does not notice that certain late Renaissance texts also associate a crisis in authorial identity with a more positive conception of shadowing, pointing to creativity's dependence on the apparent nothingness of darkness. In *The arte of Englishe poesie*, published in 1589, George Puttenham compared the poet to God, 'who, without any travell to his divine imagination, made all the world of nought'. None the less, poetic emphasis upon a 'dark' authorial vision seems often to involve an elision of the poet's relationship to the darkness of loss and death (as a ghostly or shadowy figure) with the shadowiness and insubstantiality of representation, as differences between textual subject and object are temporarily dissolved. And as the 'overshadowed' poet cedes his authority to the figurative shadows with which he works, these sometimes acquire feminine substance. Perhaps this is not so very surprising, when we consider that the darkness which intrigued Renaissance neo-Platonists – Ficino's Melancholy, Pico's Nox, Bruno's shadowy Diana – was gendered feminine. In the language of alchemy, too, the chemical process of putrefaction which was termed the *nigredo* was associated with a dominance of a 'female' influence.[20] It is to just such a feminine darkness that Donne's metaphorically annihilated poetic persona cedes his authority in 'A nocturnal upon S. Lucies day'. Even in 'Death's duell', Donne relates his theme of the 'issues from death' to man's lifelong connection with an originary (and implicitly dark) maternal space. Thereby he associates a female creative act not only with the presence of death in life, but also with a second birth which coincides with death:

> Our very *birth* and entrance unto this life, is *exitus à morte*, an *issue from death*, for in our mothers *wombe* wee are *dead* ... We have a winding sheete in our Mothers wombe, which growes with us from our conception, and wee come into the world, wound up in that *winding sheet*, for we come to *seeke a grave* ... We celebrate our owne funeralls with cryes, even at our birth; as though our *three-score and ten years of life* were spent in our mothers labour, and our circle made up in the first point thereof. (pp. 232–3)

It is in poems by Shakespeare and Marvell, however, that the implications of this theme for ideas of authorship in the late

Renaissance are explored most suggestively. In Shakespeare's *Sonnets* and in Marvell's 'Upon Appleton House,' a feminine creativity which is dark or obscure is explicitly associated with the figurative death and effective displacement of a masculine poetic authority.[21] The philosophical obscurity of this feminine darkness is clear from the different emphases of the two works. While Shakespeare stresses the materiality (and sexuality) of an authorial 'overshadowing', Marvell locates it within the spiritual context of Christian eschatology; but in each case, the significance of this association of woman and shade seems to extend well beyond the framework within which the poet attempts to define it.

As I mentioned earlier, Joel Fineman has argued that the 'poetics of praise' which is elaborated in Shakespeare's *Sonnets* privileges language over sight. I would rather contend that it sets a visionary poetics of light which is opposed to death (and which reaches its apotheosis in the sonnets to the youth) against a poetics of darkness in which poetry as 'shadowing' is closely related to 'Death's shade'. The poet of the *Sonnets* presents himself fairly early in the sequence as subjected to a process of darkening which he associates with time: he is 'beaten and chopped with tanned antiquity' (62, l. 10), and compares himself to a fading light soon to be effaced by darkness:

> In me thou seest the twilight of such day,
> As after sunset fadeth in the west,
> Which by and by black night doth take away,
> Death's second self, that seals up all in rest. (73, ll. 5–8)

As in Walton's account of Donne's last sermon, the author is here a spectacle of nothing, an image soon to be concealed in the darkness of the tomb.

But at the same time, the poet's personal attributes of age and darkness apparently enable him to produce a 'dark' art – sonnets which, in a poetic equivalent to Paracelsan homeopathy, can act as a remedy against 'age's steepy night'. When he asserts 'That in black ink my love may still shine bright.' (65, l. 14), the phrase suggests that, like that of the mystics, this poetic darkness 'dazzles', creating colour and light *ex nihilo* in a repetition of the divine creative act. In sonnet 63, the lines in the poet's face are metamorphosed into the lines of his verse, as the encroaching blackness of age becomes the very stuff of creativity:

> Against my love shall be as I am now,
> With time's injurious hand crushed and o'erworn,
> When hours have drained his blood and filled his brow
> With lines and wrinkles, when his youthful morn
> Hath traveled on to age's steepy night,
> And all those beauties whereof now he's king
> Are vanishing, or vanished out of sight,
> Stealing away the treasure of his spring –
> For such a time do now I fortify
> Against confounding age's cruel knife,
> That he shall never cut from memory
> My sweet love's beauty, though my lover's life.
> His beauty shall in these black lines be seen,
> And they shall live, and he in them be green.

Alongside this play on facial and literary lines, the sonnet alludes to the substitution of poetic lineation for that lineal succession which earlier sonnets had reproached the youth for failing to secure. The importance of darkness and shadows in this alternative inheritance (stressed in sonnets such as 53 and 61) may be associated with the homosexual subtext of the sonnets to the young man: Frankie Rubinstein has recently argued that 'shadow' was a slang term for a homosexual in the English Renaissance.[22] In his poetic (and sexual) revision of inheritance, the aged poet is rejuvenated through the poetic apotheosis of the young man as his heir. But ironically, this shadowy process of poetic inheritance is subverted by another kind of blackness: that of a female body. When, in the 'dark lady' sonnets, the 'black lines' and subtle 'shadowings' of earlier sonnets are finally embodied by a woman, the *Sonnets'* initial reformulation of inheritance in androcentric terms is abruptly challenged. The enigma of the 'dark lady's' blackness disproves the poet's claim earlier in the sequence that his 'black' writing can master loss. She it is who inherits the legacy of masculine beauty (the 'will') which earlier sonnets had aimed to preserve for a poetic posterity:

> ... now is black beauty's successive heir,
> And beauty slandered with a bastard shame. (127, ll. 3–4)

> So now I have confessed that he is thine,
> And I myself am mortgaged to thy will ... (134, ll. 1–2)

The multiple puns on 'will' in sonnets 134–6 combine themes of authorial death (since a will is read only when its author is dead) with motifs of another sexual death and resurrection in which a new, anti-Platonic vision is privileged, as the dark female body completes that 'overshadowing' or eclipse of authorial identity which had been anticipated earlier in the sequence. Through a series of sexual puns, the poet suggests that his 'black' mistress is love's other or inverted 'eye': 'Love's eye is not so true as all men's: no' (148, l. 8).[23] But whereas the dark vision alluded to in Sonnet 73 had maintained a subject–object dichotomy between the soon-to-be eclipsed author and the lover/reader who is invited to observe this phenomenon (and hence had effectively conformed to notions of the fixity and stability of identity), the bodily nature of the dark eye mentioned in the dark lady sonnets undoes the former polarity between the subject and object of a shadowy vision, for it seems that now both lover and mistress see one another in this dark fashion. If his mistress's 'eye' is untrue, so is the poet's: 'O me! what eyes hath love put in my head, / Which have no correspondence with true sight!' (148, ll. 1–2).

Hence this more bodily vision of darkness completely undermines the paradoxical authority which the poet had formerly forged from his relationship to shadows and blackness. As the hidden, genital 'eye' in which the poet recognises his own lack of any distinct identity, the dark lady actually contains and conceals everything, including the poet's assumed identities as both author and lover, that is, as her 'will':

> Wilt thou, whose will is large and spacious,
> Not once vouchsafe to hide my will in thine? ...
> The sea, all water, yet receives rain still,
> And in abundance addeth to his store;
> So thou being rich in will add to thy will
> One will of mine, to make thy large will more. (135, ll. 5–12)

The sexual 'death' which the poet undergoes here is consequently one in which his 'will' is assimilated into an originary abyss comparable to the *nihil* from which he had formerly created his 'black lines'. His wilful drive towards the establishment of a poetic inheritance ('in eternal lines to time') founders in the dark face of this capacious feminine negativity, for as his paradoxical art of blackness or 'shadowing' finally eludes its maker's control his assumed ability to master time through this black writing is also defeated. The dark lady's power over his 'will' undoes the charting of time in terms of legacies of wealth or art passed from man to man, and confronts the poet with another, bodily time, in whose shadows masculine identity is dissolved rather than confirmed. It seems that this is the 'audit' of Nature alluded to in the poem (a sonnet that is significantly incomplete) which directly precedes the first of the 'dark lady' sonnets: 'Her audit, though delayed, answered must be, / And her quietus is to answer thee' (126, ll. 11–12).

In Andrew Marvell's 'Upon Appleton House', the refiguration of poetic authorship in relation to images of death and darkness is also interwoven with questions of inheritance. And here too, a concealed female figure associated with darkness ultimately figures a break in familial as well as poetic continuity, as the vehicle of another version of time – one which is beyond the poet's control. In this Marvellian exploration of darkness, the relations between sexual and poetic authorship are figured rather differently from those in Shakespeare's *Sonnets*. Yet once again, the demands of family lineage are effectively displaced by a refiguration of poetic authority in terms of shadows. In one sense, the 'shade' towards which the poem moves is the *umbra* of classical poetic retirement – a shade which also symbolises the withdrawal of Fairfax from political affairs. But in the context of Christian eschatology, it has more mysterious and dynamic connotations, in which the contemplative arts of both poet and patron are ultimately superseded. The poem begins with a criticism of the ambitious and aristocratic arts of building which the family of Marvell's employer, the Lord General Fairfax, has apparently rejected in the 'sober frame' and 'lowness' of Appleton House. But when Marvell tells us that:

> Humility alone designs
> These short but admirable lines,
> By which, ungirt and unconstrained,
> Things greater are in less contained. (6, ll. 41–4)

His suggestion that a modest art requires a 'short' line also has veiled implications for the themes of familial descent which the poem is to treat. At the same time, of course, we inevitably associate the modest art of Fairfax with that of his poet-protégé. The recent history of Fairfax's family has, it seems, been closely associated with the Protestant search for a non-idolatrous art. Thus the poem begins by celebrating the events which made both the 'humble' construction of Appleton House and the Fairfax line possible – the dissolution of the nunnery at Nunappleton, and the abduction of the heiress Isabel Thwaites from the nunnery by William Fairfax, the Lord General's ancestor. In the course of the poem, another, courtly, art is dissolved into the many-faceted nature of Appleton House, in whose grounds Marvell reads signs of the recent Civil War interwoven with portents of the last days.

Given its initial assertion of the importance of lineage, it is no surprise that the poem reaches a climax in a wood. The apocalyptic ending of time which has been shadowed or prefigured in the meadow beyond the house prompts the poet's withdrawal to a dark regenerative space whose comparison to the biblical ark stresses the significance of the repose which it affords. This poetic shade or *umbra* is a place in which the darkness or recreated chaos discerned in the landscape of history can be made sense of. Here the poet ponders questions of familial as well as poetic continuity. The closeness of the trees in the wood suggests to him the two pedigrees of Fairfax and his wife:

> The double wood of ancient stocks,
> Linked in so thick, an union locks,
> It like two pedigrees appears,
> On th'one hand Fairfax, th'other Vere's: (62, ll. 489–92)

But immediately after, he reminds us that the wood is also a place which deceives the eye:

> When first the eye this forest sees
> It seems indeed as wood not trees:
> As if their neighbourhood so old
> To one great trunk them all did mould. (63, ll. 497–500)

And while: 'Dark all without it knits; within / It opens passable and thin.' Thus while the metaphor associates the Fairfax lineage with the creation of this dark space (affording the opportunity for contemplation which is made possible in retirement), the poet suggests that the inner meaning of this shade is much more than familial. Thus while the Fairfax line is seemingly represented by the outside of the wood, inside its darkness, the poet sees differently, as he is touched by a 'light mosaic' – a pattern of shade and light created by the sunlight falling through the leaves of the wood. This lit darkness links his poetic vocation to priestly roles which partake of the darkness of origins in that they are pre-Christian–Judaic and Druidic. The 'light mosaic' evokes a prophetic, 'Mosaic' calling, while the grove itself inspires memories of a Druidic natural religion, metamorphosing the poet into 'some great prelate of the grove'.[24] These ancient and shadowy associations enable him to trace another, non-familial process of generation and inheritance in the boughs and leaves – a more universal history.

But in this inspiring shade Marvell stresses the pleasures of masculine solitude, as he has done in several other of his pastoral poems:

> How safe, methinks, and strong, behind
> These trees have I encampled my mind:
> Where beauty, aiming at the heart,
> Bends in some tree its useless dart. (76, ll. 601–4)

Perhaps his exclusion of any principle of sexual difference from this solipsistic version of shade explains why, in a manner like and yet different from that traced in the *Sonnets*, this poet too is ultimately displaced by the dark creative process which he has described, and Moses-like, is denied participation in the paradise towards which he has pointed in his shady retreat. As in the *Sonnets*, the shadowy 'natural' art which he has discovered proves to be intimately associated with sacrifice:

> Do you, O brambles, chain me too,
> And courteous briars, nail me through.

> Here in the morning tie my chain,
> Where the two woods have made a lane
> While, like a guard on either side,
> The trees before their Lord divide.
> This, like a long and equal thread,

> Betwixt two labyrinths does lead.
> But where the floods did lately drown,
> There at the evening stake me down. (vv. 77–8, ll. 615–24)

and his progress out of the wood resembles that of a Christ-like sacrificial victim.

The scene into which the poet emerges is marked by another mingling of light and darkness. This evening landscape seemingly portends the approaching end of history, for nature has now been mysteriously renewed by the destruction of the flood. The poet tells us that 'at my lines the fishes twang'. If this is a new style of poetry to which he refers, the theme of fishing points to a possible priestly role for the poet. Yet the leisurely nature of this activity reminds us that such a definition of poetic art, while possibly appropriate to the long expanse of time between the first and second comings, is not suited to the impending advent of apocalypse. And almost immediately, the reborn poet has rejected his redefined vocation: 'But now away my hooks, my quills, / And angles – idle utensils' (82, ll. 649–50). It seems the new art appropriate to this shady apocalyptic prospect is represented not by him, but by Maria Fairfax, his charge. While the poet is Christ-like in his role of nature's victim, it is Maria who foreshadows Christ's transformation of nature at the *eschaton* or second coming. As Margarita Stocker has pointed out, it is she who walks 'to night', *into* as well as *in* the darkness, thereby ushering in the *eschaton*, which was expected to be attended with clouds.[25] Maria is both subject and object in this dark scene. Thus not only is she constructed as its privileged observer, as nature shades itself in modesty before her 'judicious eyes':

> The sun himself, of her aware,
> Seems to descend with greater care;
> And lest she see him go to bed,
> In blushing clouds conseals his head ...
> Maria such, and so doth hush
> The world ... (83–6, ll. 661–81

But she herself also embodies the new, shady aesthetic which the male poet has imperfectly anticipated. 'Her beauties' are defined by concealment: 'For since she would not have them seen, / The wood about her draws a screen' (88, ll. 703–4). And Maria's speech is clearly inspired by the Spirit, for she has the gift of tongues: 'She counts her beauty to converse / In all the languages as hers'. Since it is her purified gaze and speech which are seen as imposing order on the landscape, Maria seems therefore to represent the perfected embodiment of the dark art explored by the poet. She now wields that 'line' which was formerly associated with the modest arts of both her father and tutor, for 'she supplies beyond her sex the line'. Yet this line redefines both poetry and family. For as a female heir, Maria represents the end of the Fairfax name. As 'a sprig of mistletoe / On the Fairfacian oak' she is the progeny of a different line, a fruit of the Spirit. This mistletoe image consequently relates Maria's associations with night and shade to an impending trans-lation of masculine history and art into an altogether different frame. The order which she obscurely foreshadows is thereby intimately connected with a future heroic encounter with darkness, for the mistletoe was identified with that golden bough which was the passport of Aeneas into the underworld. With his image of Maria as mistletoe, Marvell's poem ends by pointing beyond its 'modest' frame to another, as yet unaccomplished art of shadows, which will be epic rather than pastoral. Here it seems, a feminine figure will be instrumental rather than marginal, assisting in yet another contemplation of darkness which may finally inspire successful historical action, and might even signal history's end.

These motifs of a paradoxical, dark vision can consequently provide us with new insights into the themes of authorial death which figure so prominently in late Renaissance literature. In particular, by their interweaving of a visual with a verbal crisis, the poetic texts of Shakespeare and Marvell point to an as yet unrecognised philosophical significance underlying the frequent association of the authorial crisis with themes of sexual difference. For the feminine shadows which appear in these texts define authorial death in relation to a new experience of time, one which does not conform to the assumed linearity of history and which undermines an androcentric model of the textual transmission and inheritance of authority. As figures of the future, as well as of the past, both the dark lady and Maria reveal the limitations of that authorial identity which seeks a secure knowledge of and control over the flux of human experience. At the same time, they dimly foreshadow the possibility of another kind of authorship, able to relinquish its ties to historical forms of authority along with its desire to control those shadows which inform its work of representation.

Notes

1 J. Goldberg, *Voice terminal echo: postmodernism and English Renaissance texts* (London: Methuen, 1986), 7.

2 J. Fineman, *Shakespeare's perjured eye: the invention of poetic subjectivity in the sonnets* (Berkeley: University of California Press, 1986), 297–8.

3 The importance of the echo-motif in Heidegger's work has recently been re-assessed in J. Sallis, *Echoes: after Heidegger* (Bloomington: Indiana University Press, 1990).

4 See Heidegger, 'What is metaphysics?', in D. Krell, ed., *Heidegger: basic writings* (New York: Harper and Row, 1977) and *Early Greek thinking*, trans. D. Krell and F. Capuzzi (New York: Harper and Row, 1975), 26.

5 Heidegger, 'The end of philosophy and the task of thinking', in M. C. Taylor, ed., *Deconstruction in context* (Chicago: University of Chicago Press, 1986), 250.

6 I. Walton, 'The life and death of Dr *Donne*, late Deane of St Pauls London' (1640), rpt. in H. W. Garrod, ed., *John Donne: poetry and prose* (Oxford: Oxford University Press, 1946), xl–xli.

7 J. Donne, 'Death's duell' (1631), in E. M. Simpson and G. R. Potter, eds, *Donne: Sermons*, 10 vols (Berkeley: University of California Press, 1962), vol. X, 232.

8 J. Calvin, *Institutes of the Christian religion: 1536 edition*, trans. F. L. Battles (Grand Rapids: Eerdmans, 1986), 1.7.4.

9 Walton's interpretation of this event seems consequently to be marked by the contemporary emphasis of radical Protestant sects upon the inspiration of the Holy Spirit in the interpretation of Scripture. The sects were profoundly influenced by Paul's words in I Corinthians 2:4, that the godly should speak: 'not with enticing words of man's wisdom, but in demonstration of the Spirit and power.' See N. Smith, *Perfection proclaimed: language and literature in English radical religion 1640–1660* (Oxford: Clarendon Press, 1989).

10 *Donne: Sermons*, x, 'Sermon no. 4: preached at St Paul's on Philippians 3:2', 110.

11 See I Corinthians 2:7: 'But we speak the wisdom of God in a mystery, even the hidden wisdom, which God ordained before the world unto our glory.'

12 See R. Klibansky *et al.*, *Saturn and melancholy* (London: 1964).

13 P. della Mirandola, 'Conclusiones secundam propriam opinionem ... hymnos Orphei', ii and xv, in *Conclusiones* (Rome 1486). As I have noted in 'Woman, language and history in *The Rape of Lucrece*', *Shakespeare Survey*, 41 (1991), Orphic theology is an undoubted influence upon English literature from at least 1595, when George Chapman published his philosophical poem, *The shadow of night*.

14 *Giordano Bruno's The heroic frenzies*, trans. P. E. Memmo Jr (Chapel Hill: University of North Carolina Press, 1964), part II, second dialogue, 225.

15 For a good account of the *nigredo* as described in alchemical treatises of the English Renaissance, see C. Nicholl, *The chemicall theatre* (London: Routledge and Kegan Paul, 1980), 191–200.

16 This passage is cited in W. von Loewenich, *Luther's theology of the cross*, trans. H. J. A. Bauman (Belfast: Christian Journals Ltd, 1976), 83.

17 Donne, *Devotions upon emergent occasions*, ed. A. Raspa (Oxford: Oxford University Press, 1987), 76.

18 Smith, *Perfection proclaimed*, 230–1.

19 Here I am indebted to but also in disagreement with Anthony Gash's fine essay, 'Shakespeare's comedies of shadow and substance: word and image in *Henry IV* and *Twelfth Night*', *Word and Image*, 4, 3–4 (July–December 1988), 626–62 which notes the pervasive use of 'shadow' in the literature of this time, but sees this as confirming traditional Platonic assumptions.

20 See L. Abraham, *Marvell and alchemy* (Aldershot: Scolar Press, 1990), 78–9.

21 All quotations from *Shakespeare's sonnets* are taken from the edition by Stephen Booth (New Haven: Yale University Press, 1977). All quotations from 'Upon Appleton House' are taken from *Andrew Marvell: the complete poems*, ed. E. Story Donno (Harmondsworth: Penguin, 1972).

22 See F. Rubinstein, *A dictionary of Shakespeare's sexual puns and their significance*, 2nd ed. (London: Macmillan, 1989).

23 For the sexual pun in 'eye', see E. Partridge, *Shakespeare's bawdy* (London: Routledge and Kegan Paul, 1947; rev. ed. 1968) and Rubinstein, *Dictionary of Shakespeare's sexual puns*.

24 Don Cameron Allen and Douglas Brooks-Davies have suggested that a pre-Roman, Celtic Christianity, and hence the possibility of a natural conjunction of art and religion, is figured here in an implied Druidic reference to 'some great prelate of the grove'. See Allen, *Image and meaning: metaphoric traditions in Renaissance poetry* (Baltimore: Johns Hopkins University Press, 1960), 143, and Brooks-Davies, *The mercurian monarch: magical politics from Spenser to Pope* (Manchester: Manchester University Press, 1983), ch. iv.

25 M. Stocker, *Apocalyptic Marvell: the second coming in seventeenth-century poetry* (Brighton: Harvester Press, 1986), 158–9.

PART V

Authorship and the academic world

9

What is a scientific author?[1]

Steve Woolgar

> I am not certain that the consequences derived from the disappearance or death of the author have been fully explored or that the importance of this event has been appreciated. To be specific, it seems to me that the themes destined to replace the privileged position accorded the author have merely served to arrest the possibility of genuine change. (Foucault, 1977: 117)

Introduction

Science is our most highly revered form of knowledge. In this popular perception (a perception more deeply entrenched than is usually realised), science provides the means of most reliably effecting connections between what is said and the way things are. In other words, scientific knowledge represents the apogee of relations between the text and the world. Authorship in science is therefore a key focus for the pursuit of more general questions about textuality and representation.

My approach to this (modified) Foucauldian question will, of necessity, be distinctly un-Foucauldian. Foucault usefully calls attention to the emergence and disappearance of the author in history. He notes that whereas 'scientific' texts were only thought truthful in the Middle Ages if the name of the author was indicated, the seventeenth and eighteenth centuries saw the emergence of a new style whereby 'the role of the author disappeared as an index of truthfulness' (Foucault, 1977: 126; cf. Shapin, 1984; Shapin and Schaffer, 1984; Bazerman, 1988). This neatly captures both the fact that particular forms and representations of authorship (Foucault's 'author-function') are far from immutable, and that the 'absent' author is the chief characteristic of contemporary scientific authorship. In the end, however, Foucault's analytic programme attempts to transcend our embroilment in current conventions by enquiring about the currency and modes of existence of different discourses (see also Foucault, 1972: 92–6). Foucault recognises that the significance accorded to the author figure reflects our own dependence upon a particular form of discourse. But he makes little effort to *interrogate* the author figure. In other words, he does not ask much about what happens when *we* authors ask his question; Foucault the author is largely absent from his own attempt to answer the question. In the particular case which concerns us, should we similarly adopt the guise of (absent) scientific author in pursuing our question? Can we, in any case, *avoid* any of the significant features of scientific authorship in attempting an answer to this question? I want to argue that an examination of attempts to deal with the author figure can tell us much about conventional constraints upon our analytic potential. Efforts at interrogating the author, I suggest, are an integral part of moves to tease out prospects for 'genuine change'.

This chapter pursues this argument through a brief review of recent moves in the sociology of scientific knowledge (SSK), focusing in particular on how this body of research has dealt with scientific authorship.[2] The argument starts by recalling the strategic significance claimed for relativist–constructivist perspectives on science. We then note certain key ambivalences in both theoretical and empirical work in SSK. Since these ambivalences concern the theoretical status of agency in representation, the 'problem' of the scientist–author is pivotal. Only by exploiting (instead of concealing or repairing) these ambivalences, can SSK develop some of the more radical implications of its relativist-constructivism.

The strategic significance of SSK

In an obvious sense the substantive focus of SSK is on the issues and concerns of epistemology. Epistemic practices include visual and textual representation, argumentative discourse, making interpretations, knowing, being certain, explaining, understanding, using evidence, reasoning and so on. Since such practices are (reckoned to be) foundational to a huge variety of actions and behaviour, the significance of SSK clearly goes beyond its ability to enlighten us about science. Its significance lies not just in providing more or different news 'about science', but in its potential for re-evaluating fundamental assumptions of modern thought. However, as we shall see in the example of the 'hardest possible case' argument, this potential has been stunted by the unwillingness (or inability, see note 5) to press the reflexive consequences of SSK argument.

SSK is something of a late arrival at the postmodernist ball. Although it enjoys a reputation of considerable radicalism in the context of its disputes with objectivist philosophy of science, its espousal of 'relativist-constructivism' is somewhat restricted when measured against the scope of more general questions currently being asked about textuality and reader–writer relations. Such restriction is regrettable because the field has a virtual monopoly on close, detailed, empiriral investigations of the social basis of scientific knowledge. None the less, it is instructive to examine in some detail the restrictions which SSK imposes upon itself.

Analytic ambivalence in SSK programmatics

Although the discussion takes the form of a plea for greater reflexivity, opportunities for reflexive experiments with form are passed over in what follows.[3] The form of the argument is 'univocal', apart from the passage immediately below, when the combined voices of the entire SSK community (including this author) are goaded into one brief interjection. Thus, a more provocative way of posing the central question of this chapter is to ask to what extent SSK is going to continue making the same mistakes ...
MISTAKES! WHAT MISTAKES??!
Sorry, sorry. An outrageous lapse into asymmetry, I know. I apologise. How *dare* I presume actually to be able to discern 'mistakes'?! I was just looking for a new way of raising the question of progress in the sociology of science. At the point at which SSK finds itself a 'new' object, it seems especially pertinent to enquire

about the direction, status and progress of the enterprise. The early arguments about the deficiencies and inadequacies of alternative (prior) positions (for example, of teleological accounts, of rationalist philosophy, of the 'received view', of Mertonian accounts, and so on) imply that SSK is to be preferred to its predecessors. So it seems appropriate to ask whether SSK admits that it too may in time become a predecessor to a preferred (new) perspective. To do so, would be to admit that there are features of the SSK position – unkindly referred to above as 'mistakes' – which are not as sound as they currently appear. On the other hand, not to admit that SSK can be superseded would be an extraordinary denial of the self-referential implications of SSK. It would suggest that whereas the relativity of truth holds for all other types of knowledge enterprise, SSK is to be considered a special case! This, of course, is the very thing that some advocates of SSK have said they wanted to avoid: a horrendous repetition of Mannheim's Mistake. Without admitting (this kind of) reflexivity, as Bloor (1976) has argued, the sociology of scientific knowledge would be a standing refutation of itself.

This dilemma – either admit to mistakes or claim special case (and hence self-refuting) status – is the corollary of an intriguing paradox at the heart of the programmatic claims of SSK. Although some writers suggest that SSK is (as it should be) capable of construing its own enterprise as (merely) another temporary style of knowledge production, it is not at all clear how SSK envisages the circumstances of its own demise. If SSK continus for ever, it will refute its own relativistic tenet by constituting a contrary empirical example which supports the argument of its (non-relativist) opponents. If, on the other hand, it is superseded, this will once again demonstrate its central argument about the contingency of any theory, thereby proving itself worthy of continuing.[4]

Unfortunately, this paradox (and its associated dilemma) has yet to be explored or confronted by more than a few scholars working in SSK. Instead, it has either been ignored or simply not noticed.[5] Practitioners of SSK have tended to adopt an attitude of 'getting on with the job' in preference to getting bogged down in what they view as unproductive philosophical conundra at the level of programmatics. One consequence of this attitude is that the practical correlate of the programmatic dilemma identified above re-emerges in analytic ambivalence in SSK argument.

Analytic ambivalence in SSK practice

Let us first review the essential features of the structure of a SSK argument. Without undue caricature, four main stages can be identified:[6]

1) Select the account to be ironicised.

   Typically, the account selected is a knowledge claim, a discovery, a mathematical formula, a scientific paper, a Nobel address, a scientist's interview response, and so on.

2) Assert (or imply) that accounts quite different from that selected are possible.

   The sociologist claims that it is possible in principle to supplant the selected account with another account. This is the 'it could be otherwise' move. There are various ways of achieving this assertion of alternatives; by general appeal to principles of historical and cultural relativism − in different times or in different places it could be otherwise; or by drawing upon the different accounts advanced by scientists embroiled in controversy.

3) Portray these accounts as alternative accounts of the 'same' 'reality'.

   This move is important as a rationale for juxtaposing allegedly alternative accounts. Their difference is all the more marked, it is suggested, because they relate to the same (unchanging) 'external reality'. Thus (to expand the range of examples to include relativist−constructivist explanations beyond sociology of scientific knowledge): different legal/societal definitions of the same (deviant) act; different news reports of the same events; different medical classifications of the same drug; different scientific knowledge of the same world. This invocation (either implicitly or explicitly) of a purportedly extant reality to which varying definitions (constructions) relate, is a realist manoeuvre crucial to this style of relativist argument.

4) 'Explain' the 'difference' in accounts by juxtaposing a description of antecedent circumstances.

Examples of such circumstances include social and cognitive interests, the activities of certain key social groups (or core sets) and so on. Notably, the sociologist's own account of these antecedent circumstances is not – in the course of explanation – subjected to stage 2; attention is not drawn to the fact that it is possible in principle to supplant the sociologist's own 'explanatory' account with another.

The central analytic ambivalence of this style of relativist–constructivist explanation is that the relativist argument ironically depends on a practical (that is, 'discursive' or 'textually embedded') realism, both with respect to the purportedly extant reality underlying scientists' constructions and with respect to the antecedent circumstances recruited as explanans (Woolgar, 1981, 1983; Woolgar and Pawluch, 1985). We thus see that programmatic espousals of relativism give way to a realism in practice.

One response to this ambivalence is to denounce explanatory practice in SSK as inconsistent, and to urge its abandonment. Typically, this is the response of philosophers antithetical to social studies of science (for example, Laudan, 1981). An alternative is to view such ambivalence, not as a problem or obstacle, but as an opportunity for exploring alternative modes of social science accounting (Ashmore, 1989; Woolgar and Ashmore, 1988). If current conventions of explanation constrain our attempts to explore the ramifications of relativist arguments, we need to consider what is gained by modifying our reliance upon these conventional forms. It is this line of argument which provides a rationale for recent textual experiments, 'new literary forms' and other explorations in reflexivity (for example, Ashmore, 1989; Mulkay, 1985; Pinch, 1988; Woolgar, 1988b).

The hardest possible case as contingent

We are now in a position to consider the origins of these analytic ambivalences. For it is precisely in its invocation of science as an especially significant epistemological case that SSK buys into certain key realist commitments in its own practice. To see how this occurs, let us consider one claim for the strategic value of SSK as articulated by Harry Collins:

> It would be very satisfying if the establishment of a piece of knowledge belonging to a modern mainstream science, with substantial institutional autonomy, could be described in [relativist–constructivist] terms...The impact of society on knowledge 'produced' at the laboratory bench would then have been followed through in the hardest possible case. (Collins, 1981: 7)

Elsewhere, Collins elaborates:

> When I talked about a 'hard case', I meant it in the technical sense which I thought was common usage – namely that if one wants to prove a general thesis you endeavour to prove it for the case where the thesis seems *least likely to hold*. The idea is that if you prove it for the case where it seems least likely to hold, it is fair to generalise to cases where it seems more likely to hold ... (Collins, 1982: 142; emphasis in original)

Although this argument seems straightforward, it is not hard to see that this rationale depends on a series of unexamined postulates of adequacy. What exactly is to count as 'prove', 'hold' and 'generalise' in the argumentative work of SSK itself? Are practitioners of SSK content with the observation that their own efforts to 'prove', 'hold' and so on are socially determined by the 'impact of society'?[7]

More telling for present purposes are questions about the notion of hardness. For Collins, the 'hardness' of knowledge means a low likelihood that the relativist thesis will hold.[8] And 'least likely to hold' is equivalent to 'what most people would say is this case (... the sense ... which I thought was common usage)'. Now, as befits the sceptical current of this kind of relativism, we might want to stress the interpretive flexibility of this remark. In line with the way the matter is posed in, say, the social problems and deviance literature, we could ask *for whom*, in *what circumstances*, on *what occasions*, *how* and *why* does this appear 'hard' (for example, Spector and Kitsuse, 1977)?[9] In asking these questions we would be suggesting that there is no warrant for privileging hardness as an actual, inherent property of the object of study, any more than there is for any property of natural phenomena.[10] In other words, hardness is not given, it is constructed (attributed, constituted, rendered, an occasioned accomplishment); it does not reside in the object of study, but is rather constituted through artful representation of the object.[11]

Authorship in science; authorship in social science

The literature on the empirical study of scientific discourse is far too large for justice to be done in a summary here. The important point to note for our purposes is that a large amount of work has shown the detailed ways in which representations in science accomplish relationships between the word and the world (for a recent collection see Lynch and Woolgar, 1990).[12] This vast literature can be summarised by saying that it represents an attempt to *reinsert* the absent author. Scientific knowledge (in our epoch) requires representations of reality unmediated by the presence of the human author. Discourse analysis undertaken by practitioners in SSK shows, through an examination of all the devices used to conceal him- or herself, that the author was there all along. In some work, the aim is to show that scientific authorship is not, after all, so different from authorship in other areas. For example, scientific reports are shown to deploy a familiar repertoire of 'literary' devices (Gusfield, 1976; Myers, 1990). More generally, the attempts of SSK to dig behind the mask of formal scientific literture, to reveal what science is 'actually' like (through, for example, ethnographic studies of laboratory practice), all amount to the repopulation of scientific stories. In these revelations of the messy, idiosyncratic face of science, as carried out at the laboratory bench, the scientists themselves come back into the picture.

It is clear that to the extent that SSK buys into realist epistemologies about author–world relationships, it also constitutes phenomena as 'separate from' its own authorial practice. These phenomena happen to be the practices of scientist-authors. But nearly all these attempts to recover the absent author from scientific texts seem to entail the absence of the social scientific author. The achieved presence, the reinsertion, of the scientific author depends on the achieved absence of the social scientific author. Just when we recover the scientist, the social scientist goes missing.

The reflexive application of discourse analysis thus shows that SSK constitutes its own hardness by way of a rhetorical contrast between the work of the author-analyst and the work of the scientist-authors being studied; between the representational activities of the sociologist and those of her scientist-subjects. Whereas the latter are presented as amenable to relativism, the potential application of relativism to the former is played down. This rhetorical contrast amounts to a claim that different classes of representational activity are differentially susceptible to relativism. In other words, the author-analyst, the self in the explanation, purports to operate at a level 'higher' than (different from) the objects of study. It is this practice which has been designated 'onto-logical gerrymandering' (Woolgar and Pawluch, 1985).

This practical or *de facto* assignation (in the course of represen-tation/argument) of a difference in levels, is hardness in another guise. The harder our own argument, the less likely it seems sus-ceptible to the kind of relativism we apply to the objects of study. Hardness, the lack of susceptibility to relativism, is equivalent to the distance (difference) we establish between representational practices which we portray as susceptible to relativism and those which are not.[13] The greater the distance, the harder the case. So hardness is also a measure of the work needed to indent or collapse the distance established between analyst and object. As Bruno Latour has pointed out, the conviction of the sciences is built upon just this ability to act at a distance. The most convincing argument is precisely that which allows the author-analyst to 'act upon' (explain, interpret, represent) phenomena while remaining distant from them (Latour, 1986, 1987; Woolgar, 1988b). The rhetorical requirement is that the analyst-self can speak authoritatively about the phenomenon without, as it were, being contaminated by the phenomenon itself. Hence the rhetorical tension in accounts by Nobel laureates and the like: although uniquely responsible for the discovery of a phenomenon, recipients of awards want to stress that anyone else could similarly have come upon the same phenomenon, had they been in the right place at the right time (Woolgar, 1981).

Beyond the hardest possible case

The reflexive application of relativism – constructivism shows that
'hardness' is socially contingent; it is a practical accomplishment.
This deconstruction of 'hardness' reaffirms the power of the SSK
formula. But in the same manoeuvre, as we have already suggested,
SSK ironically weakens its claim to theoretical significance. As
more and more demonstrations of the social character of scientific
knowledge emerge, so our preconceptions about the privileged
status of science slowly change. The whole objective of the SSK
project is to attenuate the hardness associated with scientific
knowledge. But the more the application of relativism to scientific
knowledge is accepted, the less it is clear that SSK is dealing with
the hardest possible case. Importantly, this suggests that there
might be a yet harder case to crack than the 'hardest possible case'.

What might this next case be? Recalling that 'hardest' means
the least likely place where the relativist thesis can hold, and that
hardness also reflects analytic distance, we might construe 'self'
as a candidate for a yet harder hardest possible case. By 'Self' I
mean the self-in-the-text, the voice of the author/analyst/writer
as it appears (or, as it conceals itself) in the course of argument
(writing, speaking, representing). Note that the application of
relativism to the embedded self-in-the-text is meant to suggest
something different from those sociological and psychological
approaches which construe self as a topic largely disengaged from
the representational work it sustains; discussions of the role of
the self; the emergence of the 'idea' of self; historical portrayals
of changing conceptions of self. While such approaches can be
valuable, they tend not to interrogate the self in action. The Self
we are concerned with is the Self which sustains representational
practice. This kind of Self can be construed as a yet harder case
than science since, I suggest, it is even less likely that the relativist
thesis can be applied to Self than to scientific knowledge.[14]

Whatever the particular merits of (this kind of) Self as a possible
yet harder hardest possible case, the important general point here
is that the reflexive application of SSK yields a further domain of
possible targets for analysis. Here, then, we come to the crux of the
matter. The theoretical significance of SSK is not (just) that it

tackles *the* 'hardest possible case'; but that *in virtue of its reflexive application* it has the capacity to generate more and more 'yet harder hardest possible cases'. One important implication of this is that 'the author' is just a temporary target for critical analysis. 'The author' is, so to speak, just a staging post, a convenient current focal point, in the wider sweep of things.

Recent work suggests it is already possible to identify a next realm of targets in the shifting critique of textuality. If we retain the generality of the term 'agent' in our earlier discussion, we recognise that the scientist-author is merely one kind of agent charged with responsibility for producing representations. Apparatus, equipment, instruments, devices of all kinds can stand as agents of representation. One might argue that such devices are rhetorical in that they further contribute to the impression of the scientific author's absence. For example, the pen trace recorder seems to record changes in electrical resistance without human intervention. Nature seems to inscribe itself automatically.

The inclusion of agents other than humans, of inanimate authors, under our critical gaze raises interesting questions about the relationship between different agents, about their relative value and reliability in representation. If recent work on representation in scientific practice is any clue, determinations of the relationship between agents and objects will depend on highly localised attributions and assignations (of origin, history, antecedent circumstances) (Lynch and Woolgar, 1990). It will become useful to construe scientific culture and practice in terms of the coexistence of animate and inanimate agents in a locally constituted moral order of representation (Woolgar, 1988a). In the light of these developments, it is likely that the preoccupation with the scientist-author, as the person responsible for the advancement of particular knowledge claims, will come to seem a very narrow definition of agent. In particular, the move proposed above, from author to Self, will appear very limited compared to the move from humans to agents (that is, humans and non-humans).

The fact that the target keeps shifting should not be viewed as a defect, but as a positive feature of the enterprise. The analytic ambivalence which stems from apprehending SSK as an explanatory formula needs to be exploited, rather than treated as an embarrassment. Then we can see that, far from being regressive, the reflexive application of SSK is thoroughly regenerative. The ultimate significance of SSK, in other words, is that it contains within itself the dynamic basis for the iterative reconceptualisation of 'epistemic matters'. It is in virtue of this dynamic that SSK has the 'potential for re-evaluating fundamental assumptions of modern thought'(Woolgar, 1993: 177).

Conclusion

We have reviewed the fate of the scientific author at the hands of a particularly virulent species of relativist-constructivism: the sociology of scientific knowledge (SSK). We see that the potential strategic theoretical significance of SSK is in danger of being compromised by an unwillingness to confront a paradox at the heart of its programmatic claims and to exploit the analytic ambivalences in its practice. The paradox and associated ambivalences can be understood to hinge around the problem of the scientific author. Modern science demands the irrelevance of the author vis-à-vis facts about the world which are (in principle) putatively available to anyone. Consequently, scientific discourse sanctions the disappearance of the author. A large body of work within SSK has been devoted to the reinsertion of the scientific author, but the corollary, under current social science conventions, is that the social scientific author is herself absent from this work. One possible step towards modifying these conventions is through the realisation that the figure of the scientific author is just one temporary focus in a series of reconceptualisations of epistemic questions.

Notes

1 For a longer version of this chapter, developing the idea of textuality and scientific authorship in a critique of recent attempts to apply the sociology of scientific knowledge to technology, see Woolgar, 1991a.
2 The discussion here focuses on the relativist–constructivist version of SSK rather than on other variants (for example, 'actor-network' theory and translation models: Callon, 1980, 1986; Latour, 1987; Law, 1987).
3 There is no justification for this last statement. There is no justification for this last statement.

4 Thanks to Diana Hicks for this formulation.

5 It is not clear whether this is a difficulty which is recognised but not taken seriously, or whether it is not recognised as a difficulty at all. In the latter possibility it is, perhaps, a 'seen but unnoticed' feature of SSK practitioners' routine accomplishment of social order, that is, of SSK arguments (cf. Garfinkel, 1967). This suggests, in turn, that the recognition of (let alone the 'confrontation' with) the difficulty will require a change in disciplinary conventions (and constraints) such that a different realm of the 'noticeable' becomes possible.

6 For a full account see Woolgar (1983) and Woolgar and Pawluch (1985).

7 For a detailed analysis of the reflexive implications of Collins' arguments, in particular, of replication in SSK's analysis of replication in science, see Ashmore (1988; 1989, ch. 4).

8 Collins (1982: 142) also says: '... there is no exact relation between the *hardness* of a case and the *difficulty* of researching it'. This seems reasonably if 'difficulty of researching' refers to the practical task of unearthing sources, organising them and undertaking analysis, since this aspect of research is distinguished from the business of persuading one's audience as to the plausibility of one's analysis. On this view, difficulty in research and difficulty of persuasion are separated. Unfortunately, this only holds good for those instances of research where oneself is already persuaded. As soon as oneself is part of the audience to be persuaded, the distinction between difficulty and hardness breaks down.

9 I am not concerned to determine whether or not it actually is hard: this is beyond my jurisdiction as an impartial observer of SSK (the tenet of impartiality: Bloor, 1976).

10 In this instance Collins appeals to an implicit hierarchy of knowledge, ranging from weak (perhaps of the kind associated with religious beliefs or political ideologies) to strong (natural sciences and mathematics). Perhaps one ground for his taking the latter as unproblematically strong is that 'most people' think of these areas of knowledge in those terms. The commonness of this conception is indicated by the observation that the superiority of the latter is taken for granted. Yet a quite different realm of objects of enquiry also comes into focus when we look carefully at what is taken for granted: namely, our ability to stand apart from phenomena.

11 This follows the SSK dictum that properties of objects are essentially equivalent to their use. Collins' (1975) example of temperature is still one of the best around.

12 Representations are essentially local accomplishments whereby the world is constituted as a phenomenon separate from mere representations 'of it'. In this process, the agent of representation is a merely passive character, simply reflecting or enabling the world to make its presence known in representation. A central contribution of the analysis of scientific discourse is the documentation of the multitude of devices and strategies used to sustain this realist epistemology. The agent of representation is thus shown to use preliminary instructions and contrast structures for 'authorising the version' (Smith, 1978), pathing and sequencing devices (Woolgar, 1981), irony (Gusfield, 1976; Woolgar, 1983), reality/appearance devices (Potter, 1983; see also Potter and Wetherell, 1987), boundary work (Gieryn, 1983) and so on. Elsewhere, we find discussions of the ways in which modalisers are used to enhance or detract from the claimed facticity of scientific statements (Latour and Woolgar, 1986), the utilisation of 'immutable mobiles' (Latour, 1986) or the textual organisation of relationships between the various semiotic characters within and beyond the text (Latour, 1988).

13 We see how the equivalence between distance and hardness pertains in at least
two different kinds of analyst–object relations. In the natural sciences, hardness
means precisely the achieved difference (distance) between scientist and the
'objects of the world': electrons are disprivileged in that they are not permitted
feelings, opinions, the capacity to 'know' (do research) and so on. By contrast,
many of the social sciences, especially those influenced by the tradition of
phenomenology, tend to sacrifice 'hardness' by stressing the similarity between
their own Selves as analysts and their objects (which become 'subjects' in the
same move). And within the social sciences, of course, there are constant debates
about the relative merits of hard and soft social science, coupled with anxious
deliberation over its (possibly) 'scientific' status. Significantly, the achievement
of distance, the robustness of the self in explanation, depends upon the judicious
use of what can variously be called technologies of representation (Woolgar,
1989); inscription devices (Latour and Woolgar, 1986) or immutable mobiles
(Latour, 1986).

14 This last proposal merits some elucidation, particularly in relation to the sense
of Self at issue here. Before tackling this task, it is worth noting that the proposal
is supported by what I call the Test of Envisaged Absurdity (the TEA test). In crude
terms, the TEA test assumes a direct relationship between (a) the degree of
horror and consternation provoked when a particular phenomenon is initially
suggested for sociological study and (b) the evident fruitfulness of pursuing
this apparently absurd perspective ('fruitfulness' means degree of debate and
scholarly attention). Hence the greater the cries of outrage, the more fruitful
the way forward. As precedent, I cite the conter-intuitive reaction to initial
proposals for a sociology of science and, in more specific detail, the degree of
consternation on the part of objectivist and rationalist philosophers at the
proposals for a strong programme in SSK. Although the test is not infallible (none
is), the apparent absurdity of the idea of deconstructing Self is encouraging.

References

Ashmore, M. (1988), 'The life and opinions of a replication claim', in S. Woolgar,
Knowledge and reflexivity: new frontiers in the sociology of knowledge (London:
Sage), 125–54.

Ashmore, M. (1989), *The reflexive thesis: wrighting sociology of scientific knowledge*
(Chicago: Chicago University Press).

Bazerman, C. (1988), *Shaping written knowledge: essays in the growth, form,
function and implications of the scientific article* (Madison: University of
Wisconsin Press).

Bloor, D. (1976), *Knowledge and social imagery* (London: Routledge and Kegan Paul).

Callon, M. (1980), 'Struggles and negotiations to define what is problematic and
what is not', in K. Knorr, R. Krohn and R. Whitley (eds), *The social process of
scientific investigation* (Dordrecht: Reidel), 197–219.

Callon, M. (1986), 'Some elements of a sociology of translation', in J. Law (ed.),
Power, action and belief (London: Routledge and Kegan Paul), 196–233.

Collins, H. M. (1975), 'The seven sexes: a study in the sociology of a phenomenon
or the replication of experiments in physics', *Sociology*, 9, 205–24.

Collins, H. M. (1981), 'Stages in the empirical programme of relativism', *Social
Studies of Science*, 11, 3–10.

Collins, H. M. (1982), 'Special relativism: the natural attitude', *Social Studies of Science*, 12, 139–43.

Foucault, M. (1972), *The archaeology of knowledge* (London: Tavistock).

Foucault, M. (1977), 'What is an author?', in M. Foucault, *Language, counter-memory, practice* (Oxford: Blackwell), 113–38.

Garfinkel, H. (1967), *Studies in ethnomethodology* (Englewood Cliffs, NJ: Prentice-Hall).

Gieryn, T. (1983), 'Boundary-work and the demarcation of science from non-science: strains and interests in the professional ideologies of scientists', *American Sociological Review*, 48, 781–95.

Gusfield, J. (1976), 'The literary rhetoric of science: comedy and pathos in drinking driver research', *American Sociological Review*, 41, 16–34.

Latour, B. (1986), 'Visualisation and cognition: thinking with eyes and hands', *Knowledge and Society*, 6, 1–40; also in Lynch and Woolgar (1990), 19–68.

Latour, B. (1987), *Science in action* (Milton Keynes: Open University Press).

Latour, B. (1988), 'A relativistic account of Einstein's relativity', *Social Studies of Science*, 18, 3–44.

Latour, B. and Woolgar, S. (1986), *Laboratory life: the construction of scientific facts*, 2nd ed. (Princeton: Princeton University Press).

Laudan, L. (1981), 'The pseudo-science of science?', *Philosophy of the Social Sciences*, 11, 173–98.

Law, J. (1987), 'Technology and heterogeneous engineering: the case of Portuguese expansion', in W. E. Bijker, T. P. Hughes and T. Pinch (eds), *The social construction of technological systems* (Cambridge, Mass.: MIT Press), 111–34.

Lynch, M. and Woolgar, S. (eds) (1990), *Representation in scientific practice* (Cambridge, Mass.: MIT Press).

Mulkay, M. (1985), *The word and the world: explorations in the form of sociological analysis* (London: George Allen and Unwin).

Myers, G. (1990), *Writing biology: texts in the social construction of scientific knowledge* (Madison: University of Wisconsin Press).

Pinch, T. (1988), 'Reservations about reflexivity or why should the devil have all the good tunes?', in Woolgar, *Knowledge and reflexivity*, 178–99.

Potter, J. (1983), *Speaking and wrting science: issues in the analysis of psychologists' discourse*, unpublished D.Phil. thesis, University of York.

Potter, J. and Wetherell, M. (1987), *Discourse and Social Psychology* (London: Sage).

Shapin, S. (1984), 'Pump and circumstance: Robert Boyle's literary technology', *Social Studies of Science*, 14, 481–520.

Shapin, S. and Schaffer, S. (1984), *Leviathan and the air pump: Hobbes, Boyle and the experimental life* (Princeton: Princeton University Press).

Smith, D. (1978), 'K is mentally ill: the anatomy of a factual account', *Sociology*, 12, 23–53.

Spector, M. and Kitsuse, J. (1977), *Constructing social problems* (Menlo Park, California: Cummings).

Woolgar, S. (1981), 'Discovery: logic and sequence in a scientific text', in K. Knorr, R. Krohn and R. Whitley (eds), *The social process of scientific investigation sociology of the sciences yearbook*, vol. 4 (Dordrecht: Reidel), 239–68.

Woolgar, S. (1983), 'Irony in the social study of science', in K. D. Knorr-Cetina and M. Mulkay (eds), *Science observed: perspectives on the social study of science* (London: Sage), 239–66.

Woolgar, S. (1988a), *Science: the very idea* (London: Routledge).

Woolgar, S. (1988b), 'Reflexivity is the ethnographer of the text', 14–36 in Woolgar, *Knowledge and reflexivity*, 14–36.

Woolgar, S. (1989), 'The ideology of representation and the role of the agent', 131–44 in H. Lawson and L. Appignanesi (eds), *Dismantling truth: reality in the post-modern world* (London: Weidenfeld and Nicolson), 131–44.

Woolgar, S. (1991), 'The turn to technology in social studies of science', *Science Technology and Human Values*, 16, 20–50.

Woolgar, S. (1993), 'What is a scientific author?', this chapter.

Woolgar, S. and Ashmore, M. (1988), 'The next step: an introduction to the reflexive project', in Woolgar, *Knowledge and reflexivity*, 1–13.

Woolgar, S. and Pawluch, D. (1985), 'Ontological gerrymandering: the anatomy of social problems explanations', *Social Problems*, 32, 214–27.

10

Master narratives:
anthropology and writing

Henrietta L. Moore

Postmodernism has arrived in anthropology: as is evidenced by recent concern with forms of anthropological writing and with the nature of representation. This 'new ethnography', as the post-modernist critique within the discipline is known, turns on two in-terrelated issues: what is it that anthropologists represent or claim to represent in their texts; and by what authority do anthropologists make these representations? The answers to these questions necessarily involve a number of considerations. Underlying the 'new ethnography' are anxieties about anthropology's role in the construction and maintenance of Western imperialism and neo-imperialism. A number of authors have expressed the hope that through new types of experimental ethnographic writing, anthro-pology can expose the global systems of power relations which are embedded in traditional representations of the 'other' and 'other cultures'. Postmodernist anthropologists call attention to the constructed nature of cultural accounts, and they seek to develop new forms of writing, such as those predicated on dialogue, intertextuality and heteroglossia to unmask and displace the unitary authority of the anthropologist as author. Anthropology as a discipline can no longer be held to speak with automatic authority for 'others' previously defined as unable to speak for themselves, being 'primitive', 'pre-literate', 'without history' (Clifford, 1986: 10). The idea that what anthropologists represent in their texts is an-'other' culture is seriously in doubt. Since all cultural and historical accounts are partial, constructed ones, there can be no question of providing a single authoritative account of another culture. Culture is a domain of contested and negotiated meanings. Anthropologists do not represent other cultures, they invent them, construct them and they do so through the process of writing or, more properly, through the process of textualisation (Wagner, 1975), since we would want to include here not only conventional written ethnographies but also ethnographic films, photographs, representations of all kinds.

It is quite clear that this process of textualisation is much more than merely a process of knowledge production; it is a process of knowledge creation. This point has been made very engagingly with regard to early writings on southern and eastern Africa. 'When we think of the so-called nineteenth century discovery of Africa, we usually think of the professional explorer and soldier, the handful of men whom Conrad called "militant geographers". Yet, ordinary literate people also discovered Africa, through their churches, mission societies and a number of written genres that were offered primarily as entertainment' (Thornton, 1983: 503). For, aside from the popular, and expensively produced, travellers' tales, there were also other texts which reached a much wider audience in Britain and Europe. Some of the most accomplished writers and ethnographers of Africa in the nineteenth century were missionaries – David Livingstone, Robert Moffat, John Roscoe. These men wrote for audiences which were essentially made up of church-goers, the ordinary women and men of the congregation. They wrote church bulletins, missionary tracts, and letters to the press, and when they were 'home' they spoke to large audiences in crowded church halls all over England (Thornton, 1983: 504). As a result, the discovery of Africa (so-called) was actually a discovery on paper. As Thornton says: 'Had the great Victorian travellers not written anything, it would not be said today that they had "discovered" anything' (Thornton, 1983: 509).

Thornton points out how neatly Conrad captures the significance of the written narrative for the European experience of Africa in *Heart of darkness*. When the narrator finally tracks down Kurtz, who is the white man in the dark interior, he learns something of significance: 'I learned that most appropriately, the international society for the suppression of savage customs had entrusted him with the making of a report, for its future guidance. And he had written it too. I've seen, I've read it. It was eloquent, vibrating with eloquence ... it gave me the notion of an exotic Immensity ruled

by an august benevolence. It made me tingle with enthusiasm ...'
(Conrad, 1902; quoted in Thornton, 1983: 509).

Tingling with enthusiasm is not the response which reading
ethnography normally produces in people. However, what is interesting about this passage is the terms in which the report is
referred to. The report itself seems to be, as it were, more significant
than the customs and peoples it describes. It is as if it is something
more than a representation of Africa. It seems as if it is Africa,
and more real for the European than the landscape and people
themselves. Hence the ecstatic: 'I've seen, I've read it, it was
eloquent vibrating with eloquence'. Somehow the experience is
not possible without the text, that is without the mediation of
the text. Thornton says part of it: 'More than a discovery, however,
writing is a bridge that connects the limited context of speech and
experience of primitive society to the larger world through the
narrative that captures the experience of the particular and makes
it available to a universal scrutiny. A new kind of understanding
becomes at least possible ... the ethnographic monograph, and other
genres shaped around similar content ... provide the crucial communicative link between cultures and between audiences that is
the hallmark of anthropology' (Thornton, 1983: 510). Thornton,
I think, intends us to take this communicative link seriously, and
to acknowledge the possibly emancipatory effects of this aspect
of anthropological endeavour. I intend this communicative link
ironically because it is in the attempt to establish a link between
cultures and audiences that much of the problematic nature of
anthropological authorship resides. Thornton's analysis of the
significance of the written narrative for the European experience
of Africa is only part of the story because he fails to explain why
Conrad's narrator should tingle with enthusiasm, why he should
feel that the report speaks so directly to him. Here, I think, we
encounter the relationship of narrative to desire. For the narrator,
the report interprets Africa in terms of his own understandings of
the purpose of Europeans, and therefore his own purpose, in being
in Africa. It reveals something to him not about the landscape and
the people of Africa, but about the landscape of the European imagination in Africa. It makes sense, simultaneously, of the practical
activities in which he and others are engaged, and of his fantasies

about what he and others are doing in Africa. The activities of the individual and the imaginings of self come together in the text in a way which eludes the narrator in a day-to-day context. It is this very function which anthropological texts so often perform for their authors and for their audiences, and it is for this reason that we cannot hope ever to come to any understanding of these texts, or of the politics of their construction, unless we start by examining the relationship between authors and readers which is established in anthropological texts.

In order to explain this statement, and in order to explain why the new ethnography has made so little impact on the acceptability or otherwise of canonical writing in anthropology, it is necessary to begin by examining some aspects of the problematic nature of anthropological authorship. A number of critics have pointed out that the distinguishing mark of the anthropologist as author is the claim to possess an authentic experience. This experience is, of course, the product of having been there. Like all claims to authentic experience, the anthropologist's claim is difficult to assess. As Clifford Geertz points out, it gives much anthropological writing a kind of take-it-or-leave-it quality (Geertz, 1988: 5). It creates also a particular problem for the anthropologist who must produce a scientifically validated text out of a unique personal experience (Clifford, 1988: 26). While no one seriously endeavours at the present time to model the social sciences on the natural sciences, the fact remains that for the vast majority of anthropologists it is still axiomatic that the society described in the text should be the society which the text claims to describe, and not some other. There must be some correspondence in 'good faith' between the anthropologist's interpretations of people's lives and the lives which those people actually lead. If we are going to agree that all cultural constructions, including anthropological descriptions and inter-pretations are partial truths, historically and politically situated, then we must recognise that as far as many anthropologists are concerned anthropology's partial truths cannot be the same sort of partial truths as those displayed on our cinema screens and in contemporary fiction. One possible response to this dilemma is simply to say that in the contemporary context, anthropology does not have a monopoly, if it ever did, of the interpretation of culture and of the discourse on difference. This means that anthropologists can carry on doing anthropology – an activity defined by specific sets of practices and forms of writing – but that they cannot claim any primacy for their interpretations over the interpretation of others (Clifford, 1988: 22, 52–4). Once the claim to primacy goes, then so does much of the anxiety. There is very little likelihood of immediate consensus on this issue either inside or outside the discipline. However, what the debate demonstrates is that the relationship between experience and text is still highly problematic, and although that relationship may be changing in response to the criticisms of the 'new ethnographers', the problem is simply displaced and not resolved.

The primacy of the anthropologist's interpretations of what was then termed 'native life' was not assured until the turn of the century – at least this is the story according to current narratives of the historical development of anthropology as a discipline. Before that moment, as I've briefly indicated, travellers, missionaries and administrators who had been 'in the field' a long time and had good linguistic skills were serious rivals (Clifford, 1988: 26). What is more, men like John Roscoe moved easily from one mode of communication or genre of writing to another. He wrote missionary accounts and he wrote scientific ethnography, and, in so doing, he moved from extensive use of the first person to a disembodied narrative voice, designed to convey objective neutrality (Thornton, 1983: 506–7). The interesting point, then, as a number of anthropologists have pointed out, is that the so-called Malinowskian revolution, where anthropology became characterised in the 1920s by long periods of research in the field, involving participant-observation, was not actually quite the revolution it was once thought to be. Many others had been living in other societies, making systematic observations, speaking the local language and writing about their findings long before Malinowski. It seems more likely that the revolution which Malinowski actually ushered in was not so much a revolution of method as a revolution in writing, in representation. What Malinowski insisted upon and what became the norm, in fact the requirement of professional acceptance in anthropology, which it remains to this day, was that anthropology should be a comparative science, and that the job of the anthropologist was to derive theory from first-hand research. Prior to Malinowski, there were men-on-the-spot (travellers, missionaries, administrators) who had extensive knowledge which they wrote about, but their work was not informed by scientific hypotheses; and there were the armchair theorists, like Frazer, who wove grand comparative theories, but who never visited the field (Clifford, 1988: 26–9). Malinowski's anthropologist was envisaged, therefore, as having a new authority – a new professionalism and a new method – and in order to convey this new authority what was needed was a new form of writing. This authority was problematic from the very beginning because while the research was to be based on the in-depth field experience of the anthropologist, the writer of the ethnographic monograph, who was one and the same person, had to convince his or her audience that the facts before them were not subjective creations, but objective pieces of information.

In order to establish the authority of the anthropologist as an author, two kinds of authorial move within the text were required, therefore. The first was that the author should appear and make a great deal of having actually been there; and the second was that the author should then promptly disappear, so as not to impugn the status of what was to follow. These two strategies in anthropological writing are now well recognised and have been much discussed. However, I would like to consider some of the stylistic strategies employed to pull off this trick in early ethnographies, not because I want to cover familiar ground, but so that I can use them as a starting-point for developing a rather different critique of anthropological writing from the one that we normally find in the work of James Clifford, George Marcus, Paul Rabinow and others.

The ethnographies of the 1920s and 1930s clearly have much in common with other forms of creative writing. The importance of travelling to another place to experience it, and the role of journeying or travelling in the Romantic imagination can be seen clearly at work in the writings of anthropologists. Much modern ethnography shows strong, and unsurprising, parallels with travel writing, and the shifts from first person narration to generalised statement which are characteristic of travel writing, right up to the present day, are evident in anthropological writing. Typically, the most obvious parallels occur in the opening passages of the ethnography, when the writer is most concerned to establish the fact that they have been there, and that therefore they have the authority to speak.

> In the cool of the early morning, just before sunrise, the bow of the Southern Cross headed towards the eastern horizon, on which a tiny dark blue outline was faintly visible. Slowly it grew into a rugged mountain mass, standing up sheer from the ocean ... in an hour or so we were close inshore, and could see canoes coming round from the south ... The outrigger-fitted craft drew near, the men in them bare to the waist, girdled with bark-cloth, large fans stuck in the backs of their belts, tortoise-shell rings or rolls of leaf in the ear-lobes and nose, bearded, and with long hair flowing loosely over their shoulders ... Almost before the chain was down the natives began to scramble aboard, coming over the side by any means that offered, shouting fiercely to each other and to us in a tongue of which not a word was understood by the mota-speaking folk of the mission vessel. I wondered how such turbulent human material could ever be induced to submit to scientific study (Firth, 1957: 1–2).

The above passage is part of the first two pages of Raymond Firth's *We the Tikopia*, first published in 1936. This passage is in no way unusual; there are many others from anthropological writings of the period which could be used to make the same point. In many such passages, there is a preference for break of day scenarios. One must after all begin at the beginning, mark a break with what has gone before, start the narrative moving forward. The metaphor of travel is important in many ethnographies, including many written in recent years. The travel metaphor sustains both the journey of the anthropologist, from home to abroad, from the familiar to the foreign, from ignorance to knowledge, and the journey of the reader which traverses much the same ground. The metaphor of travel often sustains also the theoretical discourse of the ethnography simply by incorporating it into the narrative, and thereby making it more comprehensible. There are other things happening, however, in these texts redolent with metaphors of travel, and these have to do with the topography of selves and others.

While early anthropology was influenced by travel writing, as well as utilising the metaphor of journeying, it was also influenced by the Victorian 'boy's own' story, in which the central theme is a heroic white man penetrating a dark continent at great personal risk: Rider Haggard's *King Solomon's mines*, John Buchan's *Prester John*, and many others. Anthropological imaginative discourse drew both on Romantic themes about the noble savage in Paradise, and on the heroic quests of the adventure story genre. This duality is clearly in evidence in the passage quoted earlier from Raymond Firth's book, and the fact that Firth may have intended his readers to read the passage ironically in no way undermines the general point. Discovery, adventure and difference are mixed in a most seductive fashion. Anyone with the misfortune to be familiar with the cultural genre involved, can hear, on reading such descriptions, all the sounds, tones and colours of an imaginative childhood, enlarged to fill an adult world. There is absolutely nothing surprising about this because the employment of a particular narrative form, bound together with familiar images and metaphors, was a clear necessity for an anthropological discourse desirous of making itself intelligible. There was, in a sense, no alternative to these forms of writing because these were the forms of discourse available to anthropology to handle the relationship between self and other, sameness and difference. To have stood outside these forms of discourse – even supposing such a thing were possible – would have been a guarantee of unintelligibility. Even when writing ironically, the anthropologist as author would have had no alternative but to utilise these forms of discourse. The anthropological imagination, like any other imagination, is a thoroughly textualised one.

However, the anthropological imagination of the 1930s and 1940s was a divided one, and often in conflict with itself. On the one hand, anthropologists wanted to hark back to Romantic ideas about the noble savage freed from the fetters of European Control and the anti-slavery literature of the nineteenth century. They often saw themselves as engaged in preserving alternative life-ways through recording them, and they were deeply concerned to make it clear that however different other people are, we all share a common humanity, a common capacity for rational thought and a common set of needs, strategies and motivations for living. On the other hand, the desire to develop anthropology as a comparative science of 'mankind' drew on the thoroughly Victorian images of quest, adventure and control. 'I wondered', wrote Firth, 'how such turbulent human material could ever be induced to submit to scientific study.'

What emerges from these considerations is that there is much ambiguity in the relationship of anthropology to its 'subject matter'; an ambiguity which draws on, but does not totally overlap with the overdetermined and historically constituted relationship between the West and the Rest, and between coloniser and colonised. However, the ambiguities, divisions and conflicts in the anthropological imaginative discourse actually arise from a much more complex, three-dimensional figure, one which both constitutes and is constituted by the anthropologist as author. One dimension is certainly that provided in the relationship of domination and exploitation between coloniser and colonised. A second dimension concerns the relationship between the individual anthropologist and the people she studies. The third dimension concerns the relationship between the many selves of each individual self, its other selves. These three dimensions are implicated in and implicate each other. Properly speaking, therefore, they are not simply three dimensions, but many multiples of three. The management of such multiplicity is the central concern of anthropological writing. It is, in short, the problem of anthropological authorship.

The relationship between 'self' and 'other' in modern ethnography has a distinctive mark and that mark is the desirability and the fear of 'going native'. Going native, as many have remarked, is essential if one is to carry out participant-observation correctly, if one is to acquire that level of familiarity and identity on which good anthropological writing is supposed to be based. But, it is to be avoided if one wants to write theoretical, comparative anthropology, if one wants to retain one's professional credentials, and if one wants to safeguard one's sense of self. Going native is ultimately a fear about the erasure of difference, and in that erasure the loss of self. The self constitutes and defines itself through the 'detour of the other', and for this process to take place the other must exist and, if it does not exist, it must be created. Crudely put, stable selves require stable others. The instability of self and other accounts for the sense of vulnerability and panic which characterises anthropological fieldwork for many anthropologists, and which

is much talked about in the discipline and is represented in con-
fessional writing.

Anthropologists are in the game then of creating the illusion
of stable selves through which to view stable others; a necessity
forced on them not only by the demands of a comparative science,
but by the dictates of self-identity and self-preservation. Dictates
which, I may say, are both culturally and historically specific.
One way in which the relationship between selves and others is
managed is through the creation of an authorial 'I' who authors
the text. All the literary devices and strategies used to create the
illusion of authority in the text have been widely discussed and
analysed; for example the disembodied narrative voice, alternating
with the use of the appearing and disappearing first person 'I' to
mark the text through with the authentic experience; the attribu-
tion of stable sets of beliefs, attitudes and activities to coherent
bodies or cultures, as in 'The Nuer believe that ...'; and the use
of free indirect speech to mask the arbitrary and precarious nature
of individual interpretation, and to erase the fact that the researcher
is always part of the research situation, as in, for example, 'Through
sacrifice, the Nuer make a bargain with their God'. However, what
is confusing about much so-called postmodernist analysis in
anthropology is that it often appears to suggest that this organising
'I', this authorial voice is unproblematic. In that, while it is
agreed that this authorial voice is duplicitous, if not downright
mendacious, it is assumed that what an analysis of rhetorical
devices in the text does is to reveal the strategies, intentions and
meanings of the author. This assumes, of course, an isomorphism
between the 'I', the author created in the text and the 'I', the
individual who writes the text. This is revealed most dramatically,
strangely enough, when postmodernist anthropologists come to
talk, or rather write, about what the purpose of the new experimental ethnography would be, and what it would look like.

The first point about experimental ethnography is that it is
concerned to make sure that the anthropologist is put back into
the text as part of the research process, and that the experience of
research, and its fundamentally interpersonal, communicative
nature should be revealed as the basis, and the only basis, for
anthropological interpretations. The net result of course, as Geertz

points out, is that we often end up with author-saturated texts
(Geertz, 1988: 97). There is a heavy irony here because the more
radical and experimental anthropology gets, and the more anthropologists are supposed to be seriously engaged in dispersing or
sharing the authority of authorship with others, the more we get
to hear about the anthropologist and the less we get to hear about
others. However, these author-saturated texts necessarily and
obviously presuppose that the author in the text and the author
of the text are one and the same. Furthermore, even if we examine
what many anthropologists see as the more radical proposals put
forward by the new ethnography, namely the proposals for multiple-
authored texts, where dialogue, if not heteroglossia, is the organising form (in so far as postmodernist texts are permitted to have
any organising form) we see that what is proposed is far from
radical. This is because the multiplicity of voices and the multiple
number of authors proposed for these texts would not in fact revise
the standard anthropological notion of authorship, of what it is to
author something, it would simply make it plural. In other words
the authors in the text would still be isomorphic in some way with
the authors of the text whoever those individuals might be. A further
political dimension adds weight to the desire for identity between
the authors in the text and the authors of the text and that is that
in a contemporary world where there is little sign that the combined
forces of neo-imperialism and international capitalism are on the
wane, there is every reason to argue that anthropology must faithfully represent the realities and complexities of communication
and discussion between historically situated individuals. In other
words, we must not invent characters in our dramas.

It is an irony of the contemporary moment that while international capitalism and other forces threaten homogeneity, difference
is on the political agenda more than ever. Anthropology thus retains
an anxiety about the charge of fictionalisation. This may be a displaced anxiety, but it is nevertheless there. It is, of course, the
political realisation of the fact that global systems of domination
are embedded in discourses of difference and in the representation
of others which draws postmodernist anthropology into a situation
where it imagines that the answer to anthropology's crisis of
representation – which is actually a political crisis – is to develop

a form of text in which a number of individuals have their say, and in which a number of perspectives and points of view are put forward. This may be, of course, exactly what happens in the field-work situation, in the context of interpersonal exchange, but the desire for a text which somehow faithfully represents this fieldwork situation is doomed to disappointment. It is doomed to disappointment because the relationship between the author in the text and the author of the text is not a direct and straightforward one. It is not straightforward because it is imaginary; it is fictive, in the sense, that it is arbitrary and symbolic, set up in language and culturally inscribed. When I say that the relationship between these two authors – the individual who signs the text and the 'I' or organising subject created in the text – is fictive and imaginary, I do not mean to imply that these authors have nothing to do with each other, no real connection. I mean simply that the one is the imaginary self of the other. Properly speaking, they are not two selves, but a self in process.

If we accept the poststructuralist, postmodernist argument that the unitary, rational subject is a historical product and not a universal category and if we stress that individuals construct a sense of self, a subjectivity through a variety of subject positions provided in discursive practices, some of which may be mutually contradictory, then, we can begin to make an argument about the necessity albeit under specific cultural and discursive conditions of constructing a sense of self, a unitary coherent self, that can act in the world. One way in which this unitary, coherent self is constructed is through the representation of self or selves in text. Anthropologists don't just represent their experience of an other culture in the text, they also constitute and produce their experience and themselves in the text. The constitution of self is a labour, it is work, and it is imaginary. It is achieved symbolically, through language, and, in this case, through the mediation of the text. It is through the process of textualisation that anthropologists assign meaning to their experiences and give them value. The 'I' or organising subject in the text is the fictively created, unitary self which guarantees the authentic experience and thus the verisimilitude of the cultural representation the text contains. It is a magical trick and exceptionally difficult to pull off.

When Geertz says that Vincent Crapanzano's experimental ethnography *Tuhami* (1980) turns an evocative homage of the other into a self-fulfilling homage to the self, he comes close to understanding this point (Geertz, 1988: 90–96). Crapanzano discusses the life of Tuhami, a Moroccan tile-maker, and he connects what he experiences and what Tuhami tells him to Lacan, Freud, Nietzsche, Kierkegaard, d'Annunzio, Simmel, Sartre, Blanchot, Heidegger, Hegel, Genet, Gadamer, Schutz, Dostoevsky, Jung, Frye and Nerval. There are, apparently, striking parallels between Nerval and Tuhami. It is clear that all these great men have much of import to say regarding the nature of the human condition, and, in that sense, it seems quite likely that their writings could be relevant to an understanding of anyone's life. However, we are not here learning about Tuhami, we are learning about Crapanzano. But this is much more than the comprehension of the self by the 'detour of the other', this is the imaginary constitution of self, the desire to make sense of self through assigning value and meaning to experience, the desire to capture a complete self which then becomes knowable. This is a work of extraordinary synthesis, and what is constructed in it is not Tuhami, but Crapanzano. Crapanzano is aware of this fact. For one thing, anthropology has long been very clear that the purpose of cross-cultural comparison is not just the study of 'them', but the equally important study of 'us' – whoever us might be; although this has conventionally been taken to mean the study of 'our' cultural beliefs, concepts, attitudes and behaviours, and not the study of ourselves as selves. However, Crapanzano is aware of the deeper irony, mentioned earlier, that the more the anthropologist seems to undo the authorial strategies of anthropological writing, to unmask the constructed nature of anthropological interpretations, and to examine their negotiated and contested nature, the more anthropological writing must engage with these issues, and as it becomes more self-conscious and self-critical, it expands to fill the page. The anthropological self is more in evidence than ever.

The process of constructing self through the process of textualisation has much to do with the function of narrative. It has been argued by Hayden White and Paul Ricoeur and many others that narrative is a strategy for placing us within a historically constituted world, and thus our very concept of history is dependent on narrative. If narrative makes the world intelligible, it also makes ourselves intelligible.

> What is involved in the discovery of the 'true story' within or behind the events that come to us in the chaotic form of 'historical records'? What wish is enacted, what desire is gratified, by the fantasy that real events are properly represented when they can be shown to display the formal coherence of a story? In the enigma of this wish, this desire, we catch a glimpse of the cultural function of narrativising discourse' (White, 1980: 8; cited in de Lauretis, 1984).

Desire and narrative are thus enmeshed, and this enmeshing allows us to start unpacking the anthropologist as author. I take as the starting-point for what follows the work of Teresa de Lauretis. I do not claim to say anything that she has not already said much more brilliantly, except perhaps in so far as these issues pertain to anthropological writing. De Lauretis, like others, sees narrative as a fundamental way of making sense of the world. She argues that the structure of narrative offers readers a limited set of positions within the plot space. To receive pleasure from the text, each reader must assume the 'positionalities of meaning and desire' made available by the text. For the period that the reader assumes those positions, their subjectivity, is 'engaged in the cogs of narrative and indeed constituted in the relation of narrative, meaning and desire, so that the very work of narrativity is the engagement of the subject in certain ... positionalities of meaning and desire' (de Lauretis, 1984: 196). For the reader, the text binds fantasy and affect to certain images and metaphors. The historical and ideological nature of these images and metaphors means that although the text powerfully participates in the production of forms of subjectivity which are individually shaped, these forms of subjectivity are also unequivocally social (de Lauretis, 1984: 37). The anthropological monograph is a text which constructs images or visions of social reality. But this text is involved in the production and reproduction of meanings, values and ideology at both the social and the subjective level. The anthropological monograph is thus a work which produces effects of meaning and perception, self-images and subject positions, and it does so for both readers *and* authors.

The question is that if subjectivity is constituted for both readers and authors through taking up the subject positions provided by the narrative, then what induces them to assume these positions? De Lauretis deals with this question by using the concept of identification. In order for a narrative to work, it has to please. Pleasure can simply be something of interest, whether it is aesthetic or theoretical or ethnographic. Anthropologists love knowing about new pieces of ethnography, especially when these new items are offered in the adventurous style of much anthropological narrative. Pleasure depends on a personal response, an engagement of the reader's subjectivity, and this offers the possibility of identification. This process of identification is particularly important in anthropological writing where the reader is being encouraged to identify strongly with the author or rather with the positions that the author takes up in the text. The desire involved or implicated in the narrative is the desire to know, to see, to receive pleasure, and the narrative shapes and contains that desire.

The situation is more complex, however, because readers can read a text. They can read 'against the grain' of the text. They may recognise also the way the narrative is shaping and constraining interpretive possibilities. Indeed, they may recognise, or apprehend the way the narrative shapes and continues their own desire, and they may resist this, dissenting from the text. However, resistance, dissent and even criticism require, as has often been argued, prior recognition. In fact, they are all critically dependent on such recognition. The multiplicity of subject positions proferred by the text means that identification can be partial, temporary and changing. There is no need to imagine that all readers will identify with all the positions proferred in the text, nor is there any reason to assume that the process of identification is without contradiction and conflict. Many of the Subject Positions in the text will actually be contradictory and inconsistent.

The fact that anthropological texts address readers both as individuals and as members of a social group implies that certain patterns or possibilities of identification for all readers must be built into the text (de Lauretis, 1984: 136). These patterns or possibilities of identification are directly related to the intelligibilty of the text.

It is for this reason that anthropological writing appears so wedded to conventional narrative form, and to images and metaphors, like the metaphor of journeying, which allow readers not only to identify, but to indulge in the pleasure of anticipation. The pleasure for the author is also in the familiar form of the narrative, in the pleasure of a story well told according to the conventions of narrative, in the investment in making it come out right, in the success of having described another culture, written a book, and pulled it all off without anyone realising that one wasn't somehow quite up to it. It is for all these reasons that the author creates certain positions of meaning and desire, which not only engage their subjectivity, but also engage the subjectivity of their readers in a way which will permit a considerable degree of identification between author and reader.

The identification so desired works, however, on a number of levels. The author *of* the text wishes to identify with the author *in* the text, the unitary, complete self, who has successfully done the fieldwork and written the text and is the hero of the tale. The author *of* the text also wants the reader to identify with them, through assuming that the author *in* the text is isomorphic with the author *of* the text. We all want to be the heroes of our own stories, and there is just enough of the intrepid traveller left in the popular image of the anthropologist to allow anthropologists to construct themselves in that image. We may no longer be heroic voyagers, but we are not above swopping stories about who had the most horrible time in the field and trading details of life-threatening tropical diseases. The reader of the text wants to identify with the author *in* the text or rather to identify with the positions of meaning and desire which the author takes up and makes available to the reader. To be pleasurable, the process of identification does not have to be complete and it can incorporate as I've suggested, and very often does, a component of resistance or dissent. Finally, the reader of the text wants to identify with the author of the text, through the medium of the author *in* the text. We all like to imagine ourselves as someone else, or at least as the equivalent of someone else, especially if that someone is successful or seems desirable in other ways. There are many other forms of identification which could be discussed, but with regard to the question of the identification between author and reader consider the following passage, which James Clifford has made famous as an exemplar of conventional anthropological writing, albeit for purposes rather different from mine (Clifford, 1988: 33).

> It is difficult to find an English word that adequately describes the social position of dil in a tribe. We have called them aristocrats, but do not wish to imply that Nuer regard them as of superior rank, for, as we have emphatically declared, the idea of a man lording it over others is repugnant to them. On the whole – we will qualify the statement later – the dil have prestige rather than rank and influence rather than power. If you are a dil of the tribe in which you live you are more than a simple tribesman. You are one of the owners of the country, its village sites, its pastures, its fishing pools and wells. Other people live there by virtue of marriage into your clan, adoption into your lineage, or of some other social tie. You are a leader of the tribe and the spear-name of your clan is invoked when the tribe goes to war. Whenever there is a dil in the village, the village clusters around him as a herd around its bull (Evans-Pritchard, 1969: 215).

This is a passage from Evans-Pritchard's *The Nuer*, first published in 1940 and one of the great canonical texts of British social anthropology. There are a number of rhetorical devices at work in the passage. First, the reader is identified, through elision, with the author *in* the text: 'We have called them aristocrats.' Then the reader is identified with the Nuer: 'If you are a dil of the tribe in which you live you ...' The passage also contains all the marks of authentic experience in the familiarity it implies the anthropologist has with Nuer ideas and customs; and it also carries with ease the burden of the objective, scientific gaze in the guise of a typical event: 'Whenever there is a dil in the village ...'. Sameness and difference are woven into this passage in ways which demonstrate what a past master Evans-Pritchard really was of the genre. The difficulties of translation referred to in the first sentence imply difference, but are presented in a way which also suggest the anthropologist's familiarity with this knowable, if not yet completely specified other. This familiarity carries forward into the rest of the passage where the subtle nuances of status and rank are described as if they were part of the English class system. The reader is being encouraged to identify with an aristocratic class among the Nuer, and being encouraged to do so by an anthropologist whose own familiarity with the importance and subtlety of rank and status marks him as someone who appreciates these things. It is a truly masterful piece of writing. It is seductive, it is engaging, and it has just that frisson of sexuality and power which caused Conrad's narrator to tingle with enthusiasm: 'You are a leader of the tribe and the spear-name of your clan is invoked when the tribe goes to war. Whenever there is a dil in the village, the village clusters around him as a herd around its bull.'

This passage employs in recognisable ways the discourse on self and other which is characteristic of many genres of writing. The Nuer referred to in the text in the present tense are a stable, changeless and typified entity which act as a permanent foil for English identity and English selves. However, it is also quite clear that these abstracted Nuer are male, and that the anthropologist and the reader are male also. The predominant metaphors in anthropological writing and the prominent practices in terms of the activity of anthropology – participant observation, systematic data collection, cultural description – all imply a process of looking at, examining, 'objectifying' and 'collecting'. This visualism is manifest in most anthropological writing, especially in the constant use of *mis-en-scène* techniques which writers use to convey the authentic nature of the anthropologist's experience and their description (Clifford and Marcus, 1986: 11–12). This means that it is the act of observation which is repeatedly represented in the text, and this effectively makes the reader, in one way or another, the accomplice of a voyeur (Minh-ha, 1989: 69). The voyeurism, the act of looking, is, of course, the act of othering. The people who are studied and examined begin under the gaze of the anthropologist, but as the narrative develops they are increasingly specified, brought under the control of the anthropologist, and become the property of the anthropologist. They become in the end an extension of the male self, its other looking back at it, reflecting it at 'twice its normal size'. The male and female discussed here do not, of course, refer directly or straightforwardly to individual men and women. This is clearly the case since many people studied by anthropologists are male, and their 'feminisation' through the process of objectification and the assumption of the position of other in relation to the male self, still proceeds.

In similar vein, we have the problem of the woman anthropologist, and the woman reader of the anthropological text. The straightforward response to this is simply to say that the processes of identification under discussion are not the unproblematic outcome of the known gender identity of historical individuals. Identification is not single or simple. Identification is a relation, part of the process of becoming a subject, and it involves the identification of oneself with something other than oneself, so that subjectivity is constituted through a series of such identifications (de Lauretis, 1984: 141). Women anthropologists and women readers identify with the desiring subject, the hero, and they simultaneously identify, of course, with that hero's other, with his object of desire. Women readers and authors are able to take up and partially identify, at best partially, with the male position in the text, with those positions which are given particular value and meaning; and in so doing, they construct a sense of self, a self which is imaginary. Subjectivity is, of course, social and historical, as well as individual, and therefore through the process of identification one acquires a social as well as an individual subjectivity. Women anthropologists and women readers do not float free of their social and historical contexts, of the particular discourses available to them for the construction of self. To be successful anthropologists, women have to identify with the valorised male position. They are also historical beings and they cannot necessarily stand outside the discourses available to them for constructing relations between self and other. This may be one reason why, until very recently, there was very little which was distinctive about the writing of women anthropologists. The tension between objectifying gaze and authentic experience is there, the rhetorical devices for establishing authorial authority are there. However, the process of identification is never complete, never perfect or finished. The writing of women anthropologists is not actually *the same* as that of their male colleagues. With the notable exception of Margaret Mead, women anthropologists, like Audrey Richards, Lucy Mair, Monica Wilson and Phyllis Kabbery – all of whom did fieldwork in the 1930s and 1940s – do not use the as 'I was standing under the palm tree' approach to ground their authentic experience. They avoid the travel writing style and the metaphors of journeying. Their overall style is often very distant and slightly cold. They aim, perhaps, for a markedly scientific status in their writing, and thus it often lacks the evocative detail of their male colleagues. This is no doubt, in part, because they were under particular pressure to demonstrate their scientific abilities and professional rigorousness, being prone to lapses in objectivity and to subjective interpretation on account of their gender. But, it is also, in part, that they seem to have more difficulty in constructing that easy familiarity with the other which is part of the process of creating a unitary male self, an imaginary self who acts as the organising consciousness of the text. The imaginary male author *in* the text eludes the female author *of* the text and the woman anthropologist thus retreats into objectivity and distance to cover over this lack. This may be one reason why women anthropologists are so often accused of writing very boring ethnography.

The question then at this stage is whether the postmodernist turn is going to offer anthropology any hope: will it provide it with sufficient grounds for self-reflection in the endless process of meaning deferred to work against its historical role in the discourses and practices of domination; will the new experimental anthropology provide modes of shared authorship, shifting perspectives and fragmented domains of partially shared cultural meanings, in a way which will allow other people to speak alongside the anthropologist, from within the same text, in a manner direct, equal and independent? Have we grounds for anticipating the imminent demise of the traditional anthropological author?

There are as yet very few postmodernist texts in anthropology; one, however, which has received much acclaim is Michael Taussig's *Shamanism, colonialism and the wild man*. As we might expect, Taussig is against traditional anthropological modes of authorising and authenticating texts. He inserts himself into his discourse, and he builds up the argument using refraction, displacement and the repetition of powerful images. This seems a truly decentred and deconstructed text, full of shifts, fragmentation and polyphony. However, more than one reviewer has remarked that the average professional anthropologist, never mind the average person, finds it almost impossible to comprehend this text precisely because there is no story to follow. In a text of this kind, as Kapferer

(1988) has so brilliantly pointed out, the idea is that the author builds up images and metaphors one on top of the other, capturing the sense of a complex, shifting reality, so that the 'facts' can speak for themselves. The authority of the anthropologists as author is decentred. The problem, of course, is that the facts speak for themselves, and this carnivalesque form of empiricism gives very little meaning or import to the experience of the anthropologist or to the experiences of people living in Colombia. In spite of Taussig's professed antagonism to traditional modes of anthropological writing, he frequently uses *mis-en-scène* techniques. 'From the vantage point of his house by the river in the foothills beyond the sugar plantations and the great groaning mass of humanity sustaining them, Don Benito can afford to be a little snooty. "Nothing but pig sties" he says of the sugar cane towns, rural slums one and all, created by the new agribusiness systems. "Pure filth" he exclaims. And by filth he means sorcery' (Taussig, 1986: 274). Don Benito no more speaks for himself in this context than he might have done in one produced by Malinowski. He is still presented as representative, and we are being encouraged to understand or comprehend Don Benito by visualising him. This passage is in no way atypical of the book as a whole. However, the more important point concerns the argument about the dispersion of the anthropologist's authorial authority. It is not just that he can be seen setting the scene, as in the above quotation, but consider the following passage:

> In his uncompleted manuscript on commodity fetishism and the modern European city, Walter Benjamin wrote that 'in the dream which every epoch sees it images the epoch which is to succeed it, the latter appears coupled with elements of prehistory – that is to say classless society'. Certainly, there was a passion for classlessness among one set of 'prehistoric elements' in the modern agribusiness town of Puerto Tejada, and that was the large grouping of black migrants from the trackless jungles of the Pacific Coast (Taussig, 1986: 282).

Whose dream are we in here, whose reality is this or whose illusion of reality is this? The association of European thought with the experiences of black migrant workers is cavalier rather than illuminating, such an association can only be understood as an attempt to make sense of a European self. Taussig's concern with decentring and deconstruction in the text looks very like a reworking of a metropolitan crisis in the context of Colombia. Long passages in this book read like scenes from *Apocalypse now*, the imaginative reworking of the nightmare of Vietnam. This is the context in which we should be reading this text. These are the metaphors and images which are replacing the images of travel and the metaphors of journeying. Perhaps the chaotic, fragmented nature of the relationship between order and disorder which the shamans of Colombia manage means that they are true deconstructionists or perhaps it means that they are the other selves of the anthropologist, working in the text to produce his imaginary self.

It seems that the dispersion and fragmentation of authorial authority, and perhaps even of the authors themselves, is not really about a change in anthropological authorship that is in the nature of the anthropologist as author. It has more to do with changing concepts of the self, and most especially the anthropological self. The definition of the anthropological hero has changed. We are no longer objective, comparative scientists, but self-reflexive, self-critical, connected individuals. This newly valorised subject position is no less male than the one which preceded it, and its liberal credentials should be viewed with the same scepticism.

However, there have been significant changes in the genres and styles of anthropological writing. As anthropologists and as authors, our imaginations are now textualised and contextualised very differently from the way they were for anthropologists writing in the 1940s, 1950s and 1960s. The sources of our images and metaphors themselves have altered. The changes in disciplinary fashions and the sheer volume of anthropological writing produced have provided us with a larger number of models on which to base our own writing as individuals, even if this process works through contradiction and dissent, as it does for many feminist anthropologists. There is now no single way to write anthropology. However, even in our moments of greatest self-reflection, there is very little sign that we have relinquished our authorial authority. We are just recreating and rewriting our relationship with ourselves – our many selves – and with others. Our writing continues much in the image of ourselves, as must inevitably be the case, if we are to establish any kinds of relations with others.

References

Clifford, J. (1986), 'Partial truths', in J. Clifford and G. Marcus (eds), *Wring culture* (Berkeley: University of California Press).

Clifford, J. (1988), *The predicament of culture* (Cambridge, Mass.: Harvard University Press).

Clifford, J. and Marcus, S. (1986), *Wring culture* (Berkeley: University of California Press).

Crapanzano, V. (1980), *Tuhami: portrait of a Moroccan* (Chicago: University of Chicago Press).

de Lauretis, T. (1984), *Alice doesn't* (Bloomington: Indiana University Press).

Evans-Pritchard, E. (1969; 1st ed., 1940), *The Nuer: a description of the modes of the livelihood and political institutions of a nilotic people* (Oxford: Clarendon Press).

Firth, R. (1957; 1st ed., 1936), *We, the Tikopia: a sociological study of kinship in primitive Polynesia* (London: Allen and Unwin).

Geertz, G. (1988), *Works and lives: the anthropologist as author* (Cambridge: Polity Press).

Kapferer, B. (1988), 'The anthropologist as hero: three exponents of post-modernist anthropology', *Critiques of Anthropology*, 8, 2, 77–104.

Minh-ha, T. (1989), *Woman, native, other: writing, post-coloniality and feminism* (Bloomington: Indiana University Press).

Taussig, M. (1986), *Shamanism, colonialism and the wild man: a study in terror and healing* (Chicago: University of Chicago Press).

Thornton, R. (1983), 'Narrative ethnography in Africa, 1850–1920: the creation and capture of an appropriate domain for anthropology', *MAN*, 18, 502–20.

Wagner, R. (1975), *The invention of culture* (Englewood Cliffs: Prentice-Hill).

White, H. (1980), 'The value of narrativity in the representation of reality', *Critical Inquiry*, 7, 1 (autumn), 8.

Index